Alfonso Gálvez

The Feast of Man and the Feast of God

Second Edition Revised

Translated from the Spanish by
George Kearns and Lope Pascual

New Jersey
U.S.A. - 2025

The Feast of Man and the Feast of God by Alfonso Gálvez, translated by George Kearns and Lope Pascual from the Spanish *La Fiesta del Hombre y la Fiesta de Dios*, Burgos, 1987, Editorial Monte Carmelo. Copyright © 2025 by Shoreless Lake Press. American edition published with permission. All rights reserved. No part of this book may be reproduced, stored in retrieval system, or transmitted, in any form or by any means, electronic, mechanical, photocopying, recording or otherwise, without written permission of the Society of Jesus Christ the Priest, P.O. Box 157, Stewartsville, New Jersey 08886.

CATALOGING DATA

Author: Gálvez, Alfonso, 1932–2022
Title: The Feast of Man and the Feast of God

> First edition: December 1987
> Second edition: November 2025

Library of Congress Control Number: 2025922054

ISBN: 978-1-953170-56-9
    978-1-953170-57-6 (e-book)

Published by
Shoreless Lake Press
P.O. Box 157
Stewartsville, New Jersey 08886

Editorial note for the second edition

The first English edition was published in 1994, based on the 1987 Spanish original. The second edition is now presented, preserving the text, as well as the poems translated into English at that time. References to similar poems in Cantos al Final del Camino, published—only in Spanish—during the author's lifetime in 2020, Shoreless Lake Press, 2025, have been added.

Shoreless Lake Press, 2025

FOREWORD

It is both an honor and a challenge to introduce the thought of Father Alfonso Gálvez to English-speaking readers. The author's prose, as the reader will discover, moves rapidly among several modes or registers, from precise philosophical and theological argument to an exalted and deeply-moving lyricism, from observations on the state of the Church and society in our time to meditations in verse inspired by two of his favorite texts, *The Song of Songs* and the *Spiritual Canticle* of the great sixteenth-century poet, mystic and saint, John of the Cross. His language, as in the case of all great preachers, not only talks *about* the spirituality and love-relationship with God he urges us towards, but it enacts and embodies that spirituality and love, as well. I have followed Father Gálvez's Spanish as closely as possible —at times sacrificing more idiomatic English constructions— because I believe that the reader should experience not only the author's ideas, but his voice and rhythms, the flavor, as it were, of his very personal expression.

In 1957, Father Gálvez founded, in Spain, the Society of Jesús Christ the Priest, as a new association of Christian Faithful.

The Society, which includes priests, laymen and laywomen, was recognized as a canonical association in 1981. Each year, since 1982, several members of the Society have been ordained to the priesthood. Although the Society is young, it has members in Europe, South America and the United States, the North American Region having been established in 1984. Its members are active in parish life as pastors, assistant pastors and CCD instructors, and devote themselves as well to a broad range of spiritual and educational activities. Following the precept and example of its founder, the Society places a special emphasis upon working with young people.

In addition to his work with the Society, Father Gálvez has been a teacher and spiritual force in Spain and in South America. For five years, he served as a missionary priest in Ecuador and Venezuela, as seminary professor, pastor, and minister to the Indian peoples of the Andes. In Spain, he has written and spoken widely, his books including a meditation on *Prayer* and an extensive commentary on *The Song of Songs*.

The Feast of Man and the Feast of God, which appeared in Spain in 1987, is a thematically unified collection of talks and meditations based on Biblical texts. They reflect the author's warm and profound spirituality, as well as his analysis of practical, ecclesiastical and philosophical problems confronting the Christian in our time. Father Gálvez is a poet, as well as priest and philosopher, and later chapters in this book contain passages from his devotional verse, which pays homage to John of the Cross. I have decided to leave Father Gálvez's poetry in Spanish, supplying English translations in the notes. All passages from Holy Scripture are taken from the English translation published as *The New Jerusalem Bible* (New York, 1985).

George Kearns
Highland Park, N.J., April 1990

PREFACE

This book is the result of putting together several talks about the Gospel delivered some time ago. The author acknowledges that he has always felt a certain prejudice on reading in a preface that the book was composed originally for oral presentation. The prejudice against that form of writing books is still alive in the author, aggravated in this case, moreover, by the time that has elapsed since these talks were heard by those for whom they were intended. Nevertheless, the author is convinced that they can still be useful for anyone, because they are timely. The title of the book refers to the last of these talks, on The Wedding at Cana, and tries to be an expression of what these talks wanted to say: the feast of man remains something very poor if God does not intervene to change it into a true feast; it is even in danger of becoming no feast at all. Indeed, since God is not an enemy of man's festivity, but quite the contrary, what He wishes for His creature is precisely Perfect Joy. Man cannot be such a man without God, and love and joy cannot? be real without Him.

The author is neither exegete nor theologian, and his intentions are purely pastoral. These meditations were compiled for publication but have remained put away for almost ten years. Except for a few explanatory notes and omission of occasional references that would not be clear to the English-speaking reader, the text remains as originally written, nor has the bibliography been brought up to date. Leaving the text as it was first conceived has, at least, the advantage of demonstrating that many of the problems pointed out in these talks have come to pass in all their harshness; therefore, these talks were not spoken to no purpose. Gathered, as has been said, with pure pastoral purpose and without scholarly claims, they deal, nevertheless, with the more serious problems of human existence in light of the Gospel, trying to offer them solution from it. The author is utterly convinced that the Gospel, as all Sacred Scripture, is the inspired word of God, and therefore fully actual; it is a word that ponders all the problems of modern man and offers the solution for them. For the Gospel can be illuminated and made real with scholarly analysis, but much more, perhaps, in a practical and true sense, with prayer. It is in the light of prayer that one can verify that, "The word of God is something alive and active: it cuts more incisively than any two-edged sword; it can seek out the place where soul is divided from spirit, or joints from marrow; it can pass judgement on secret emotions and thoughts." (Heb 4:12) Without that light pure scientific exegesis turns into a cold laboratory product that is useful for nothing, and pastoral preaching is reduced to a dull monologue detached from reality that interests no one and bores everyone.

The book is destined now for the same kind of people as those to whom the talks were given, simple people, but those with a sincere desire to find God and to savor the wonders of His word. To those who possess good will and the firm conviction that the Bible is *truly* the word of God, the author would almost dare to guarantee that they will profit from the attentive reading of these meditations, uttered with so much love, even when they point out the evils that exist in the Church, and with only the desire to do good to all men.

I

THE SIGNS WHICH THE WORLD DEMANDS

The Pharisees and Sadducees came, and to put him to the test they asked if he would show them a sign from heaven. He replied, "In the evening you say, 'It will be fine; there's a red sky,' and in the morning, 'stormy weather today; the sky is red and overcast.' You know how to read the face of the sky, but you cannot read the signs of the times. It is an evil and unfaithful generation asking for a sign, and the only sign it will be given is the sign of Jonah." And he left them and went off.

(Mt 16: 1–4)

"A sign from heaven"

The Pharisees and Sadducees approach the Lord asking for "a sign from heaven." It must deal with something extraordinary which would guarantee the authenticity of the mission which the Master has assumed. To deduce from the text, it seems that these demands are for signs within the purely natural realm, that is, that the extraordinary sign must be considered so according to human measure.

If this interpretation is true, we are facing the world's intention of assuming to itself the right before God to decide which are to be the criteria of guarantee. Things are valued with reference to a norm; however, here the world sets the norm. That is to say, even in regard to God, it should be the world which determines that which is or is not; thus it is no longer God who judges the world, instead it is the world who judges God. Carrying this attitude to its final consequences, as often happens, leads to claiming the right to decide whether or not God exists.

This attitude implies *a priori* the rejection of the supernatural. The world is ready to accept a sign but according to human measure. It demands a marvelous and convincing sign but within what the world understands as marvelous and convincing. The supernatural is not admitted as sign since from the beginning the supernatural is ruled out.

However, God cannot be measured by man. Moreover, if God wants to raise man to the supernatural order, He should then give him testimony of Himself with criteria of credibility sufficient to whoever wants to see; but such criteria cannot be determined by human measure.[1] It is true that this testimony will be inspired by His deeds,[2] but these deeds must be divine. That is to say, it is unlikely that they will be what the world has expected; rather they are the deeds that the Father "has given" the Son "to perform."[3]

This is why Jesus Christ does not yield to the demands of those who speak to Him. We are dealing with the same attitude when He refuses to perform miracles at Nazareth,[4] or to throw Himself down from the tower of the Temple,[5] or to perform miracles before Herod.[6]

It seems that our Christianity has forgotten all this. It persists in presenting itself to the world with the kind of credibility that conforms with what the world demands, hoping that its message will be accepted. The whole actual moment of desacralization ends up here. A reversal has been made, with the consequence that the attitude of going out into the world with a spirit of converting it[7] has been followed by another attitude of pleading where Christians beg for acceptance. Maritain calls this a kneeling before the world.[8] It can be said that the yeast has lost its strength, the salt has lost

---

[1] Jn 8:18; 1 Jn 5: 7–9.

[2] Jn 5:36; 10: 25.37–38.

[3] Jn 5:36.

[4] Lk 4:16 seq.

[5] Mt 4:5 seq.

[6] Lk 23:8.

[7] Mt 28: 19–20.

[8] Cf. J. Maritain, *Le Paysan de la Garonne*, (Paris, 1966). Also, Raymond Aron ironizes this attitude in *L'Opium des intellectuells*, (Paris, 1968).

its taste and the lamp has been placed under the bushel.[9] That is why many Christians are engaged in a tremendous effort not to appear strangers to the world,[10] and to offer signs of credibility that are acceptable to it.

How have we arrived at this situation? Because this attitude, besides being contradictory within itself, encloses a mortal trap.

If Christianity means anything, it must be strange to the world.[11] Otherwise it is nothing. Furthermore, it must be said that if the signs given as a guarantee must be valued by human measure, then they have nothing to say to the world, as they are not different from it. Nevertheless, Christianity presents itself transcendent to the world. Due to the fact that the world hates what is not its own as well as what presents itself as different from the world,[12] if Christianity is voluntarily carried away by fear, then it will consent to be reduced to the world.[13] But then Christianity will be nothing and it will have nothing to tell the world.

If we try to find an explanation for this situation, perhaps it may be said that it does not seem enough to allude to a tactical error on the part of Christians or to the weaknesses of human nature. The situation is so grave that we seem rather to be before a tremendous cooling off of charity and a strong crisis of faith, all this inflamed by

---

[9] Mk 9:50; Mt 5:15.

[10] To *strange* toward the world is an essential characteristic of the Christian. The *lex incarnationis* will never suppress that condition. There is a tension here, one of many found in Christianity, between the real fact that the Word assumes all which is human and *comes to his own* and the no smaller reality of the abyss that separates the supernatural from the natural.

[11] Jn 8:23; 15:19.

[12] Jn 15:19.

[13] About this reduction process, first from the divine to that which is purely human and, secondly, from the human to solely material, refer to the very interesting book by R. García de Haro–I. de Celaya, *La moral cristiana*, (Madrid, 1975).

a superhuman power, a mystery of iniquity which we cannot doubt is already in action.[14] It is true that the moment of the last days is hidden from us;[15] but the Lord spoke of some signs which would foretell His coming, and, among other things, He said that by then faith would hardly be found on the earth, and that the charity of many would have grown cold.[16] Nonetheless, the moment being totally hidden, it is very certain that we can neither speak of the imminence nor of the remoteness of the last days.

If we wish to specify with some instances the diminishing attitude of which we have already spoken, we may refer to the case of the priest determined to appear as a leader of social, political and economic concerns of his community;[17] or to the excessively socialistic tone of certain magisterial actions on one part of the Hierarchy; or to the theology of the death of God, in trying to present a rationalized Christianity in which God is no longer needed; or to the philosophies of Rahner and Metz which practically reduce faith to something made by man himself instead of being a gift from God;[18]

---

[14] 2 Thess 2:7.

[15] Acts 1:7; Mt 24:36.

[16] Lk 18:8; Mt 24:12.

[17] Authentic concerns at times, and at other times artificially fostered by the leaders themselves, following the principles of the Marxist orthodoxy of the class struggle.

[18] H. U. Von Balthasar strongly criticized that line of thinking in *Cordula ou l'épreuve décisive*, (Paris, 1968). There is a Spanish translation of this book entitled *Seriedad con las cosas*; however, it is not a good one. We could add to the aforementioned, the intent of Rev. Schoonenberg for making a Christ more *understandable*: "Too understandable," Rev. Renwart tells us, 'since this Jesus is none other than the greatest among us, which empties all His mystery and all the richness of the salvation He came down to bring us." Cf. *Nouvelle Revue Théologique*, 95 (1973), pp. 1137ff., quoted by C. Pozo in *María en la obra de la salvación*, (Madrid, 1974), p. 293.

or to the swarm of theologies of liberation, or to many other tentative theologies, of which many have said that we are facing a true Neomodernism, more serious than the Modernism at the beginning of the century.[19]

Modern Christians are afflicted with a sort of inferiority complex which seems to have been brought about by a serious crisis of faith. For when charity cools down then faith disappears, and fear makes its appearance as a byproduct.[20] The blameworthy fear St. John refers to surfaces in man when love is lacking; and it is capable of compelling him to yield to the worst evasions.

"They came, and to put him to the test"

It is evident that those Pharisees and Sadducees who approached Jesus asking him for a sign did not have good intentions. The Sacred text itself tells us so, and that is why the Lord Himself refers to them as an "unfaithful and evil generation." They have more than enough intelligence to know the natural things, but they lack the will to open themselves to the supernatural,

> "You know how to read the face of the sky, but you cannot read the signs of the times."

---

[19]Cf. R. García de Haro, *Historia teológica del Modernismo*, (Pamplona, 1972). Cf. also about Neomodernism, A. García Bañón, 'Persistencia de la crisis modernista," *Scripta Theologica* VII (1975), pp. 203-246. Regarding theologies of liberation, cf. the interesting book by A. Bandera, *La Iglesia ante el proceso de liberación*, (Madrid, 1975).

[20]1 Jn 4:18.

Those are precisely the same signs by which they would have known the Lord. Because God may be known with certainty by the intellect alone, even though in a very imperfect way, providing that the will does not prevent it.[21]

Neither the Pharisees of that time nor those of today, who demand a human measure to convince themselves, have ever had good intentions, and that is why they shall never be convinced, even if they witness the most extraordinary wonder.

Many Christians today are frightened. This is because they have been led to believe two things which they have admitted rather too easily. First, that the temporal city is being built without them. Second, that the future city they await is a utopia, an alienation which even hinders them from collaborating as they should in the building of the earthly city. We are speaking of two falsehoods. These, however, are not as extraordinary as the fact that some Christians have consented to believe them. All this because charity cooled off and, in consequence, they have been chastised with a weakness of faith. Without faith Christians can no longer be conquerors of the world, but will be conquered by it.[22]

Men who with bad faith look for signs ought not to be pleased. Nonetheless, the Lord offers a sign to the Pharisees and Sadducees: that of the prophet Jonah, without doubt referring to His death and three days in the sepulcher followed by the definite victory of the resurrection. Thus we are moved to believe that the last and definite sign which God wanted to give to the world is none other than that of the cross. A sign that, because it is foolishness and a stumbling–block to the world, this world is not ready to accept.

---

[21] Rom 1:19 seq.; 1 Cor 2:14, cf. Den–Sch. 3026, 3004.
[22] 1 Jn 5:4.

Saint Paul tells us of the reason for this mysterious behavior on the part of God,

> "Since in the wisdom of God the world was unable to recognize God through wisdom, it was God's own pleasure to save believers through the folly of the gospel. While the Jews demand miracles and the Greeks look for wisdom, we are preaching a crucified Christ."[23]

In fact, the Lord had already foretold that He would only draw them all towards Him when He was lifted up from the earth, meaning the cross.[24] Only then would people of good will recognize that sign and believe in Him.[25]

The only sign

If modern Christians wish to convince people of good will, they must be willing to offer that same sign. But this will be a cross that cannot remain in a world of ideas or words. On the contrary, it ought to take shape in their own lives,[26] and, therefore, in labor to the point of exhaustion, in a total and true surrender of the will, in chastity earnestly lived, in a sincere charity[27] towards all, in true poverty, in joy when we are not understood, in humility of not ever feeling forgotten and in the absence of all earthly ambition.

---

[23] 1 Cor 1: 21–23.
[24] Jn 12: 32–33.
[25] Jn 3:14; 8:28.
[26] Gal 2:19; 5:24; 6:14; Rom 6:3 and passim
[27] 2 Cor 6:6.

It has been said, in regard to the evangelical passage in which John the Baptist sends a message to the Lord asking whether He is the Messiah or not,[28] that the most important sign that the Lord offers to the Precursor is that the poor are evangelized:

> "Go back and tell John what you hear and see; the blind see again, and the lame walk, those suffering from virulent skin–diseases are cleansed, and the deaf hear, the dead are raised to life and the good news is proclaimed to the poor."

In this a certain hierarchy of signs appears, the last one, even higher than the resurrection of the dead, being the evangelization of the poor. It is as if the Lord wanted to say that the main sign by which His disciples would be recognized is love towards others, above all towards those most needy, expressed by announcing the Good News to them. That love must be fulfilled in the giving of one's own life, for only then love is shown in its whole fullness.[29] That was the sign that the Lord gave to His disciples by which they would be recognized.

> "It is by your love for one another, that everyone will recognize you as my disciples."[30]

In this stage of the pilgrim Church, love goes together with death and the cross, because no one shows greater love than one who gives up his life for his friends.[31] The cross continues to be the supreme sign.

---

[28] Mt 11: 2–6; Lk 7: 18–23.
[29] Jn 15:13; 13:1.
[30] Jn 13:35.
[31] Jn 15:13.

Unfortunately, love exposes itself to many forgeries. Many today defend as the principal task of Christianity that of securing a better distribution of temporal goods. Nonetheless, we should not forget that the Lord already warned that He was not a distributor of goods.[32] As a matter of fact, the giving of one's own goods does not suffice in the search of a greater social justice and one must advise that, according to the Apostle, such action is not necessarily true charity.[33]

Our modern Christianity is putting so much enthusiasm into the improvement of the material conditions of the life of mankind that very often it forgets all else. If anyone dares recall that after all, "there is no permanent city for us here; we are looking for the one that is yet to be,"[34] one is ridiculed and accused of alienating others. The exclusive preoccupation with the earthly city is offered by some as the authentic sign of true Christianity.

Even though it seems incredible, it takes some courage nowadays to say that the famous *opium of the people* is really furnished to man when we make him forget his eternal destiny; or when one tries to satisfy him with earthly goods, without hope of anything else; or when he is left without an answer to the problems which are imbedded in his heart and spirit; or when, under the pretext of service to society, he is deprived of his rights as a person,

> "They have abandoned me, the fountain of living water, and dug water–tanks for themselves, cracked water–tanks that hold no water."[35]

---

[32] Lk 12:14.
[33] 1 Cor 13:3.
[34] Heb 13:14.
[35] Jer 2:13.

It is not true that we arrived at this situation by the desire to live our faith with greater sincerity. On the contrary, we have arrived at it due to a crisis of faith. It is said that one wants to furnish man with the immediate, that which is tangible; but everything else is left in second place, in the dim shadow of whether it is or is not. It is not true that man's entire well-being is sought, and that Social Justice is only a preliminary stage. The real truth is that those who assert this are convinced that there is nothing else to look forward to; their thought and speech always remain with what belongs to this world, precisely because they do not believe in the other.[36]

Love that is not accompanied by faith is not Christian love. Charity, which is Christian love, believes everything,[37] and faith is ever fulfilled through charity.[38] The charity mentioned in the New Testament is always a fruit of the Holy Spirit, and the greatest.[39] The Holy Spirit, however, can only dwell in man through faith.[40] At the same time the crisis of faith the world suffers today is the consequence of a choice freely taken against God;[41] Saint Paul already said that the failure of faith is the result of having lost good conscience.[42]

Conclusively, the only sign which Christians can give to the world as a guarantee of their message is love. We are speaking of a genuine love. Love is genuine when it gives its life in Christ.

---

[36] 1 Jn 4:5.
[37] 1 Cor 13:7.
[38] Gal 5:6; cf. Rev 2:19.
[39] Gal 5:23.
[40] Heb 11:6; Gal 3:14; Eph 3:17.
[41] Cf. C. Cardona, *Metafísica de la opción intelectual*, (Madrid, 1973).
[42] 1 Tim 1:19.

Because, on one hand, it is said in the New Testament that he who lays down his life is the one who truly loves;[43] on the other hand, it is also said that the sign of the Son of Man is the cross.[44] The Lord Himself affirms that He is willing to give no other sign except that of Jonah. With the cross as the expression of divine love consummated,[45] from then on, all genuine love passes through the cross. It should be also said that any love which does not spring from the cross of Christ, which does not lead to it, is not love, no matter how many labels it carries for social causes.

The best sign that Christians can offer to the world is that of love crucified, without minding too much that the world would have preferred another sign. And without being fooled; for if the world finally accepts a sign, it should be precisely that of love crucified, which is the only one that can convince people of good will. Regarding the rest of mankind, they will not accept any sign, and, of course, will not be convinced by the earthly signs.

It is unthinkable that Christians can conquer the world on its own ground. The signs shown, no matter how marvelous they are, will not convince the world as long as they are of its own kind. The New Testament clearly tells us that towards the end of time many deceivers shall appear, claiming to be prophets who will carry out great signs and wonders.[46] Without doubt these signs shall be of the sort wanted and awaited by the world. However, it should not be thought that these signs will be like juggling or fireworks, to cause admiration or fun; without a doubt, they will deal with something more serious; perhaps it will be something that will fulfill the

---

[43] Jn 15:13; 1 Jn 3:16.

[44] Mt 24:30.

[45] Jn 19:30; 13:1.

[46] Mt 24:24; Mk 13:22; Rev 13: 13–15; 2 Thess 2: 9–10.

earthly wishes of humanity, will satisfy its hopes, and will reach the attainments which up to that time had been considered unattainable, making mankind startled at its own power, and leading people to the certainty that God is no longer necessary. Placing, therefore, oneself in a worldly line with accomplishments which might be good, but which remain on a strictly natural level, means playing the game of the enemy of salvation, precisely by not realizing that those signs cannot be strictly Christian, due to their ambiguity.

There is a place that is strictly Christian where the enemies of salvation cannot situate themselves. This place is the cross. This is why, to Christians, this is the only authentic sign, while the rest are misleading. As long as Christians remain on a solely human plane, they shall not be able to offer to the world that which is proper to them and which makes them different from the world.[47] If Christians only had what is strictly natural to offer as merchandise, then they would have nothing to present to the world but the sad and grotesque show of desertion.[48]

Christians cannot conquer the world fighting with its weapons. The only thing with which you can confront the pride and power of the world is the weakness of the Cross:

> "Consider, brothers, how you were called; not many of you are wise by human standards, not many influential, not many from noble families. No, God chose those who by human standards are fools to shame the wise; he chose those who by human standards are weak to shame the strong, those who by human standards are common and contemptible —indeed those who count for nothing— to

---

[47] Jn 17:16; 15:19.
[48] Mt 5:13.

reduce to nothing those that do count for something, so that no human being might feel boastful before God."[49]

The most authentic *witness* to Jesus Christ will never be the champion of earthly vindications, but the martyr,[50] as Christ is called in the New Testament "the loyal witness" precisely because He is "the first-born from the dead..., He who loves us and has washed away our sins with his blood."[51] Going down into the arena with weapons chosen by the adversary, abandoning what one's own strength is made of, was always considered recklessness. If the Christians of today wish to offer something *marvelous* to the world, that something can be none other than the love of the cross. In all truth, it is all that the disciples need as a viaticum for the journey, just as the Lord clearly warned.[52] What is surprising is that it seems to have been forgotten.

We must go, therefore, where God wishes to take us, even if no one wants to go there, allowing others to go ahead of us in the distribution of worldly gifts. We must remember that it is better to give than to receive, and that we have not come to be served but to serve. We must not receive injustice with amazement, but as something expected, which offers us the unmerited honor of partaking in the Lord's cross. We must not seek the labors which people can reward, but those which only God can repay. We must understand people when they do not understand us, and rejoice with the feeling that God does understand us. We must always keep in mind the fact that we can neither wait for mankind to love us first, nor can we wait for them to love us later.

---

[49] 1 Cor 1: 26–29.
[50] Acts 22:20; Rev 6:9.
[51] Rev 1:5.
[52] Mt 10: 9–10; 16:24.

We must always remember that the Lord taught us that in many areas it is better to lose than to win, to give up our life rather than to take it, to prefer the last place to the first, to offer our coat when they beg for a shirt, or to walk two miles with him who asks us to walk one...

Maybe someone will say that all this is beautiful. Without a doubt, it is; but isn't beauty also truth? Saint Paul called Christ's testimony beautiful, or the testimony given in His name.[53] In all truthfulness, that is the only sign which Christians can give to the modern world.

---

[53] 1 Tim 6: 12–13.

II

THE NAME OF JESUS

The seventy-two carne back rejoicing. "Lord," they said, "even the devils submit to us when we use your name." He said to them, "I watched Satan fall like lightning from heaven. Look, I have given you power to tread down serpents and scorpions and the whole strength of the enemy; nothing shall ever hurt you. Yet do not rejoice that the spirits submit to you; rejoice instead that your names are written in heaven."

(Lk 10: 17–20)

"Lord, even the devils submit to us when we use your name"

The name designates and represents the person, and sometimes even acts like the person. For the New Testament the name of Jesus is endowed with the same qualities as the Person of the Lord (Acts 3:6). Sometimes it interchanges the generic and substantive expression of *name* for Jesus Himself or for the personal pronoun. To the angel of the Church in Pergamum it is said,

> 'I know where you live, in the place where Satan is enthroned, and that you still hold firmly to my name, and did not disown your faith in me..."[1]

Likewise to the one of the Church in Philadelphia,

> 'I know about your activities,... and I know that though you are not very strong, you have kept my commandment and not disowned my name."[2]

Generally speaking we may affirm that the use of the expression *name* referring to God is quite frequent in biblical language.[3]

Thus, faithfulness to the name of Jesus amounts to faithfulness to Jesus himself, and that is the meaning of the texts from the Book

---

[1] Rev 2:13.
[2] Rev 3:8.
[3] Ps 8:1; 72:17; Mt 6:9; Acts 4:12; Jn 17:6; etc.

of Revelation which emphasize the fidelity to Jesus in the midst of difficulties, these hardships being the touchstone of faithfulness.

Our epoch is one of widespread apostasy and unfaithfulness to the name of Jesus. Orlandis says that the statement uttered by the anti–clerical politician, Azaña, in 1931, according to which Spain was no longer Catholic, was at that time only a boast, but has now become a reality.[4] We ought to admit that Europe as well as Spain are no longer Christian. Orlandis refers also to Italy, with its laws about divorce and its social and moral chaos. The environment is becoming an obstacle for any Christian who wants truly to be one, to an extent previously unknown in the history of Europe.

The disciples returned with joy after having experienced that the name of Jesus was almighty, accomplishing what seemed to be most difficult, power over the demons.

The Acts of the Apostles tells us about the lame man who begged alms at the Temple entrance called the Beautiful Gate. When Peter and John were passing by, he extended his hand in the hope of receiving *something* from them. Peter's answer was unexpected,

> 'I have neither silver nor gold, but I will give you what I have: in the name of Jesus Christ the Nazarene, walk!'[5]

The name of Jesus gave that unfortunate man much more than what he could have expected.

Men's lowness itself prevents them from thinking that they are able to receive a lot. But God wanted to give man much more than man could ever have fancied. When men approach the apostle, they ordinarily do it with the hope of getting from him *something*; perhaps the answer to some material problem, or the relief of their con-

---

[4] J. Orlandis, *Historia y espíritu* (Pamplona, 1975), p. 172.
[5] Acts 3: 5–6.

science, or even a reconciliation with God, when the apostle happens to be a priest. But in general, they do not demand much. They are not usually thirsty for true holiness nor do they wish that anybody unfold great horizons for them. It seems as if men are comfortable with the role of beggars, and, being used to give little, they do not expect to receive much. It seems that they are not capable of wishing or dreaming for what is high; some would even gladly content themselves with the pods that the swine eat (Lk 15:16).

This is why the apostle should begin by whetting men's appetite,[6] so that when they open their hands waiting for some alms, they encounter the name of Jesus along with all that name means and connotes.[7]

Yet the worst occurs when meanness in giving merges with the lack of appetite; and this happens when the one who should give is as needy as the one who is to receive, or even more. That is, when you can say to the apostle that which was said to the angel in Laodicea,

> 'Never realizing that you are wretchedly and pitiably poor, and blind and naked too."[8]

Thus we face the grand drama of a great part of the modern ecclesiastic world: it has become hollow. And that happened perhaps because salvation has been sought not in the name of Jesus,

---

[6] That is the way the Lord acted when urging us to "ask, and it will be given to you; search, and you will find" (Mt 7:7; 21:22; Mk 11:24; Jn 16:23).

[7] "Give, and there will be gifts for you: a full measure, pressed down, shaken together, and overflowing, will be poured into your lap..." (Lk 6:38). All this is normal, because, "when someone is given a great deal, a great deal will be demanded of that person; when someone is entrusted with a great deal, of that person even more will be expected" (Lk 12:48).

[8] Rev 3:17.

but in the name of other teachers who called themselves prophets of this earth. This has brought about desertion for many Christians and boredom for others. The low quality of pasture offered to the sheep in some places has cast discredit on Shepherds. We ought even to say that the pasture which has sometimes been offered was poisonous or at least tasteless. For instance, many Christians are tired of hearing speeches exclusively about human rights and social claims. The same happens when it comes to the peace theme, about which Shepherds talk very often but mean human peace or pacific coexistence, rather than that peace promised by the Lord,

> 'Peace I bequeath to you, my own peace I give you, a peace which the world cannot give, this is my gift to you."[9]

Saint Peter solemnly proclaimed before the Sanhedrin that there is no salvation except in the name of Jesus,

---

[9] Jn 14:27. Accordingly, the Lord distinguishes between both kinds of peace. A distinction we frequently miss in some Shepherds' exhortations. It seems that they only contemplate worldly peace, which is the only one the world cares about and admits, and, furthermore, it seems that those Shepherds feel at peace with such reductive meaning. The words of Jeremiah already rebuked bad prophets who spent time after time promising and talking about peace to those who, after all, were despising God's word (Jer 23:17). On the other hand, we ought to say that worldly peace is not an absolute value, as proved by the Lord's words: 'It is not peace I have come to bring, but a sword" (Mt 10:34), which would be enough to disprove more than one modern speech. What happens is that peace is one of those concepts which have an ambiguous meaning in the New Testament (the same happens, for instance, with the concept of world), and thus requires, whenever it is used, a clarification of the sense in which it is to be taken. But that clarification is not always supplied, which might lead one to suspect its omission through ignorance, if not through the animus of wishing to deceive the listeners.

"Only in him is there salvation; for of all the names in the world given to men, this is the only one by which we can be saved."[10]

If that is true, they are cheating the People of God who try to shepherd it to salvation through another path. For Saint Paul there is only the name of the One Who humbled Himself and saved us dying upon the cross, "And for this God raised him high, and gave him the name which is above all other names: so that, all beings in the heavens, on earth and in the underworld, should bend the knee at the name of Jesus."[11]

Faith in the Name as a premise to the "power over all enemy power"

Faith in the name of Jesus is the cause of power over the devils,

"Lord, even the devils submit to us when we use your name!"

And the Lord certifies it,

"I have given you power over the whole strength of the enemy."

The power that an apostle can exercise over the enemy of salvation is, therefore, linked to his faith in Jesus. Even more, if we think that Satan is the adversary who is always behind any obstacle in the

---

[10] Acts 4:12.
[11] Phil 2: 9–10.

way of the apostle (Eph 6:12), and that there is no other name with which Satan can be defeated, it is obvious that faith in Jesus is of the essence of all apostleship. All power over the devil depends on it in direct proportion.

Even more, faith in the Name as a means to fight against the devil is not only essential but also exclusive. It means that other things are not useful for that fight, and, still more, they should be taken away to whatever extent they might induce us to forget, even momentarily, that faith is the only effective thing in this task.

Things do not help in the fight against the devil. Nevertheless, their use is not always counter-productive. Everything created by God can and must be employed in the work of hastening the coming of the Kingdom. What is meant here is that things, by themselves, are ineffective for that purpose, and are even self-defeating when they distract the apostle's mind or heart from the only necessary thing. Thus Peter's lovely exclamation to the crippled man at the Beautiful Gate of the Temple,

> 'I have neither silver nor gold, but I will give you what I have...'[12]

We see here that sheer lack of human goods arouses in St. Peter sheer faith in the Name, and, as a consequence, complete success in his imprecation. Most likely, this is also the sense in which the Lord's advice to his disciples should be understood,

> 'Provide yourselves with no gold or silver, not even with coppers for your purses, with no haversack for the journey or spare tunic or footwear or a staff.'[13]

---

[12] Acts 3:6.
[13] Mt 10: 9–10.

Employment of human means is, for the apostle who lives in the world, not only something legitimate but compulsory. But that will be on the condition that those means create a tension in the apostle which should take shape as follows:

The apostle must be firmly convinced that those means are useful only insofar as they are instruments to lead men to God, because He is the only efficient and final cause of all apostleship and of all power over the devil.

The apostle ought also to be aware that the instrument will be useful as long as it neither overshadows nor hinders the principal cause; which would happen the very moment that the apostle trusted the effectiveness of the instrument *on its own*. In fact, if that occurred the instrument would turn against the apostle; it would be not only inefficient but also harmful. That phenomenon came to pass in the Church when human means were given too much importance. Therefore, they came to be seen as having value in themselves, and obscured the very end which they should have served.

The apostle must use those means convinced that they are useful and convenient, but not indispensable. There is only one thing necessary for the apostle (Lk 10:42), and everything else is, therefore, accidental. The word *accidental* should be placed here in between the concept of evil or useless and the concept of essential. In reality *accidental* refers to neither concept, judging by what seems to follow from the Lord's words addressed to Martha. Accordingly, to condemn human means as if they were evil would be as out of place as to believe them indispensable. Therefore, we should perhaps consider unsuited for the secular apostleship those who do not understand this. Because should any apostle consider human means something more that what is merely convenient or useful, these means would end up neutralizing the apostle's life and message. If he thinks them evil in themselves, pretending to live a certain *wild* and Manichean poverty, which is very fashionable nowadays, the apostle will wind up preaching an empty and unreal message which will lead him, first to inefficiency, and then to a frantic return to those things he abhorred.

Perhaps the poverty, which the apostle is called to, is not so easy to live as some would like to believe. In reality, Christian life is never simple. It does not seem that poverty can be conquered once and for all. On the contrary, it looks as if poverty must be constantly reconquered. The same happens with chastity, obedience and, in general, with all virtues. It is sound to remember that what is easy is not always better. To solve the question by not using human means might appear easiest, but surely not most convenient.[14] The apostle —we might say the Christian— is compelled, once again, to live under a strain and to assume a risk. Thus on the one hand he must live true poverty, while on the other hand he must use things to the extent it is convenient and helpful. There is no contradiction here but certainly a tension. And the Christian —at least the one who lives in the world, as is the case with the secular priest and the laymen— should take it with all risks. It is not even acceptable to say that, in case of conflict or doubt, it is better for the Christian to lean toward this or that side; truly speaking, the Christian should not incline toward either of the two, but live the tension that flows from this situation and in which his condition as a Christian places him. Surely the Lord alluded to that situation when He said,

> "How blessed are the poor *in spirit*: the Kingdom of Heaven is theirs."[15]

---

[14] Cf. J. Danielou, *El cristiano y el mundo moderno*, (Barcelona, 1967).
[15] Mt 5:3.

And in another place,

> 'I am not asking you to remove them from the world,
> but to protect them from the Evil One."[16]

This tension is not exclusive to poverty, but is, as we have said, a characteristic of the whole Christian life. Obedience, for instance, is a tension between death to my own self and personal autonomy. Faith itself is in the middle way between rational knowledge and knowledge by vision.

Franciscan poverty should not be raised as an objection to what we have said above. To do so would be to confuse once again, within Christian life, the religious and the secular, something that has happened too frequently in the life of the Church, and has brought about serious harm. We should recall that a member of a religious order has removed himself or herself from the world, and should bear witness to something in itself astonishing: the victory over things through their loss. This does not imply that things are evil in themselves, no. We are dealing here with a testimony to God's transcendence over things, and, really, with a testimony to the wonder of the Cross given in a *wondrous manner*.[17] Thus, when the style of life of a member of a religious order loses this astonishing character, it also produces astonishment among people, but now of a quite different kind. The ideal of Franciscan poverty is an ideal for members of

---

[16] Jn 17:15.

[17] The layman, as well as the secular priest, should bear witness, in his or her own way, to the wonder of the Cross. What we mean to say is that the member of a religious order must do it in a doubly wonderful manner, or, if we prefer it so, in a wonderfully wondrous manner.

religious orders, but it cannot be proposed to a normal Christian.[18] It would make no sense to try to solve the question about which one of the two ways of living poverty is more heroic. Surely the reference point is not the degree of heroism or perfection, but the fact that the Holy Spirit, Soul of the Church, inspires in each moment of History the way in which He wishes the gospel to be lived and, accordingly, to be witnessed. Therefore, many discussions about states of perfection appear to be idle and meaningless.[19]

The efficacy of the apostle's action "over all the powers of the enemy" depends, therefore, on the depth of his faith, and, consequently, on living a poverty within which he does not think of human support as indispensable. Demoniac power will grow in the world insofar as that way of life fails. And if a time of crises of faith and poverty among Christians arrives —that is to say, if we recur to worldly things because we have lost the sense of the supernatural— that means that we will have ended up in a situation in which demoniac power is utterly deployed.

---

[18]To propose to the people impossible utopias is to lead them toward a failure in their entire Christian life (because failure in a sector expands to the whole), for which those responsible will have to render account before God. All this happens because of the confusion of some, who are not able to realize that the richness of the content of the gospel (poverty in this case) is lived in the Church through a variety of ways, according to each person's different vocation or *status*.

[19]In our opinion, both ways of living poverty accomplish perfect and true poverty, as long as they are seriously lived and tempered with sufficient compromise.

"Rejoice instead that your names are written in Heaven"

The gospel passage finishes with the Lord's exhortation to his disciples to rejoice, reminding them what must be their deepest reason for joy,

> "Yet do not rejoice that the spirits submit to you; rejoice instead that your names are written in Heaven."

The apostle ought to rejoice at the destruction of evil and at the good which are brought about by his passing by. How could it be any other way? Wearing always his faith (Eph 6:16) he experiences how people listen to him and keep his word (Jn 15:20), how he gathers his abundant harvest (Mt 13:8), and that he can perform greater deeds than those He did (Jn 14:12). That is why the disciple must rejoice. It is too beautiful to contemplate the offspring of one's own faith and effort growing around one,

> 'Like arrows in a warrior's hand are the sons you father when young. How blessed is the man who has filled his quiver with them; in dispute with his enemies at the city gate he will not be worsted."[20]

That is so, and an apostle who does not possess happiness may very well be called unsuccessful, because it will be due, without doubt, to his not reaping any fruit. Though God kindly reminds his disciples that the true motive for happiness is deeper,

> 'Rejoice instead that your names are written in heaven."

---

[20] Ps 127: 4–5.

The apostle should retreat very frequently to the intimacy of prayer, which is where all is contrasted and all is clarified. Only there he will realize the deepest cause of his happiness. Because success in the apostolate and victory over evil are not enough, by themselves, to keep the apostle joyful; and that is what the Lord seems to say here. It is as if He is saying that the apostle will indeed be happy, but for the deeper reason from which happiness springs. In all truth, it is because he knows himself as a child of God (Jn 1:12); because he knows that he is no longer a servant but a friend (Jn 15:15); because also for him these extraordinary words were pronounced,

> "Whoever eats my flesh and drinks my blood lives in me and I live in that person."[21]

Or those, which fill him with joy,

> "And look, I am with you always; yes, to the end of time."[22]

But above all, the apostle will be happy because he loves Love Himself and feels himself loved by Him.

This is the joy in which is based and from which springs any other joy. This is the joy the Spirit makes blossom within us like a fruit–tree (Gal 5:22), the joy which Chesterton said was the gigantic secret of Christians.

---

[21] Jn 6:56.
[22] Mt 28:20.

III

ZACCHAEUS

He entered Jericho and was going through the town and suddenly a man whose name was Zacchaeus made his appearance, he was one of the senior tax collectors and a wealthy man. He kept trying to see who Jesús was, but he was too short and could not see him for the crowd; so he ran ahead and climbed a sycamore tree to catch a glimpse of Jesús, who was to pass that way. When Jesús reached the spot he looked up and spoke to him, "Zacchaeus, come down. Hurry, because I am to stay at your house today." And he hurried down and welcomed him joyfully. They all complained when they saw what was happening. "He has gone to stay at a sinner's house," they said. But Zacchaeus stood his ground and said to the Lord, "Look, sir, I am going to give half my property to the poor, and if I have cheated anybody I will pay him back four times the amount."

(Lk 19: 1–8)

It seems as if there are only two characters in this episode: the Lord and Zacchaeus. The rest would be ornamentation: the crowd thronging to see the Lord passing by, the people murmuring, the deceived poor... a backdrop against which the two characters and what happens between them take shape.

That is what we find when, in the silence of prayer, we go back to ourselves: the Lord and us... Truly, it is there that all begins and ends for each of us. There are also the circumstances of everyone's life, other people, and all the elements of our environment; but everything revolves upon that axis which is the Lord and each one of us. Nobody will ever find another thing more important for him.

The Lord and each one of us; this relationship is what principally appears in the first commandment. For this commandment —the one truly decisive for each person— everything else is *other things*. Which does not mean to diminish them, but to put them in the place they ought to be.

This relationship sets the Lord face to face with each person who comes into this world. Of course, the more important of its two terms is the Lord. He is the determinant for each of us. Because the Lord is not just another thing in our life, not even the most important: He is the only truly decisive one, the fundamental one, the whole, the "my God and my All" of Saint Francis of Assisi, or "my life itself," in the words of Saint Paul.[1] Nicolas Cabasilas, the 14th century blessed theologian, put it very graphically: "The Savior is present in everybody who lives in Him, in such a way that He provides for all their needs and He is all for them. He does not

---

[1] Phil 1:21.

let them turn their gaze to anything else, nor search for anything in a place other than Him. The upright are not in need of anything which cannot be found in Him: He begets them, makes them grow, feeds them and is for them the light and the breath they breathe. He is the eye which in them contemplates, the light thanks to which they see and the object in the vision contemplated. Being the One who feeds, He is at the same time the food. It is He who gives the Bread of Life and is Life for those who live in Him. He is balsam perfume for those who inhale Him, and clothes for those who wish to don Him. He is the foot on which we walk, and, at the same time, the way, the inn in which we rest on our pilgrimage, and the end of our pilgrim journey."[2]

The Lord is the first and only All in our life. Only from this point can things be seen in their true worth, no more no less. If this were not the case, we risk either giving them excessive value, as it happens to all those for whom God is not the first, or not estimating them for what they really are.

The latter also occurs very frequently. The lazy and superficial person tends not to give enough importance to things. For things were created by the Word, ''Through him all things came into being, nothing came into being except through him."[3] Saint Paul adds to this that all things were created for Him and in Him all things hold together.[4] Therefore, it is unsuitable for the Christian not to take

---

[2] N. Cabasilas, *La vida en Cristo*, (Madrid, 1958), p. 94. Saint Paul says that it is no longer he, but Christ who lives in him (Gal 2:20), that neither our life nor our death belong to us, but they are for the Lord (Rom 14:7; 2 Cor 5:15). Perhaps the most important text is the one of Jn 6:57 which contains the words of the Lord Himself, ''As the living Father sent me and I draw life from the Father, so whoever eats me will also draw life from me."

[3] Jn 1:3.

[4] Col 1: 16–17.

seriously things like work, happiness, sacrifice, love toward others and, in general, everything. Things *hold together* for the Christian —that is to say, are taken seriously— when he does them *in Him*. If we do not love God we are doomed to remain on the surface of things without ever understanding or savoring them. Without Christ love itself, for instance, withers as an inconsistent reality in which even that little entity it holds soon fades away.[5] The drama of our generation, which has lost Christ, is that it does not find coherence in things; consequently it has taken refuge in Marxism, sex and drugs, only to find there a greater emptiness and a greater incoherence. That is why it has been called the bored generation, and the alien plants of Marxism and Existentialism have grown up within it.[6]

---

[5] Françoise Sagan admits that she was unable to spend more than three months with a man without getting bored. Cf. interview by H. Goier-Marvier, *Bonjour Françoise*, (Paris, 1957); cited by Ch. Moeller, *Literatura del siglo XX y cristianismo*, vol. 5, (Madrid, 1975), p. 46.

[6] The diagnostic literature about the present situation is rather abundant. Let us choose a text: "We find ourselves in the most strange situation in which man lives exactly opposite to how he should objectively live. In the most peaceful and secure society that ever existed, man lives, nevertheless, immersed in a growing uncertainty and fear. In a scientific society man lives in an irrational way, and in the most liberal society, man experiences *repression* and even ultra repression. In a society where communications have reached their highest degree of development, man lives in a kind of phantasmagoria; in a society in which everything is done in order to establish relationships, man lives in loneliness... Technology has offered him a marvelous universe of possibilities and objects. Man accepts the possibilities, even without his noticing, and starts fearing the objects because his life has no sense and he is afraid of being displaced by things. But as getting more objects is the only possible value that the System offers him in compensation for his work, man purchases things constantly, and his anguish increases as he is invaded by objects." J. Ellul, *L'espérance oubliée*, (Paris, 1972), p. 20. You may also refer to the curious and interesting book by G. Suffert, *Les intellectuels en chaise longue*, (Paris, 1974).

"And behold there was a man named Zacchaeus; he was a leading publican and a wealthy man"

Here we have a character with his personal circumstances. It does not seem to be true, as Ortega would have it, that circumstances added to each person are valid to define that person; nevertheless, we cannot doubt that they are of great importance. Because it has been through them that the Lord has wanted us to find Him, and then, once we have found Him, to sanctify ourselves. That is why circumstances are beautiful. For each one of us, it was our beloved circumstances which have brought us to the Lord. They are to each one the mysterious ways of God's Providence through which we meet Him: our home, the education we have received, our environment, places, people, successes and failures, happiness, as well as sufferings. If we look backward in our life, we will understand that our encounter with the Lord was the result of a series of accumulated circumstances; but they were lovingly prepared by Him so that we might find Him, in an interweaving, mysterious to us, of His providence and our freedom. The problem here is not to find those circumstances, because, in reality, all of us meet them (1 Tim 2:4); the problem for each person is to know how to use them, which amounts to knowing how *to see* into them. Circumstances are for each one of us our own surroundings, the door on which the Lord knocks (Rev 3:20), and it is up to us to open and recognize Him. How can we not love the circumstances, if they have been the way through which Jesus came into our lives? And, why should we not rejoice, whatever they might have been, if we know that they have been arranged by Him for us to find Him and achieve holiness in them and through them?

"He kept trying to see who Jesus was"

There is surely a great difference between hearing about Jesus and meeting Him personally. Zacchaeus had heard about Jesus, but he wanted to know Him personally.

Indeed, all Christians know Jesus by hearsay, for, according to the Bible, faith comes from hearing.[7] But we do not mean that. What we want to express here is that for many Christians, their knowledge about the Lord is very superficial: it is confined to the little they have heard in the Sunday sermon, if they listen to it; to which some occasional readings may be added from time to time.

Nevertheless, even in ordinary life it is difficult to get to know a person just by what you have heard about him, without having dealings with him. It is no different with Our Lord. To this you should add the fact that, in our time, preaching is often of low quality, while good spiritual books are not always readily available to the average Christian.

Zacchaeus wanted to meet Jesus personally, to see Him with his own eyes. It should be emphasized that it is impossible seriously to know the Lord without making His personal acquaintance. It must also be stressed that preaching is in itself insufficient, though it is clear that good preaching will finally bring the listener to prayer.[8] To find what personal acquaintance with the Lord means is the most important discovery of our life. The Samaritans, for instance,

---

[7] Rom 10:17.

[8] The New Testament is filled with exhortations to pray. But today this has disappeared from the horizon of our Christian Pastoral care. The number of priests who think that they must somehow lead their people to prayer, as an essential means for the knowledge of Christ, is rather few. Perhaps the immediate cause of this phenomenon ought to be sought in the fact that prayer is no longer practiced in the private life of the priest.

understood it so, and that is why they noted the difference between what the woman at the well had told them and what they themselves had experienced.[9]

The obstacles

The personal, or first hand, knowledge which Zacchaeus pursued seemed to be impossible. A vast crowd had gathered, and, were that not enough, he was too short. But let us try to understand his problems and transfer them to ours.

First, he was small of stature. Indeed, you cannot doubt that our small moral stature is a very important obstacle to reaching true friendship with the Lord. The Lord is too great and too good, whereas we are too small and too wicked. But in reality this problem is just apparent..., to the extent that there are good will and a serious attempt, on our part, to fight to overcome our spiritual smallness. Zacchaeus made the effort and did not hesitate to climb a sycamore, which implies his exerting some physical effort and transcending some human considerations. But the important thing was to see who the Lord was. We can be certain, on our part, that without that effort to prevail over material and moral obstacles, we will never come to know the Lord personally. Those efforts will not be sufficient; but we can be sure that if we make them, then He will supply the rest; which is exactly what happened to Zacchaeus.

The other obstacle between this man and the Lord was the huge crowd. Thus it happens in the same way now: for the man who earnestly wishes to know the Lord also finds many things which get

---

[9]Jn 4:42.

in the way, trying to hide Christ from him. The Church herself, which is the sacrament of salvation, at the same time that she gives Christ to him, hides Christ from him. Really, it is impossible to find the Lord without the Church, that Church which was wanted and founded by Him, and which now is holy and sinful at the same time. Without her He is never there. But we cannot overlook the grave barriers which she herself may erect, and which in fact she places all too often.

We referred before to the mediocre preaching in our time. But we can also talk about the frequent practice of reducing religion to politics; and, in connection with that, about the pulling of strings and fickleness of so many Pastors. Politics and opportunism are damaging the Church very badly. We may also mention here the inferiority complex before the modern world which has overtaken so many clergymen, and which, at base, has been caused by a crisis of faith. It would be much more painful to talk about the crisis of authority and obedience, the abandonment of responsibilities, the moral, spiritual and cultural misery of the clergy, the bursting of Marxism and Protestantism into Catholic doctrine with the complicity of sheer passivity on the part of the Shepherds, the scattering of religious and priests, the secularization of what is religious and the clericalization of what is secular...

"He climbed a sycamore tree to catch a glimpse of Jesus"

Nevertheless, all those things, and many more, may and must be surpassed. Zacchaeus did what he had to: he climbed higher, to be above the crowd. It did not occur to him to start kicking his way through the people.

You ought to love the Church as Jesus did; and in order to do that you must overcome her defects by placing yourself above them. Because to wage a war against the Church, even under pretext of reforming her, does not lead to anything good. Before the evident miseries of the Church we can follow no other path than to love her, carrying those miseries upon our own shoulders (Mt 8:17; Is 53:4) and suffering for them; as the Lord did, in which He was seconded by the Apostles (Col 1:24).

The miseries of the Church and of the world only can be redeemed if they are assumed by someone.[10] Christ did it once and forever, but with a redemption which has to be continued now and completed by Christians (Col 1:24). To assume means here to embrace human misery from its root, from inside and from the bottom, to suffer it in one's own flesh; the true apostleship abides more in personal suffering than in accusation. The Lord begins his public ministry by accepting John's baptism in the Jordan,[11] that is to say, mingling with those crowds of people who acknowledge themselves sinners and prepare to receive the Kingdom of Heaven which is close at hand. It is true that the Lord was the Just whom nobody could convict of sin (Jn 8:46); but by wishing to be baptized by John, He took upon Himself the condition of sinner, without being one, and became one among many, "He was reckoned among the wicked"[12] and, furthermore, "He bore the sins of many."[13] The epilogue of

---

[10] "Quod non est assumptus non est sanatus." *S. Th.*, III^a, 5, 4, where Saint Thomas quotes Saint John Damascenus: "Quod enim inassumptibile est, incurabile est."

[11] Cf. Acts 1: 21–22.

[12] Mk 15:28.

[13] Is 53: 11–12.

his public ministry was similar: to be judged as guilty and crucified between two thieves. Ever since, possibility of redemption from sin does not exist except through the death of the apostle (Heb 9:22; Jn 12:24). Therefore, attempts of redemption which try to follow a different way arouse suspicions. Prophetic accusations which point at others as the guilty ones, at the Church, at institutions, at the system, would be false were they not accompanied by death to himself on the part of the accuser and by a clear conscience of his own sins: "I thank you, God, that I am not... like everyone else."[14] The true prophet is ashamed of himself and filled with compassion towards others when he accuses, because he is aware of his limitations (Jer 1:6). The real prophet must do violence to himself in order to realize a mission which he never assigned himself, because he knows that the mission will lead him always to death. If the Just took on the condition of sinner without being one, nobody can claim the condition of redeemer without having a clear conscience that he is a sinner. When this is forgotten, it is no longer the Spirit who speaks there (Jer 14: 14–15); consequently, the listeners are exposed to the greatest deceits. To deem Jesus Christ's baptism in the Jordan as a mere act of humility with only pedagogic intentions is not to understand the profound meaning of the kenosis: we are not dealing here with a lesson in humility, but with the assumption upon oneself of the deepest human misery, sin. Christ shows himself as a sinner before the crowd at the Jordan, and He dies on the cross as a sinner. But we should not think that it is a phenomenological appearance without any base in reality; that would mean falling into Docetism. It is true that the Person of the Word is Holy with essential holiness, as well as it is true that His Humanity possesses a certain plenitude of holiness because of the hypostatic union. But

---

[14] Lk 18:11.

Christ is Head of the Mystical Body too, and He not only took a human body and soul but He also united Himself with the all Humanity, a Humanity which is completely under sin. Christ being the new Adam (Rom 5:14), Head of the new creation and Head of the Body which is the Church, the sin of humanity is His; it belongs to Him as his own, though He did not commit it personally. That is why the agony in the Garden or the abandonment on the cross is something more than mere words. The author of the Letter to the Hebrews notices that Christ was put to the test in all things exactly in the same way as we are, apart from sin;[15] but he goes on to say, "Every high priest... is appointed... to offer gifts and sacrifices for sins... because he too is subject to the limitations of weakness. That is why he has to make sin offerings for himself as well as for the people."[16] Now, it seems that the author does not distinguish between Christ and a merely human high priest, for two verses below and without changing the subject he adds, "And so it was not Christ who gave himself the glory of becoming high priest..."[17] The

---

[15] Heb 4:15.

[16] Heb 5: 1–3.

[17] Heb 5:5. Surely we cannot say that Christ became a sinner for our sake in the same way we can say that He became obedient (Phil 2:8) or that He, being rich, became poor (2 Cor 8:9). Saint Peter, for instance, says that "The Just died for the unjust" (1 Pet 3:18). Saint Paul says that Christ for our sake "was made a victim for sin" (2 Cor 5:21), not that he became sinner. But insofar as we give real value to texts like Rom 6:6, "Our former self was crucified with him, so that the self which belonged to sin should be destroyed," or Rom 8:3, "...sending his own Son in the same human nature as any sinner to be a sacrifice for sin, condemning sin in that human nature"; and, above all and as definitive, the text of 2 Cor 5:21, "For our sake he made the sinless one a victim for sin, so that in him we might become the uprightness of God"; to the extent we give real value to the marriage of the Word with Humanity and the assumption of the members of the Church as members of His own Body, in that same measure we will be able to understand the reality and depth of the kenosis.

Baptist's resistance to baptizing the Lord in the Jordan (Mt 3:14) is our resistance to understanding the profound significance of the kenosis; a resistance or stumbling block which the Lord took good care to warn the Baptist about (Mt 11:6; Lk 7:23).

In the face of the misery of the Church it has to be firmly said that this misery may and must be denounced by any member of the Church, whether he belongs to the Hierarchy or not, in whatever way is most convenient to each one's condition. But that denunciation will only be legitimate and valid if the sin of the Church and the world has been assumed by the person who makes it. If not, the critique will be useless and dishonest.

This assumption supposes, first, that we experience with Christ anguish for the sin of the world (Mt 26: 37–38). Secondly, it implies an earnest fight in order to die to sin and to oneself (Rom 6: 2–4), which includes total obedience to the Church. As far as all that is said above is real for the Christian, his critique will be just and efficient. Because the apostle cannot pretend to follow a different way from that of his Master, Whose apostleship, life and death he shares: He is not only the starting point and the end of the way (Rev 1:8 passim), He is also the Way Itself (Jn 14:6). But Christ took upon Himself the sin of the Church and of the world, which is exactly what the disciple will have to do since it is enough for him to be like his Teacher (Mt 10: 24–25).[18]

But all these things are far from what happens with certain kinds of critique which nowadays take place in the Church.

Such critiques are not urged by the anguish of sin. No, for in those quarters sin has been banished from sight within the human

---

[18]We should note that, according to the Lord, no disciple is above his Master. Accordingly, the Christian who commiserates in Christ or suffers with Christ is certainly a sinner, but does not take up sin more than does his Lord.

horizon. Truly enough, today's Church feels in anguish, but we are dealing here with another kind of anguish: sociological anguish,[19] or perhaps an inferiority complex, the anguish of not being late.[20]

If what we have said is true, it is improbable that we shall find a serious attempt to die to sin. Because that dying would require prayer, personal asceticism and, in regard to the problem we are concerned with, the firm will to love and to obey the Church. But prayer has disappeared from the horizontal vision Christianity offers today, and personal asceticism finds no room within a new morality demolishing of taboos and repression. We have obedience to the Church but only in those matters in which each individual decides that she must be obeyed. It seems no longer a matter of going to the world to proclaim the Good News to it, but, as Jacques Ellul says, to tell the world that what it is doing is well done. And so, the Church is in tow to the world. Therefore, preaching is not done with happiness, but with complexes, when preachers are hanging on what the world wants; it is preaching done also with anger when ad-

---

[19]"The Church, fully aware of her extreme misery, of her deficiency, unable to remain living in uncertainty because she no longer finds in herself the reference to the Strong of Israel, feels the necessity of clinging to the world. She feels an urgency to be confirmed by the approval of society, trying to find her strength in number, in the multitude, finding only one way to achieve it: to attempt to justify the world, to give the world reasons in order to make it believe that what it does is good and just. Lost in herself, the Church strives to witness, in the midst of a powerful yet insecure world about what it pursues, that in which she does not believe any more. She becomes the blind guiding the blind." Jacques Ellul, *op. cit.* These undoubtedly hard words should be read within the context of the whole book which, all in all, we believe is objective and filled with love for the Church.

[20]For the banquet of the world, not the banquet of the Lord.

dressing the Christian who resists accepting the new Christianity.[21] About pretentious denunciations in behalf of social justice, fostering the struggle among classes, it should be said that they belong to the most vulgar conservatism; they spring, indeed, from a certain desire of not losing what is thought to be the train of History and of continuing in control of certain systems of power.

Once we have reached this point, we have to admit that we are criticizing the critique, precisely when we have just said that no critique is efficient or honest if it does not share Christ's feelings (Phil 2:5). Do we perhaps share them? We can only say that we would like to have them and that we suffer when we see the situation of our Church, with a suffering which is, at the same time, deep and quiet, filled with hope and nostalgia for that Kingdom where there will be no opportunist politics, nor unfair play, nor a forgetting of the upright, nor disloyalty, nor any sin. As the Book of Revelation has put it so beautifully, 'He will wipe away all tears from their eyes; there will be no more death, and no more mourning or sadness or pain. The world of the past has gone.'[22] The Apocalypse is a book full of hope which was written for very hard times, and who knows? Perhaps in years to come it may become all too real. Although we have to truly confess that we cannot stone that Sinner, for who would dare to cast the first stone (Jn 8:7), she being a sinner because

---

[21]Christianity is a joyful proclamation of Good News. From the announcement of the angels to the shepherds, passing through the Beatitudes and Saint Paul, to the Book of Revelation, we see that happiness is of the essence of the Christian message; it is not necessary to pile up texts to confirm it. Cf. N. Beaupere, *Saint Paul et la joie*, (Paris, 1973). Zacchaeus himself welcomes the Lord "joyfully." Even the dogma about Hell is but the other side of that joyful proclamation: Hell is the fact of the real possibility of losing that joy, but it does not overshadow the happiness of the Christian, who knows that everything has been desired by God who is Love.

[22]Rev 21:4.

we are all sinners? The Lord did not condemn that woman caught in adultery although He was entitled to do so. On the contrary, He saved her life and cleansed her from her sins (Jn 8:11).

We have to be willing to do as Zacchaeus did: to pass over obstacles in order to be able to see things from above, from the stand-point furnished by faith and love of the Church.

"Jesus looked up..."

And both stared at each other for the first time. That encounter would have been impossible, if will of overcoming obstacles had not existed. That occasion was, surely, unforgettable for Zacchaeus, because the first time we find the Lord is always unforgettable. The first gaze of God–made–Man remains in the memory and provides a lifelong strength. So it happened to Saint Paul on his way to Damascus,[23] and to John and Andrew when they first found Jesus, a certain day, "about the tenth hour."[24] The Lord's gaze, if we will it so, has power to change the bearing of our life. We men always look inward in order to receive and count the poor stock of our assets, compelled as we are by our need and our deficiency; but Jesus always looked outward, to give, moved by the plenitude of His Being. That is why the look of men leaves us empty, whereas the Lord's gaze fills us, for it flows from the One Who is Plenitude Itself, from which plenitude we all receive (Jn 1:16).

---

[23]"He appeared to me too" (1 Cor 15:8).
[24]Jn 1:39.

IV

THE RESURRECTION OF THE YOUNG MAN OF NAIN

It happened that soon afterwards he went to a town called Nain, accompanied by his disciples and a great number of people. Now when he was near the gate of the town there was a dead man being carried out, the only son of his mother, and she was a widow. And a considerable number of the towns people was with her. When the Lord saw her he felt sorry for her and said to her, "Don't cry." Then he went up and touched the bier and the bearers stood still, and he said, "Young man, I tell you: get up." And the dead man sat up and began to talk, and Jesús gave him to his mother.

(Lk 7: 11–15)

They were carrying a young man to his grave, the only son of his mother; she was a widow, and the procession was formed by a large crowd. There were the mother, relatives, friends and neighbors, flute and zither players and moaning women. In one word, the whole village, probably not too large. We all know how it is in little villages: everybody is related or knows each other. There the real pain of the mother blended with the pretended one of the moaning women, and with the desire to fulfill one's obligation on the part of most of the villagers.

At the front of the procession, carried by some, was the corpse of the young man. Would it be too much to see in this corpse the figure of the youth of today? Certainly, many will not want to admit it, but the real truth is that today youth is lost to the Church and is dead to God. Saying this, we will be shocking, and many will accuse us of pessimism, bitterness, defeatism and of living contrary to the modern world. That will happen, but they will know that they are lying. Though they do not want to admit it because they are afraid, they need be on the side of the world so that they may go on living according to their whims.

That is why they spend time flattering and justifying youth, adapting themselves, at the same time, to the fashions and customs of the young, and talking about what they think young people are interested in. They wander in life begging to be accepted by youth, without courage to proclaim their faith, even disowning it, and without daring to confess that they do not believe any more. They put on airs of reformers and advanced thinkers; for they know that they would not be accepted with their true renegade faces.

This is the great truth: that youth, highly indulged and flattered by politicians, new leftist Catholics, clever clergymen, opportunist Shepherds and merchants who know their craft, are dead. It is a very well dressed and perfumed corpse, yet a corpse. If this provokes indignation, we shall remember the old story: they can say what they want, but I say that the king has no clothes on, for that is what I am seeing.

One cannot say that the youth of today are better because they rebel or carry an anxiety which previous generations did not know. Those are adulatory and easy phrases. It is only in the gospel that we can find true rebelliousness and real novelty; but most of modern youth do not know the gospel. As for their social anxieties, one could believe in them if one could see young people working and practicing sacrifice and poverty. On the contrary, one sees them idle, challenging a consumer society of which they are the first customers, wreckers without spare parts, nor with anything new to substitute. They take refuge in a gregarious Marxism, or in sex, or in drugs, or in all of it at the same time, thus suffering the anguish of a spiritual emptiness which grows more and more.

For all that, the grown–ups should be blamed, especially the conventional Christians, the clerical establishment, and, in general, the complacent middle–class Catholicism. No doubt we are hitting the target. But we cannot deny that youngsters have also compromised their freedom and, therefore, are responsible for themselves.

For many, today's young people are neither better nor worse than those of yesterday, though more sincere and authentic. But this new cliché cannot stand up to an analysis of the terms authenticity and sincerity. Nor does the gravity of hypocrisy take away any of the cynicism or spiritual emptiness which is willfully sought out and lived for.

Sometimes it is said that they want to tear down so as to build a better world. But then it should be asked where the materials for the new construction can be found; because, so far, only destructive devices have been shown.[1] And if it is Marxist ideology that is pretended to be brought forward as a new element, then we are about to see the world transformed into a termite nest: the singular and personal reduced to a number on the lapel of the uniform.

The dead young man of Nain was accompanied by a great multitude. As it happens most of the time, some were there just for profit, like the musicians and the moaning women, whereas others escorted the corpse out of a friendship or a kinship which put them under obligation to the mother. In that way some earned some money and others met their social obligations. Man has always profited from everything, even from that which is mournful.

It happens the same way with a great part of modern youth, away from God, marching like corpses toward the tomb, unaware of the new man who was given to us in Christ. It is accompanied by a big cortege of opportunist rogues very interested in fattening their businesses. They fill the air with their shouts and the sound of their flutes, but actually they do not feel any suffering. Some hound the youngsters, stirring them up to protest, in order to sell them their consumer products: songs, records, cassettes, music (Jesus Christ Himself has been reduced to a consumer product, with a *Nihil obstat* too), good luck charms, glass beads, garments, with many millions of

---

[1] "Les valeurs de l'humanisme ne sont plus reçues comme autrefois. Souvent, elles sont contestées; plus souvent encore, elles n'intéressent même pas. Est-ce le signe que d'autres valeurs se préparent? Peut-être, mais, pour le moment, c'est la negation qui domine: 'Pour la première fois dans l'histoire, une génération débouche dans l'existence sans référence aux valeurs' (A. Malraux)." Cf. lecture delivered by J. M. Domenach, director of *Esprit* in the Third Symposium of European Bishops, *La Documentation Catholique*, 58 (1976), pp. 80–83.

dollars at stake. Others sell them sex: women's liberation, knocking down of taboos, authenticity, naturalness, spontaneity, street theatre, intimate (bedroom) cinema and a flood of literature of a similar kind, with another stream of millions to earn for very little effort. There are also others who make them instruments of political purposes: here the propaganda is made up of a great number of commonplaces like freedom, democracy, social justice, socialism, sharing, the struggle of the proletariat, etc., without omitting to spice it with the needed amount of sex so that everything looks good. There are also those who join the procession in order to keep the status they enjoy. Here we could include a number of people: politicians who recently changed sides, the wealthy who have felt attracted to socialist ideas, and certain opportunist clergymen. All of them are escorting a youth which is dead; even though its death causes noise, merrymaking, life, business and satisfied merchants. And so it has always happened with real funerals as well.

In the midst of that turmoil the mother was the only one who accompanied the corpse of the young man with real pain. For her sake the Lord had pity, and because of her the young man was restored to life. In our modern world, we see a great number of people concerned with the *youth problem*. They suffocate us with an outpouring of studies, essays, surveys and wordy speeches. But we should ask ourselves: how many are really suffering for the young? And sure enough, it is not the scientific analysis, nor the brilliant essays that are going to raise up those young men and women; only the Lord Who will be determined to do it upon contemplating the pain of those who truly suffer with the problem. But in Nain there was only one person like that among the multitude.

"He felt sorry for her"

If there were truly compassionate people today, the Lord would also have pity on our youth, just as He did with the dead young man of Nain. The Lord becomes compassionate very easily. Really, He came for that, to suffer–with us. Let us remember the episode of the woman Saint John tells us about,[2] who was hurled at the Lord's feet to be judged by Him because she had been caught in adultery. They wanted to get rid of Jesus and her at the same time; justice can be invoked as a pretext to destroy both the upright and the poor. But the Lord had pity on her and, at the same time, unmasked the hypocrisy of those who considered themselves just:

> "Woman, where are they? Has no one condemned you?"
>
> "No one, Lord."
>
> "Neither will I condemn you. Go your way, and from now on sin no more."

He also had pity on the woman who, because of her generosity, caused murmurs among the right–thinking,[3] in this case those who think that what is given to God is taken from the poor. They pretend to accuse God under the pretext of justice for the oppressed. To the eyes of some present at the meal, that woman had not understood that love must be *horizontal* and that it cannot be wasted on God when it is needed by the suffering of men. But the truth is that love is neither horizontal nor vertical, but circular, which is to say comprehensive: it includes everything without excluding anything (1 Cor 13:7); neither God nor men, nor any particular man; and if

---

[2] Jn 8: 1–11.
[3] Mt 26: 6–13; Mk 14: 3–9; Jn 12: 1–8.

it excludes it is no longer love. That is why the Lord felt sorry for her and saved her from ridicule, saying the truth at the same time,

> "Leave her alone. Why are you upsetting her? What she has done for me is indeed a good work! You have the poor with you always, and you can be kind to them whenever you wish, but you will not always have me. She has done what she could: she has anointed my body beforehand for its burial."

The Lord also pitied that crowd which was following him for several days without being able to eat,

> "I feel sorry for all these people; they have been with me for three days now and have nothing to eat."[4]

The Lord's compassion seems to have reached its limit at the death of his friend Lazarus.[5] He wept before the tomb, where He had already arrived very moved and troubled,

> Jesus said, "Take the stone away."
>
> Martha, the dead man's sister, said to him, "Lord, by now he will smell; this is the fourth day since he died."
>
> Jesus replied, "Have I not told you that if you believe you will see the glory of God?"
>
> So they took the stone away. Then Jesus lifted up his eyes and said: "Father, I thank you for hearing my prayer. I myself knew that you hear me always, but I speak for the sake of all these who are standing around me, so that

---

[4] Mt 15:32.
[5] Jn 11:33 seq.

> they may believe it was you who sent me." When he had
> said this, he cried in a loud voice, "Lazarus, come out!"

Saint Paul exhorted us to have the mind of the Lord, to 'make your own the mind of Christ Jesus.'[6] It is necessary that we have pity on those young people who have died because they have drifted away from God or perhaps because they did not know how to reach Him. But we should analyze the nature of our feelings: do we belong to those who escort the corpse just to prosper, or to look good; or do we belong to the curious and indifferent crowd which looks at the corpse passing by; or do we truly suffer? And even in the latter case we should ask ourselves how or to what extent. If ours is a real suffering, it will lead us to think and to keep alive our worries over the youth; it will compel us to be better and we will shed tears. Besides, those sufferings will appear always in our prayers, moving us to importune the Lord constantly; and the plea will give earnestness and weight to our prayer life as we cry, persist, groan, weep and sigh (Heb 5:7). Then our prayer may be tormented or difficult, but never cool or indifferent. Real suffering will force us to bring up the theme of our works and sacrifices for young people; first of all, the faithful accomplishment of our professional duty; then we shall have to think about how much time we dedicate to work and how much time to rest, and also how far we are willing to go in relinquishing our money, health, future, independence, happiness, honor and even our own life.

Political commitment, often Marxist, is nowadays frequently offered as an ideal to youths who live deceived. But if we ask many young people how those commitments take shape for them, they will answer with some more or less blurred ideas about the class struggle; with commonplaces such as the alliance between the Church

---

[6]Phil 2:5.

and the middle class; and with a few badly learned theories that pretend to be scientific. With such things, they justify what they call liberation, an idea which, in reality, has no content in their lives.[7]

"And he went up and touched the stretcher"

The Lord comes near and touches the stretcher. That youth who has died to supernatural life will not rise unless the Lord approaches and gets in touch with it. Both things: that the Lord approach and get in touch. Without that, nothing.

What must we do for that to happen? For the Lord to come to close quarters with the world of youth and get in contact with it? Without a doubt we have to think, to work, to pray and to suffer, because the Lord is not going to put a magic remedy into our hands. But something is very clear: the approach will have to be something the Lord does, and He will do it when moved by the true pain of the really compassionate.

The younger generation, by itself and despite all that might be said, will never rise to go toward the Lord. It is a corpse, and corpses do not walk nor take initiatives. The most men can do for them is to escort them with their music and tears, true or pretended, and to organize a great din around them, even a *Council of Youth*, if you wish. But the young will still be corpses and aliens to all that, and they will only be present there physically: the organization of the

---

[7]The Christian commitment is a thousand miles away from political commitment. A classic text about Christian commitment, which expresses very well all its radicalism, could be the one of Rom 9:3, 'I should wish to be anathema myself from Christ, for the sake of my brethren."

funeral will be entrusted to others, whatever is talked or done there will be thought by others, and, of course, the very idea of *Council* —or of burial— will always be an initiative of others. When it is over, everyone will leave, and the corpse will still remain there: "My God, how lonely the dead are!"

The Lord will have to come closer and touch the coffin. For that to happen, people will be needed who, like that mother of Nain, are able to weep sincerely, without hidden interests for a young person, or for a young generation which has died.[8]

"The bearers stood still"

It will also be necessary that the bearers of the corpse stop and the clamor cease. This also happened at Jairus' house:

> So they came to the house of the president of the synagogue, and Jesus noticed all the commotion, with people weeping and wailing unrestrainedly. He went and said to them, "Why all this commotion and crying?"[9]

The organizers of the tumult will have to quiet down. That is to say, all the uproar of the merchants, opportunists, those who take advantage of anything in order to prosper, smart and selfish clergymen, opportunist politicians, and the vultures gathered to eat

---

[8]It is understood that the initiative is entirely the Lord's. Also the truly compassionate are roused by Him. But man's freedom, and therefore his cooperation, are not excluded, in the sense that God has decided to answer human good will with His grace; that is why He has really given man freedom, that is to say, the true capacity to choose or to reject.

[9]Mk 5: 38–39.

the corpse (Mt 24:28). The Lord will talk to the corpse, but not to them, because He has nothing to tell them, since they are already judged (Jn 3:18); besides, they would never believe Him, because the corpse, according to them, is dead, and quite dead, and it cannot get up: "But they ridiculed him."[10] In fact He will be heard rather by the corpse than by them, because the voice of the Son of Man can reach even to those whom death has stricken, but never to those voluntarily deaf.

Thus the Lord got closer to the young dead man, but before addressing him He had all the noisy escort stop and be silent. Perhaps He wants to do the same now: before returning life to the younger generation He probably wishes to drive away from it the multitude of selfish and official mourners. Then He gave the boy to his mother. Not to them, but to his mother who was the only one who truly wept over him.

"Young man, I tell you: get up"

Dialogue with a considerable part of the younger generation is impossible nowadays. Because it is not possible to hold a conversation with a corpse. Nevertheless that is not true when it is the Lord who talks, for His voice can be heard even by the dead,

> 'In all truth I tell you, the hour is coming —indeed it is already here— when the dead will hear the voice of the Son of God, and all who hear it will live."[11]

---

[10] Mk 5:40.
[11] Jn 5:25.

The Lord's voice can be heard even beyond death, for not without reason He is the Lord of life and death (Jn 11:25). When the dead do not listen to us it is because we do not use the voice of the Master, but our own. As apostles of the Lord we must never speak with our own voice, but with His. When we talk to the people with our own voice, it always sounds alien. It is not recognized and rather causes withdrawal (Jn 10:5).

The lost generation will only get up if it hears the Lord's voice, and no other voice will do it.

The Lord's expression "I tell you" means something like "in spite of everything." It is the recognition of human impotence before death. Man can never give life to a corpse, and if he talks to that corpse his word will fall into emptiness. But the expression of the Lord carries the will to address the emptiness, the nothing, with the purpose of His word being heard and answered (Is 55:11).

"The dead man sat up and began to talk"

Once he was returned to life, the young man started talking, thus communication with others was resumed. Return to the life of grace is the required condition before any valid dialogue may be established.

"And Jesus gave him to his mother"

He gave him to his mother. For the Lord is the only one who can end the gap between generations. Love and friendship between parents and children, between the old and the young, are only possible with Christ.

Attempts made to pursue other ways end up in failure and have always left the clash between generations still there: the young have still felt misunderstood, considering the adults as reactionary, and adults have kept on thinking that youth was wrong.

The true meeting in Christ between young and old does not rule out tension (Mt 10:35). But we are dealing here with another kind of tension which is even necessary and contemplated in the budget of human pain, always capable of being overcome —though not annulled— by charity.

V

THE BLIND MAN AT BETHSAIDA

They came at Bethsaida, and some people brought to him a blind man whom they begged him to touch. He took the blind man by the hand and led him outside the village. Then, putting spittle on his eyes and laying his hands on him, he asked, "Can you see anything?" The man, who was beginning to see, replied, "I can see people; they look like trees as they walk around." Then he laid his hands on the man's eyes again and he saw clearly; he was cured, and he could see everything plainly and distinctly. And Jesus sent him home, saying, "Do not even go into the village."

(Mk 8: 22–26)

"They came to Bethsaida, and some people brought to him a blind man whom they begged him to touch"

The whole history of all apostleship is condensed in this passage of the Gospel. They brought Him a man; and apostleship is that: to bring people to the Lord. Of course, God does not need us for Him to get in touch with people, but the fact is that He wanted it to be so, and here lies the foundation of any doctrine about apostleship.

Besides, this man who is brought to the Lord is blind. That is why men have to be taken to Him for them to see, because they are blind. He Being the light (Jn 1:9), the one who does not follow Him walks in darkness (Jn 8:12; 12:46; 1 Jn 1:7).

The people who brought the blind man did it so that Jesus might touch him and so that he might get in contact with Jesus, which is the goal of all apostleship.

To achieve such a goal they begged the Lord. For any apostleship is inoperative when not accompanied by prayer.

The blind man was brought to the Lord. As we have already said, that is what apostleship is about. We may suppose that, in order to do so, they first talked to the blind man about the Lord. Actually, the Christian must talk about his Lord. The priest and the layman will do it in different ways. The priest must do it at any time, even when it is not opportune (2 Tim 4:2); in fact he is the man of God, and the people must not seek in him another thing or another theme to talk about; he is the only man in the whole world who can talk about his proper business at any time and under any circumstance, and only in doing so does he prove himself a good professional. On the contrary, should he not do it, he proves his mediocrity. The layman sanctifies himself by achieving worldly works, preaching not being his occupation; nevertheless, he will have to bear witness to the Lord with his word: through his views about people, things, the world and life, and even with direct testimony when required by occasion and circumstances.

The blind man at Bethsaida became convinced, and allowed them to take him to the Lord, surely because they had spoken enthusiastically with him about the Lord. Enthusiasm is essential when it comes to bear witness to the Lord. The people who told the blind man about the Lord were probably convinced that He was the only one who could cure him; perhaps they had even experienced it themselves or in others close to them. Apostleship cannot be carried out if not with enthusiasm, which is to say with great love and great confidence in the Lord. Otherwise people will never be convinced, and that is why so many apostleships fail. On the contrary, the Lord warned us that our lamps must be always burning,[1] and He Himself set His listeners' hearts afire whenever He spoke.[2] It is beyond doubt the Lord's wish that apostleship be done in an audacious, interfering, even violent manner, with the violence and the sweetness of a love which always knows how to respect freedom. Thus, for instance, in the parable of the great banquet, the Master says specifically to the servant, when sending him to look for guests,

---

[1] Lk 12:35.
[2] Lk 24:32; Jn 7:46.

"Go to the open roads and the hedgerows and press people to come in, to make sure my house is full."[3]

That expression "pressing them to come in" belongs to the Lord Himself. Yet if it were used nowadays, it would not fail to shock certain ecumenical people and others. There are many in the Church today who have lost enthusiasm for apostleship, maybe because they have lost the fervor for their faith. These people want to demand from others a neutral attitude regarding the apostolate, as if it were truly evangelical, without taking into account that such an attitude is far from being shared by other Christian faiths and even less by militant atheism.

The tragedy of many priests today is that of having lost fervor for their ministry once they have let go of their interior life. Their attitude is the opposite to that of the first Apostles, who abandoned serving at tables so that they could devote themselves to prayer and to the ministry of the word;[4] whereas there are many today who abandon prayer and priestly ministry to devote themselves to serve at tables.

The attitude they saw in the Lord reminded the first Apostle of the passage from the psalm: "I am eaten up with zeal for your house."[5] This does not seem in accord with the neutral attitude some would like to see in apostleship.

The Christian must talk about the Lord with fervor and joy, with that same enthusiasm with which Andrew brought the news to his brother Simon, or Philip to Nathanael,[6]

---

[3] Lk 14:23. Saint John of the Cross gives the same interpretation to this passage in his work *The Living Flame of Love*, 3, 62.

[4] Acts 6: 2–4.

[5] Ps 69:9, quoted in Jn 2:17.

[6] Jn 1: 41.45–46.

> "We have found the Messiah... we have found him of whom Moses in the Law and the prophets wrote, Jesus son of Joseph, from Nazareth..."

These are words that seem to reach out to us vibrating with joy and filled with enthusiasm. There was no need to repeat them to Simon or to Nathanael; there was something in the expression of the countenance and in the tone of voice of their friends, which filled them with wonder and curiosity, and they were determined to follow their friends at once; which is praiseworthy, for Andrew as well as Philip knew at that moment very little about Jesus, as proved by the fact that they had just met Him and called Him Messiah, but also knew Him as the son of Joseph of Nazareth. Nevertheless something is very clear: both of them had already given Him their hearts.

There the secret for apostleship lies. Neither the rudimentary knowledge of fresh apostles, nor their defects, nor their heedlessness as beginners will matter greatly so long as the surrender of the heart goes first. On the contrary, a pastoral office with more than enough technique, but lacking in love and enthusiasm is to be feared. Nowadays we see an apostleship overly concerned with organizational technique, very often reduced to this: studies, meetings, surveys, conferences, updatings, consultations with the common people, committees and subcommittees. Techniques are deemed to be more important than love. Even preaching itself has become extremely technical: everywhere we have prefabricated homilies in the form of file cards, notebooks, cycles of preaching; or "pastoral letters" with dubious content and timeliness, which the poor priests are frequently told to read at Sunday mass. Certainly, priests should supplement their preaching with theologically serious material. And perhaps it would be convenient that now and then they get together to study some basic ideas upon which homilies may be worked out. But preaching must always be the fruit of prayer, study, and personal suffering; and only after having humbly asked for the grace of understanding the Word so that you may expound it later and reach the listeners' hearts can preaching be achieved. Christian preaching cannot be anything but testimony through which you convey an experience, never the recited reading of a product made by others in laboratories of pastoral alchemy. "We are declaring to you what we have seen and heard,"[7] said the first Apostles. Thus we understand the merry spontaneity in Andrew and Philip's words saying they have found the Lord. But what have certain modern apostles found to announce? Sometimes just social and political anxiety fostered by Marxism; and with it, as almost exclusive viaticum, they pretend to reach a degraded world filled with politics and ideologies; a world that seems to have made its own Feuerbach's idea that politics is the only religion.

That is why it is necessary that the apostle first finds the Lord. It is impossible to talk about Him if one does not put Him into one's own life. Only in that way will Jesus' life be able to appear in our time and through us (2 Cor 4: 10–11).

*　*　*

They begged the Lord to touch the blind man. They took him, indeed, to get him in touch with the Lord, convinced that this was the only remedy. This is the goal all apostleship must pursue: to get people in touch with the Lord. For men to experience the happiness, unsuspected by them until now, of intimacy with the Lord, "We are declaring to you what we have seen and heard..., so that you

---

[7] 1 Jn 1:3.

too share our life..., so that our joy may be complete."[8] Incredible intimacy already announced by the Lord,

> "I shall no longer call you servants, ...I call you friends."[9]

And when He prayed to the Father in the great priestly prayer,

> "May they all be one, just as, Father, you are in me and I am in you, so that they also may be in us... With me in them and you in me, may they be so perfected in unity."[10]

"He took the blind man by the hand..."

The blind man, by letting Jesus lead him, was in a way not blind any more, according to what Jesus said, "Anyone who follows me will not be walking in the dark."[11] That man did not see yet; but he set out on the right road.

They had to walk for a while, and all that time the blind man trusted himself to the Lord. The blind man did not ask any question or put forth any conditions: he just put himself in the hands of the Lord, being led by Him. It is impossible to abandon blindness if we are not ready to follow the Lord wherever He may want to take us, even though if, at the moment, we do not recognize the way nor understand why.

---

[8] 1 Jn 1: 3–4.
[9] Jn 15:15.
[10] Jn 17: 21–23.
[11] Jn 8:12.

"And He led him outside the village"

To be in the midst of too many people and turmoil is not the best circumstance in which to see clearly. The Lord wished to be alone with the blind man. The blindness of the spirit demands silence for its cure, and is in need of peaceful intimacy with the Lord. But if one has reached a certain degree of blindness, then one should manage to achieve a more intense solitude and a deeper silence if one wants to see again clearly. For that, ordinary prayer is not enough; we must get away from our daily tumult and surroundings. We must withdraw and, forgetting about routine works, come to terms with the unique problem, with the Truth Who speaks to us alone in silence,

> A mighty hurricane split the mountains and shattered the rocks before Yahweh. But Yahweh was not in the hurricane. And after the hurricane, an earthquake. But Yahweh was not in the earthquake. And after the earthquake, fire. But Yahweh was not in the fire. And after the fire a light murmuring sound. And when Elijah heard this, he covered his face... Then a voice came to him...[12]

Silence will have to be sought inside no less than outside. Imagination and the capability of thinking can get blocked by the terrible shrillness that comes from outside, at the same time that the pounding and overinformation of the mass media may destroy interior serenity.

---

[12] 1 Kings 19: 11–13.

> "The man, who was beginning to see, replied, 'I can see people; they look like trees as they walk around.' Then he laid his hands on the man's eyes again and he saw clearly; he was cured, and he could see everything plainly and distinctly"

The former blind man started seeing things, but only blurred shapes; the Lord had to act again so that at last he could finally see clearly.

If we meet the Lord and allow Him to guide us, conversion has already taken place. But then a long stage must elapse before we end up seeing things with their distinct contours; that is to say, until we have acquired supernatural criteria. Only when one sees things as God sees them does one know reality as it is. This second stage, in fact, unlike the first which is more or less instantaneous, lasts for a lifetime, and needs as materials from which to develop itself: prayer, study, spiritual direction, patience, tenacity. In fact it requires a lifelong effort to achieve our transformation into Christ.

But one comes to see with great clarity when one looks at things that way, because they are seen as God sees them. An earnest Christian, not even one of average education, comes to judge things with great common sense: after all, the Lord gave thanks to the Father for He had hidden "these things" from the learned and the clever and had revealed them to little children (Mt 11:25). The former blind man at Bethsaida got to see things "plainly and distinctly." Based on this we can think that those who allow the Spirit to guide them end up by seeing things distinctly and in perspective, even things of the future. Some words of the Lord Himself give clear basis for that:

> 'However, when the Spirit of truth comes he will lead you to the complete truth, since he will not be speaking of his own accord, but will say only what he has been told; and he will reveal to you the things to come."[13]

According to this, the Spirit will reveal to us the things to come. Surely we are not dealing here with the charisma of prophecy, but with that sense of knowing and judging justly, about the past as well as the future, which each Christian possesses and which results from having been anointed by the Holy One (1 Jn 2: 20.27). This spirit of discernment is very important in the Christian faith. It is useful to distinguish truth from error, an ability which nowadays is of the greatest importance. Because the fact is that, too frequently, the content of faith is falsely presented. There are many bad shepherds who deceive the simple faithful. Bad shepherds who, in turn, have been deceived through many ways: the development of Marxist philosophy, the crisis of faith, the desertion of so many Christians and what has been called *the treason of the clergy* are daily topics. This defection took place at the precise feasible moment, because a part of the Hierarchy had *lowered its guard.* Some resolutions taken as a result of Vatican II —such as the suppression of the Sacred Congregation of the Holy Office, or of the Index— were understood by some to mean that a door had been opened to doctrinal as well as moral relativism. At the same time, many Shepherds were troubled by a strange complex of permissiveness mixed with an ill–understood concept of freedom. It is possible that a day may come when the Church will have to reconsider dispositions of a disciplinary nature taken at that time. Be that as it may, what is true is that the Church cannot be Mother and Teacher of the truth without pointing out directions and warning about misguided

---

[13] Jn 16:13.

ways. The new Testament assumes that Shepherds have a duty to watch in the strictest sense. And for Shepherds to give enlightening teaching does not seem to be enough, for a governing function will be necessary too. The Shepherds will have to lead the faithful away from dangerous pastures, even with threats and punishments, and nobody may say that this is not the mind of the New Testament. Institutions born with the Council, such as National Conferences of Bishops, later became instruments ripe for manipulation by groups, manipulations which naturally reached, later on, all the faithful. This is not to say that such institutions are harmful or incompetent, but that the Church will have to face the problem of how they may better function. During the Second Vatican Council much was said about limiting papal power and mending the so-called abuses of Vatican I. But perhaps the problem should not have been focused so much upon setting limits as in seeing to it that the various offices of the Church all fulfill their missions with a higher supernatural sense. At any rate, in the Church, an excessive centralism would be as bad as would be the Pope's refusal to act as head, or to exercise his authority. In liturgy, for instance, they have gone from excessive centralism and demands for uniformity to the folkloric: you can hardly attend two masses that are similar to each other, either in ritual or in language; and you don't have to move to another nation or another region; sometimes it is enough to go to two churches in the same city.

* * *

The gradual giving of sight to the blind man is an example of the way Divine instruction works with us. God is teaching us and leading us to Him through a whole life; it could have been no other way, given our natural way of being. Total and instant illumination and transformation does not occur, and one has instead to suffer through pains of giving birth, until Christ is wholly formed in us (Gal 4:19); birth that really continues for an entire lifetime: that is why our birthday is the day of our death, not the day on which we are baptized. We are disciples all our lives (Mt 10:24; Lk 14: 26–27, passim). Therefore, we can never ever abandon the means for our formation, nor ever call ourselves masters (Mt 23:8). The race is ended only when you reach the goal (2 Tim 4:7); only then Christ will have been formed completely in us, and only then, like the blind man at Bethsaida, shall we see distinctly (1 Cor 13:12) without mistaking men for trees, but seeing things as they are, under the light of God and for all eternity. In the meantime, our condition as pilgrims entails patience, without which we never will be able to see realized the plan God has designed for us (Lk 21:19); with it we will endure our own deficiencies and those of our neighbors, temptations, sufferings, and, above all, the waiting. To accept the condition of discipleship forever means also to accept forever prayer, spiritual direction, study, or fraternal correction. To accept for one's whole life the condition of pilgrim, of being a person who has not yet arrived at the goal, is a proof of humility, and finally of love. That means accepting and recognizing oneself as a child, which is an imperative condition if we are to enter into the Kingdom of Heaven (Mt 18:3). In fact, as long as we live we have only walking (Jn 9:4) without ever stopping, rising each time that we fall, so that our falls do not turn themselves into setbacks (Jn 11:9). Only in the evening of our life will we be examined about whether we have accepted our condition as pilgrims, children, and disciples who left room for love (Mt 20:8).

* * *

The Lord was the first man seen by the newly opened eyes of the man who had been blind. Surely he always felt nostalgia for that face, the first one his eyes saw, and which no other would match thereafter. The Lord would be for him the pattern by which to measure everybody according to the first one he had seen. We really start knowing people when we begin to know the Lord; Saint Augustine already warned us about the necessity of knowing the Lord so as to be able to know ourselves and others. The mystery of human being can only be clarified in the light of the mystery of the Man–God.

"And Jesus sent him home"

Jesus sent him home, back among people. Now he will have to work, to live his own life, the one God wanted for him. It is not in God's plans that we open our eyes to the light to keep it for ourselves (Mt 5: 14–16).[14] God sends him to work now, so that he does not forsake that great adventure: each one's life lived in the Lord. Those formerly blind people, now able to see, are not taken away from the world; on the contrary, they are sent back home to their work, to their everyday life, to live among people bearing witness to Him in a struggle that will last until the end. The blind man was brought to the Lord; but from now on he must walk alone, without any guide to release him from the responsibility of his own steps. Among his own and in the midst of the world is where he will now have to shed the light he has received.

---

[14]"Go on your way while you have light" (Jn 12:35).

"Saying, do not even go into the village"

It appears that the Lord did not wish the former blind man to expose the wonder worked in him to the marketplaces of the world. There is too much vain curiosity in the world, willing to see and to hear, but not to believe in the deeds of the Lord.

When he who was blind tries to tell about his experience before a curious multitude of ill faith, they will not believe him; they will tend to look for twisted interpretations and to accept weird explanations, but never what is clear, simple and evident. With that, the one who was blind will waste his time, and even his happiness from having recovered his sight, as men are quite capable of terminating his joy. One will have to be very careful not to expose God's deeds to the voracity of dogs (Mt 7:6; 15:26). Apostleship demands a little bit of good will in those to whom it is addressed; but should that good will be missing, the apostolate should stop, and the apostle go elsewhere (Mt 10:14), with the assurance that there will be no shortage of places to work in before He comes back again (Mt 10:23). The Lord departed from a place when requested to do so.[15] Acting differently would be to waste time and happiness, and even to participate in a scorn for holy things and in the turning of men against the apostle himself and killing him. The Lord clearly warned about this in almost those very words (Mt 7:6).

---

[15] Cf., for instance, Lk 8: 37–39 and parallel passages.

VI

A DAY IN THE LIFE OF THE LORD

And at once on leaving the synagogue, he went with James and John straight to the house of Simon and Andrew. Now Simon's mother-in-law was in bed and feverish, and at once they told him about her. He went in to her, took her by the hand and helped her up. And the fever left and she began to serve them. That evening, after sunset, they brought to him all who were sick and those who were possessed by devils. The whole town came crowding round the door, and he cured many who were sick with diseases of one kind or another; he also drove out many devils, but he would not allow them to speak, because they knew who he was. In the morning, long before dawn, he got up and left the house and went off to a lonely place and prayed there. Simon and his companions set out in search of him and when they found him they said, "Everybody is looking for you." He answered, "Let us go elsewhere, to the neighboring country towns, so that I can proclaim the message there too, because that is why I came." And he went all through Galilee, preaching in their synagogues and driving out devils.

(Mk 1: 29–39)

In this passage of the Gospel according to Saint Mark we can contemplate an entire day filled with the Lord's activities. It is a cycle of approximately twenty-four hours, and we can see in it how the Lord distributes His time and takes care of all His works: He exercises His office of teaching —"And at once on leaving the synagogue..."—; He socializes at His disciples' house —"he went with James and John straight to the house of Simon and Andrew"—; He performs many healings, devotes a great part of His time to prayer —"he went off to a lonely place and prayed there"—; and, of course, also to rest —"long before dawn, he got up." We may say, to begin, that the Lord teaches us to distribute our time in order to avoid idleness, so that we can accomplish all our obligations. "There is a season for everything, a time for every occupation under heaven," said Ecclesiastes.[1] It is true that disorder in scheduling our time is, after all, laziness; as it is also true that it is not enough merely to work all day long; the work must be done well (Mk 7:37).

* * *

The text of the gospel shows us Jesus healing. His healings are of two kinds: some are corporal, whereas others are the castings out of devils.

The Lord, by curing bodily illnesses, shows us His power and that He has delivered us from them. This liberation has just begun, yet is real and effective. First of all, it implies the possibility of

---

[1] Eccles 3:1

living illness in a co–redemptive way. When the Christian shares the death and sufferings of Christ, he finds meaning for his own sorrows, which makes it possible to carry illness not only with acquiescence, but with happiness. Thus sickness becomes a gift from God. It is no longer only a punishment due to sin, but in it and through it the deeds of God are now shown plainly (Jn 9: 1–3). As for the final victory over disease and death, it was gained by the Lord for us through His resurrection, and we will enjoy that victory when our bodies are also glorified into the likeness of His body (Phil 3:21).

The healing of the possessed that appears in this passage and others in the Gospel refers mainly to bodily diseases. Those diseases are the devil's actions in the body of the possessed person, through the organs or faculties, but do not imply a dominion over the spirit. Nevertheless, those cures may remind us of the total victory of the Lord over the illnesses of the spirit, that is to say, over sin. Christ delivered us from sin which had turned us into slaves of the devil. Here liberation is conclusive and brought to completion at once (Rom 6: 10.14; 1 Jn 3:5; 2 Cor 5:21, passim). Contrary to what happens with bodily diseases, guilt is always found in sin and in the moral disorders which follow from it. The Lord wants to set us free from all that right now. And He will do it by casting from us any domination by Satan, any that may cause the smallest disorder. It is up to us to let the Lord cure us in that way. Any moral disorder deprives us of happiness and is, therefore, an obstacle to the development of the spiritual life. Indeed, wherever the Gospel mentions diabolic possession, there sadness, despair and what is dark are present: the Gerasene demoniac who lived in the tombs,[2] a young man whose father was begging Jesus to cure him, was possessed by a spirit which ''takes hold of him, throws him to the ground, and

---

[2] Mk 5:3 and par.

he foams at the mouth and grinds his teeth."[3] Sometimes, a devil makes its victim dumb, isolates him, prevents him from any communication or social interaction with others.[4] Even when an unclean spirit is expelled, it wanders through arid places never finding rest.[5] Therefore, it is important to let God cleanse our heart. We will have lost our happiness and our freedom at the precise moment that any love not encompassed by that love spoken of by the first commandment comes to dwell in our heart.[6] Saint John of the Cross said that appetites not only deprive the soul of the spirit of God, but also exhaust, torment, darken, defile and weaken it.[7] The Lord Himself links happiness to the living of spiritual poverty: "Blessed are the poor in spirit."[8] The saints loved God above all things, that is why they enjoyed happiness as no one else, happiness which is a heritage kept only for them, a token of eternal beatitude and a sign of predestination. Who thinks that holiness can be sad? Our God is a God of happiness: "He is God, not of the dead, but of the living," Jesus said, adding, "You are very much mistaken."[9] That is why Jesus Christ asked the Father in His great farewell prayer that His disciples might share His joy to the full (Jn 17:13), making them, at the same time, a wonderful promise: "And that joy no one shall take from you."[10]

---

[3] Mk 9:18 and par.

[4] Lk 11:14.

[5] Mt 12:43 and par.

[6] "Are you sad? Then consider that there is an obstacle between God and you." J. Escrivá De Balaguer, *The Way*, n. 662.

[7] *The Ascent of Mount Carmel*, 6, 1.

[8] Mt 5:3. Psalm 97:11 reserves happiness for honest hearts.

[9] Mk 12:27.

[10] Jn 16:22. Cf. 15:11.

The passage also tells us about the Lord's prayer: "In the morning, long before dawn, he got up and left the house and went off to a lonely place and prayed there." It is the prayer raised to God long before dawn: "I muse on you in the watches of the night."[11] Prayer is the first undertaking before starting all the others of the day. It is first in time because it is first in importance, even as God is more important than anything else. It is the sacred, still and quiet silence of that beautiful moment of the night which just precedes the day,

La noche sosegada
en par de los levantes de la aurora,[12]

It is a solemn moment in which time seems to pause and God appears close to us. Whoever has not talked to God in such moments will not know what a dialogue of love is. The silence of dawn is majestic, beautiful, suggestive, eloquent; it briefly encloses things in parenthesis, so that we may seclude ourselves within that silence to talk to Love. To parenthesize things does not mean to take away their importance, but to allow us the possibility of turning towards their Author, who is more important and beautiful than all of them. We people easily learn how to talk, but hardly how to remain silent. Nevertheless, God talks better to us in silence. Thus silence becomes resonant, allowing us to listen to a music impossible to be performed on or conveyed through man-made instruments, music that is more quiet, secret and silent the more one tries to explain it to others,

---

[11] Ps 63:7.

[12] Saint John of the Cross, *The Spiritual Canticle*, 15: The tranquil night / At the time of the rising dawn.

> *la música callada*
> *la soledad sonora...*[13]

But if one is capable of hearing that voice and is so generous as to open the door of his heart, then a wonderful thing occurs: friendship and intimacy with God. To fall in love with Love and to be loved by Him: "Look, I am standing at the door, knocking. If one of you hears me calling and opens the door, I will come in and have supper with him and he with me."[14] And we should notice that the Lord does not say, "We will have supper together," but "I will have supper with him and he with me." There is love, offering equality, becoming intimate, making the you-to-you real, giving and receiving everything, erasing differences, leveling obstacles, annulling distances and bringing about reciprocity. Love is beautiful when human, but divine when Love Himself falls in love. It is unbelievable and fascinating for a human: to feel oneself the object of the love of an enamored Love. That is why Saint John of the Cross wrote of

> *La cena que recrea y enamora.*[15]

The Apostles search for the Lord who is praying, and tell Him to go to tend the people, because they all are looking for Him. But the Lord prefers to head for another place: "Let us go elsewhere, to the neighboring country towns, so that I can proclaim the message there too, because that is why I came." Why this attitude in the

---

[13] Saint John of the Cross, *The Spiritual Canticle*, 15: Silent music, / Sounding solitude...

[14] Rev 3:20.

[15] Saint John of the Cross, *The Spiritual Canticle*, 15: The supper that refreshes and deepens love.

Lord? He is within sight of those people who already know Him and longingly search for Him and with whom His success is secure, yet He takes another road. Why?

"Let us go elsewhere." The apostle does not look for success, but to be heard by the largest number of people. He is also a pilgrim, and his destiny cannot be but the wide world: "Go out to the whole world; proclaim the gospel to all creation."[16] "You will be my witnesses not only in Jerusalem but throughout Judea and Samaria, and indeed to the earth's remotest end."[17] He can settle neither heart nor feet in any place: "If they persecute you in one town, take refuge in the next; and if they persecute you in that, take refuge in another. In truth I tell you, you will not have gone the round of the towns of Israel before the Son of man comes."[18] That is why Saint Paul enthusiastically quoted the words of Isaiah, "How beautiful are the feet of the messenger of good news."[19] Because the heart of the apostle is as large as the world, and, as it happened with Saint Teresa of Lisieux, will find no final rest so long as there are people who do not know or love God. It happens the same way in western movies or films: the hero or the shrewd detective, once he has pacified a town or solved a difficult case, moves elsewhere. There remain behind celebrations, a happy people and restored justice. But the hero is gone, for they are waiting for him in another place. "You will not have gone the round of the towns of Israel before the Son of man comes..."[20] Certainly, there is too much to be done, though time is brief (1 Cor 7:29). That is why pretty soon we will have to move elsewhere: because that is why we came.

---

[16] Mk 16:15; cf. Mt 28:19.
[17] Acts 1:8.
[18] Mt 10:23.
[19] Rom 10:15.
[20] Mt 10:23.

VII

PARABLE OF THE TEN VIRGINS

Then the kingdom of Heaven will be like this: Ten virgins took their lamps and went to meet the bridegroom. Five of them were foolish and five were sensible: the foolish ones, though they took their lamps, took no oil with them, whereas the sensible ones took flasks of oil as well as their lamps. The bridegroom was late, and they all grew drowsy and fell asleep. But at midnight there was a cry, "Look! The bridegroom! Go out and meet him." Then all those virgins woke up and trimmed their lamps, and the foolish ones said to the sensible ones, "Give us some of your oil: our lamps are going out." But they replied, "There may not be enough for us and for you; you had better go to those who sell it and buy some for yourselves." They had gone off to buy it when the bridegroom arrived. Those who were ready went in with him to the wedding hall and the door was closed. The other virgins arrived later. "Lord," they said, "Open the door for us." But he replied, "In truth I tell you, I do not know you." So stay awake, because you do not know either the day or the hour.

(Mt 25: 1–13)

To begin a parable saying that "the kingdom of Heaven is like this..." is tantamount to saying that "it happens the same with the kingdom of Heaven as it does with..." It is an analogy between situations from which some moral or principal lesson is drawn along with some secondary ones of great importance as well. In order for us to better understand this parable, it would be convenient to move ourselves in imagination to a wedding of ancient times. The beginning of the parable is solemn and beautiful in itself, "The kingdom of Heaven is like this: Ten virgins took their lamps and went to meet the bridegroom." But we must give two warnings before beginning to comment.

The first is to point out that whatever we are going to say here about the virgins should really be thought of as referring to the bride. The virgins were the retinue, but the transposition is correct, for the Bride of the Lamb is the Church of which we are members. The text itself brings the virgins into the wedding banquet when it says that those who were ready went in with the bridegroom to the wedding. So, in the following considerations, we can see ourselves personified in the virgins as well as being the object of the love of the Groom.

The second ought to make clear that, though the virgins appear in the parable as going to meet the groom, truly speaking the initiative belongs to him. If the virgins walked to meet the groom it is because he had called them and was waiting for them, "No one can come to me unless drawn by the Father who sent me."[1] Merely going out to meet the groom is already in itself a grace (Jn 15:16).

---

[1] Jn 6:44.

The Song of Songs tells us about the Groom's initiative, and puts into his mouth the words with which He is calling the bride:

> *Come then, my beloved,*
> *my lovely one, come.*
> *For see, winter is past,*
> *the rains are over and gone.*
> *Flowers are appearing on the earth.*
> *The season of glad songs has come,*
> *the cooing of the turtledove is heard in our land.*
> *The fig tree is forming its first figs*
> *and the blossoming vines give out their fragrance.*
> *Come then, my beloved,*
> *my lovely one, come.*
> *My dove, hiding in the clefts of the rock,*
> *in the covets of the cliff,*
> *show me your face,*
> *let me hear your voice;*
> *for your voice is sweet,*
> *and your face is lovely.*[2]

The calling, the initiative and the gift of the possibility of answering the call belong to the Groom. But the generosity and the answer are also ours; and it is precisely with these that the parable is going to deal. For although many were called, nonetheless not all answered in the same way (Mt 20:16; 22: 2–14). We will immediately see how the parable is going to classify the virgins according to their generosity in answering the call. Some were sensible, whereas

---

[2]Sg 2: 10–14.

others, on the contrary, were foolish: approximately half and half according to the parable.

"Like this: Ten virgins took their lamps and went to meet the bridegroom"

We ought to start pointing out something very important which could pass unnoticed. The virgins went to meet somebody, but that somebody is, precisely, a Groom.[3] We should not forget this. The one who calls us, whom we go to meet, does it as Groom. Thus the story the parable is going to tell us is a love story. We go out to meet somebody who is calling us; but that calling, as well as the answer, refers to the same thing: to love and to be loved; and not in any way, but as total union in a consummated love: it is a real wedding feast. If we have faith, or rather, if faith possesses us, it is because we have been called and chosen; it is a calling and a choosing of love, and for no other thing. We have been called by Love for love. That is to say, to love Love and to be loved by Him.

Christian life cannot be lukewarm. It is not an attempt to fulfill a minimum or merely to avoid sin. It is not an attempt to be better either, nor even, as it were, to achieve holiness. Christian life is a calling to love and an affirmative answer to love. Prayer, for instance, cannot be reduced to a routine practice; nor to an examination of conscience in which we review our defects; nor a

---

[3]The Vulgate says that they went to meet the bride and the bridegroom. But the bride seems to be an addition to the original. At any rate, the question is of no interest to us. Long after the composition of this meditation, the Neo–Vulgate was published, and the text was actually corrected as follows: The virgins 'exierunt obviam sponso."

working-out of more or less sincere intentions. Prayer is a fight with God (Col 4:12). It is a combat in which those who love each other struggle to give themselves in mutual and total acceptance. It is a combat of hearts and generosities in which we will achieve victory when we have been defeated by the Groom. That is the way Jacob wrestled with the angel, that is to say, God.[4]

Christian life is a fight of love between us and God, a story of bride and Groom: Christian life is a love story. The Song of Songs puts on the bride's lips some words, referring to the groom, which are the key of our relationships with God,

His banner over me is love.[5]

It is a true challenge in which the Lord wants to give Himself to us and hopes to be requited in the same way. Christian life implies a morality and a fidelity, but these always come afterwards and as a consequence; before that, and above all, is love. First comes loving, then, and as a consequence, fidelity and keeping the word we have received from Him (Jn 14:23).

In this combat of love, mediocrity, mere *fulfillment*, stinginess, calculation, measurement, wretchedness and meanness are left in a sorry state. Love loves without measure or it is not love. The Lord

---

[4]Gen 32: 25–32. Cf. M. Molinie, *Le Combat de Jacob*, (Paris, 1967).

[5]Sg 2:4. The reductive interpretation of the Song made by *La Bible de Jérusalem*, (Paris, 1973), p. 946, according to which this book is but a collection of songs celebrating human love in marriage, does not seem acceptable. The allegorical interpretation, also extending to the love between man and God, is held by many. A. Feuillet rejects the restricted interpretation of *La Bible de Jérusalem* in "Jalons pour une meilleure intelligence de L'Apocalypse," *Espirit et Vie*, 85 (1975), p. 220; cf. also by the same author, *Etudes d'Exégèse et de Théologie Biblique (Ancien Testament)*, (Paris, 1975), p. 281ff.

Himself teaches us how our conduct should be and that His reply will depend on our generosity.

> "Give, and there will be gifts for you: a full measure, pressed down, shaken together, and overflowing, will be poured into your lap; because the standard you use will be the standard used for you."[6]

When the Lord tells us to use a "full," "pressed down," "shaken together," and "overflowing" measure (notice the accumulation of adjectives), He is undoubtedly encouraging us to love without measure. It is very important to point out the admonition that He will give Himself to us in the same measure we do: the standard you use will be the standard used for you. Although it is clear that He being greater than we, when He gives Himself away to us, we will receive much more than we give:

> "And everyone who has left houses, brothers, sisters, father, mother, children or land for the sake of my name will receive one hundred times as much, and also inherit eternal life."[7]

Sometimes Christian life becomes monotonous, reduced to a few pious practices which leave the soul cold and indifferent. Prayer can become distressful and dull before it is completely abandoned. Sacrifice in fulfilling one's duties can become unbearable. But all this happens for lack of love, because when we are stingy with God, we hinder Him from being generous toward us. Instead of the relationships between God and us the Song of Songs talks about — relationships of love, gathering of bride and groom, mutual giving

---

[6] Lk 6:38.
[7] Mt 19:29.

and surrender— all is reduced to minimal relationships that could exist between two strangers: "I do not know you," said the Lord to the foolish virgins, who will not be able to go in with Him to the wedding.[8]

Once the Lord complained about our wretchedness in our relationships with Him. They were words addressed to Simon the Pharisee, who invited Jesus to have a meal at his home, but they could fit us as well:

> "You see that woman? I came into your house, and you poured no water over my feet, but she has poured out her tears over my feet and wiped them away with her hair. You gave me no kiss, but she has been covering my feet with kisses since I came in. You did not anoint my head with oil, but she has anointed my feet with ointment."[9]

It is a complaint about love. For the maximum we manage to do, when we do something, is a minimum. Perhaps we even think about being better, but never about loving: "You gave me no kiss..." How suggestive those words are! Simon, the Pharisee, who took Jesus to his house, met a minimum, but only a minimum. His motives, undoubtedly good, for inviting the Lord to his house are unknown to us; but we can be sure that none of them was true love.

The Lord does not want to have mere polite relationships with us, but relationships of love. The One Who comes to meet the virgins does it as a Groom, the same One Who told us: "I shall no longer call you servants, I call you friends";[10] or the One of Whom the Apostle said: "It is no longer I, but Christ living in me.";[11] or

---

[8] Cf. Mt 7:23.
[9] Lk 7: 44–46.
[10] Jn 15:15.
[11] Gal 2:20.

the One about Whom the bride of The Song said: "His banner over me is love."[12]

We Christians get to love God, but only the saints fall in love with Him. That is why, very often, ecclesiastical Curias, institutions, clerical proceedings and speeches present a polite and artificial, as well as sad, air; they lack the light and joy which only the saints can radiate: Saint Paul, Saint Francis of Assisi, Saint Teresa, Saint Francis Xavier... of whom it has been said that they, like Elijah, will have to come a second time; unless God chooses to raise other saints, supposing the world deserved them.

* * *

We have already said that the story of the ten virgins, as the story of any Christian life, is a love story. But it also is a story of joy. For if we have been called to love, it is because we have been called to joy: He Who comes to meet us is the Groom, and He does it as a bridegroom. The Lord has clearly told us,

> "Surely the bridegroom's attendants cannot mourn as long as the bridegroom is still with them?"[13]

The Groom's presence and His intimacy make sadness impossible. Unspeakable and mysterious is the saints' joy! For if it was said, in all truth, that there is but one sadness: not to be a saint; it is true then that there is but one joy: that of holiness. But, because the world, in its search for happiness, is running away from holiness, it condemns itself to perpetual sadness.

---

[12] Sg 2:4.
[13] Mt 9:15.

Christian life is not only an absence of sadness, an impossibility of weeping. That would be something negative, whereas Christian life is complete positiveness. Truly speaking, the presence of the Groom entails happiness, total joy. The Gospel says it also, while speaking through the mouth of the Baptist,

> 'It is the bridegroom who has the bride; and yet the bridegroom's friend, who stands there and listens to him, is filled with joy at the bridegroom's voice. This is the joy I feel, and it is complete."[14]

Christian joy is not the quiet peace of a tranquil conscience. It is an overflowing, stormy, and inebriating joy, and, most of all, a joy which is unutterable by him who possesses it and incomprehensible for those who have never known it.

In married human love there is, at first, the physical–spiritual love of the marriage. Although time changes its character, love between spouses need not diminish, but may, on the contrary, increase. But the love between God and man, which also grows and becomes more pure within the latter, does not change its character: it is always the primeval love of the marriage, the eternal wedding banquet. In marriage spouses see their mutual love increasing, while with the passage of time that love changes in character. In the divine–human wedding, the Bridegroom and the bride always are two lovers; here the passing of time does not change the character of that love *of the first days*. Quite the opposite, for time makes that love grow in depth and novelty: in the divine–human love, each passing day is more the morning following the first meeting of lovers. And because this love does not depend on the flesh in the same way conjugal love does, it always keeps the beauty, the excitement, the tenderness, the

---

[14] Jn 3:29.

joy and the wonder of the love of the two lovers as they were at first: 'Let us be glad and joyful and give glory to God, because this is the time for the marriage of the Lamb. His bride is ready... Blessed are those who are invited to the wedding feast of the Lamb.'[15]

At this point, the theme should be abandoned. For the love between God and man cannot be depicted, except through analogies and approximations which always are deficient. One could say that it is not this or that, or that it is different from human love in certain aspects; but it is impossible to say what that love consists of. Because it was never grasped by our knowledge —which is in need of our senses— there is nothing that appears like it. Because our mind, in this world, has no precise and fitting concepts for it, what God has prepared for those who love Him remains, for the present age, as an incommunicable secret in the heart of those who are His (1 Cor 2:9).

"Five of them were foolish and five were sensible: the foolish ones, though they took their lamps, took no oil with them..."

The virgins answered the Bridegroom's call, but not in the same way. For not all of them were the same: five, indeed, were foolish, and the other five wise. The reason for their foolishness or prudence is given in the gospel immediately afterwards: some brought flasks of oil as well as their lamps; yet others, though they brought their lamps, brought no oil with them. In other words, some worried about what was needed to meet the Bridegroom, whereas others did

---

[15] Rev 19: 7.9.

not do so. It is tantamount to saying that some had a true interest in welcoming Him, but not the others. In other words, some were in love with the Bridegroom, but the others were not. For, though all were equally called, and all arrived together, and all were waiting, not all were in love. The fact that some did not take with them flasks of oil proves it. They did not want to use the necessary means which would have allowed them to meet the Bridegroom.

A lamp cannot burn without oil, and it cannot yield light and warmth without burning. That is why the person in love with God, like a lit lamp, sheds light and warmth around him —light that guides the understanding and warmth that kindles the heart— whereas the one who is not enamored illuminates and warms nobody. The latter is an extinguished lamp that is neither burning nor shedding light because he is not in love. The Lord enthusiastically exhorts us to shine, "In the same way your light must shine in people's sight..."[16] The Apostle beautifully reminds us, "Now you are light in the Lord; behave as children of light."[17] That is why a technical apostleship is a useless task if the apostle is not in love with God: "I have come to bring fire to the earth."[18] The reason for the unrest, more or less conscious, caused among the faithful by certain exhortations, speeches or documents of some shepherds can perhaps be found in the fact that they are as bloated with technicalities as they are lacking in love. Or sometimes they are so worried about the diagnosis of the ailment of the sick that they forget to talk about the Doctor Who could cure it; or they are so anxious to show concern for people that they forget the only love people really need and look for: the love of God. Men are growing tired of shepherds

---

[16] Mt 5:16.
[17] Eph 5:8.
[18] Lk 12:49.

talking only about mere human affairs, and that is why they are searching more and more to be told about God, though they might not admit it.

The absence of God can bring about the greatest void within the apostle, all the more since, according to Saint Augustine, the human heart possesses an endless receptivity. This void will turn the apostle into a creature without hope. If he is a priest, for instance, he will try to stun the people with a great din: he will constantly talk to them about themselves, putting before them their problems and wounds, deepening them even more by so doing. But he will not be able to hide his own emptiness, deepening, at the same time, the void within his brethren. An apostle who has failed in loving is like a schizophrenic, a split being in self-contradiction, who will only bring forth divisions and ruptures. That is why to become an apostle one should meet the challenge of love.

When one deals with the formation of priests, perhaps one should not give so much emphasis to being good at pastoral work, although we do not despise, by any means, their preparation. But it is more important that they succeed in being simple men in love, true apostles able to tell people much about God and to tell God much about people. To truly love people one ought to be in love with God (1 Jn 5:2). Access to the priesthood should be banned to the candidates who have no heart with which to fall in love with Love, right to the very end (Jn 13:1). Were that the case, the fact that they might eventually become good theologians, excellent at pastoral tasks, bright exegetes or renowned preachers should not be an obstacle. The candidates may be men of good heart, interested in improving things; they may be troubled over people's problems, suffering for the poor and oppressed; they may wish to be poor, making a burnt offering of their lives; they may be wise and know the human heart. All such things are good, but will avail them nothing if they do not know how to love (1 Cor 13: 1–3). It would be better, in such cases, to look for humble and simple men who are incapable of looking after their own lives, but very capable of giving them up: men, finally, who know how to fall in love.

"The bridegroom was late, and they all grew drowsy and fell asleep"

This verse makes two facts clear: first, that the bridegroom keeps people waiting. The second is a consequence of the first; the Groom's delay suggests a danger for those who are waiting: tiredness, sleepiness and the possibility of resting content with the present situation and not waiting any more. Let us go into detail.

It ought to be warned, first of all, that the situation suggested by the first part of the verse is necessary, in the present economy of grace. On the other hand, that suggested in the second part is accidental, in the sense that it should not happen. This second situation may happen, and often it does; the first, nevertheless, is bound to happen of necessity.

The delay of the Bridegroom coincides, in a certain way, with the span of our life. We have said *in a certain way* because, as we will see later, the Lord in some manner foreshadows His coming. There is a definitive coming in which the wedding is totally and forever consummated; but there is also an earlier possession of the Bridegroom, in the form of a token or pledge, which occurs during the stage of our earthly pilgrimage. At any rate, in both cases the Bridegroom keeps people waiting. In the meantime the enamored human, because he is in love, believes in the Bridegroom, and because he believes in Him, confidently waits for Him. The time of waiting is always a time to live the three theological virtues.

Let us set aside the reasons for the Bridegroom's delay, and let us rather see what our attitude ought to be during that waiting. It should be one of longing and loving. As the deer yearns for the running waters (Ps 42:2), so the bride is always yearning for the arrival of her Groom, nostalgic because of His absence, with eager desires, craving for a love that can only be contented with the bliss of the Bridegroom's presence; all that is so well expressed by the Illumined Doctor:

> *Iba el Amigo deseando a su Amado,*
> *y se encontró con dos amigos, quienes,*
> *con amor y llanto, se saludaron, se abrazaron*
> *y besaron. Desmayóse el Amigo, pues tan*
> *vivamente le hicieron memoria de su Amado.*[19]

When the Gospel tells us about the delay of the Bridegroom, warning us about the possibility of getting tired and forgetful, it is calling us to think of our situation: How are we waiting for the Bridegroom? Are we even waiting for Him? For in a world which perhaps no longer waits for the Bridegroom, despair, bitterness, sadness, emptiness and lack of love can be a shadow of hell, just as grace is the beginning of heaven. A Christian who is not waiting earnestly is not ready to face a world which seems to have lost all hope.[20] An apostle —with more reason if he happens to be a priest— who does not feel in his heart an overwhelming impatience for his meeting with the Lord will only disconcert his brothers. The Gospel does not even

---

[19] Raimundo Lulio, *Libro del Amigo y del Amado*, p. 59: Wandering was the Friend, longing for his Beloved, / When he met two friends. They with love / And among tears, embraced and kissed. / And the Friend fainted, for they made / So vivid a memory of the Beloved.

[20] Cf. J. Ellul, *op. cit.*, (Paris, 1972).

allow a tranquility born from confidence in the Bridegroom's delay; it is a false and treacherous tranquility that leads those who have it to partake in the fashions and manners of the world. Those are called hypocrites by the Lord (Mt 24: 48–51), because there is no other epithet to be laid on those Christians, that is to say apostles —whether they are lay people or priests— who dare to appear as such in front of their brothers and are not consumed by the yearning for meeting their Lord. Saint Paul said that the prize is only for those who want and long for His coming (2 Tim 4:8). And the Book of Revelation utters through the mouth of the Spirit, the Bride, and of all who want to listen, the same urgent desire, the desire of the Bridegroom's coming:

> 'The Spirit and the Bride say, 'Come!' Let everyone who listens answer, 'Come!'... Amen; come, Lord Jesus."[21]

The virgins of the parable, even the sensible ones, fell asleep. Nevertheless, their attitude should have been that of a longing, waiting and looking for the Bridegroom, as it was for the bride of the Song of Songs:

> *I opened to my love,*
> *but he had turned and gone.*
> *My soul failed at his flight,*
> *I sought but could not find him,*
> *I called, but he did not answer.*
> *The watchmen met me,*
> *those who go on their rounds in the city.*
> *They beat me, they wounded me,*
> *they took my cloak away from me:*
> *those guardians of the ramparts!*[22]

---

[21] Rev 22: 17.20.
[22] Sg 5: 6–7.

And not long before she also says,

> *So I shall get up and go through the city;*
> *in the streets and in the squares,*
> *I shall seek my sweetheart.*
> *I sought but could not find him!*
> *I came upon the watchmen —*
> *those who go in their rounds in the city:*
> *'Have you seen my sweetheart?'*[23]

The search is anxious, eager; the waiting one of craving and nostalgia for that absence. All because the bride is truly in love,

> *I charge you,*
> *daughters of Jerusalem,*
> *if you should find my love,*
> *what are you to tell him?*
> *—That I am sick with love!*[24]

It cannot be just any kind of love, not even a great love, but much more than that: it is a love which kills, with a death caused precisely by the absence of the Beloved. In a world like ours, dying for love is still the most beautiful sort of death; and the only one worthy of man, since the Lord also died on a cross, in love and for love.

* * *

---

[23] Sg 3: 2–3.
[24] Sg 5:8.

But the attitude of an eager waiting and a loving search for the Bridegroom cannot take place if man is not in love with his God. Saint John of the Cross said it beautifully in the first stanza of his *Canticle*:

> *Como el ciervo huiste,*
> *habiéndome herido;*
> *salí tras ti clamando, y eras ido.*[25]

Here the bride goes out beseeching the Bridegroom because she first felt wounded by Him, with the wound of love.

But God never lets anybody down. He always shows Himself to those who lavishly give themselves to Him.

All people have to choose between being for or against God. Some easily acknowledge that they are not self–sufficient, and admit, without shame, their dependence. They are fully aware that they do not thoroughly possess either goodness in itself, beauty in itself or truth in itself, yet rejoice to recognize them wherever they may be found. That is why these people are humble and simplehearted, and do not hesitate to put their trust in Someone Who, somehow, they discover is greater and better than they. They see themselves small and limited, and find their joy in that; for they love truth, and they are like children who have not yet learned how to lie. And let us not forget that the Kingdom of Heaven was said to belong to the children (Mt 18:3).[26] Thus he who does not receive the calling from Love in such a way, shall never fall in love (Mk 10:15), nor shall he ever comprehend the enamoured waiting of those virgins longing

---

[25] Saint John of the Cross, *The Spiritual Canticle*, stanza 1: ...You fled like the stag, / Once you wounded me; / I ran after You beseeching, and You were gone.

[26] Cf. Mt 11:25; Lk 10:21.

for the coming of the Bridegroom. Since Love became a child, only those who are like children will ever get to understand it.

This being so, no one who has not learned humility, or better, how to be a child, should dare approach the priesthood. For one must acknowledge his smallness, so that one has no inconvenience in vanishing and allowing Christ to replace his own life.[27] Nevertheless, becoming like children is something to be achieved only by grown people; a great maturity is thus needed. For this reason some say that one of the causes of the great crisis clergymen are going through lies in the rush to ordain youngsters who are not yet mature.[28]

"But at midnight there was a cry, Look! The bridegroom! Go out and meet him"

The characters of *Waiting for Godot* by Samuel Beckett are waiting for somebody who finally never comes. It seems as if the author wanted to tell us that God may be waited for, but all in vain, because He will never arrive. But it is not true. God always comes, even when He is not expected. The parable of the ten virgins tells us that the Bridegroom finally arrived precisely at midnight, when it seemed He would not arrive and was barely expected. The author of the Letter to the Hebrews said it with great joy, "Only a little

---

[27]"Through that sacrament, priests, by the anointing of the Holy Spirit, are signed with a special character, and so are configured to Christ the Priest in such a way that they are able to act in the person of Christ the Head," Vatican II: *Decree on the ministry and life of priests*, n. 2. In number 6 it is also said: 'Priests exercise the function of Christ as Pastor and Head in proportion to their share of authority...' etc.

[28]L. Bouyer, *La descomposición del catolicismo* (Barcelona, 1969).

while now, a very little while, for come he certainly will before too long";²⁹ whereas the Book of Revelation proclaims it emphatically, 'I am who is, who was, who is to come, the Almighty.'³⁰

God comes at last. For each one, His final coming coincides with the ending of the period of trial. And He arrives, according to the parable, about midnight; at an unexpected and, at first sight, inopportune moment. At midnight seems to mean in the middle of life, or at least in the middle of what we thought our life could have been. It is said that He surprises us at midnight for, when He comes, we shall be always half way into our chores: with our plans, projects and dreams half finished. In fact, our life will be taken away —or stolen, as the Bible appears to express itself— at the hour we least expect (Mt 24: 42–44).³¹

But, as we said above, we can also talk here about a foretaste of His coming, to which the parable undoubtedly refers as well, because, before His final arrival, God reaches us in many ways. We have been called to enjoy His friendship and intimacy, beginning now, though later on these have their fulfillment in the Kingdom. The parable refers to a relationship, already real, already begun, at the same time that we may speak of waiting, delaying, arriving.

Thus the Bridegroom is already on His way, but, according to the parable, will arrive at midnight. Saint John of the Cross, the great master of *The Dark Night of the Soul*, said that midnight is the darkest point of night, equal in distance between the dusk of evening and the dawning light of daybreak. During our earthly pilgrimage, indeed, the Bridegroom comes and makes Himself known in the midst of darkness, in the hour of gloom. The parable presupposes

---

[29] Heb 10:37.
[30] Rev 1:8.
[31] Cf. Mk 13: 32–36, and Lk 21: 34–36.

it so, for the Bridegroom arrives at midnight, and only afterwards the virgins come into the wedding feast. To Saint John of the Cross, the light of faith is dim at the same time, but it is a dimness that can guide man with certainty. In this world, God cannot be for man anything but shadow, but a shadow which is brighter than the most luminous day. God talks to Moses from a cloud, and it is in this same darkness of faith in which God begins to make Himself known to man, and man communicates with Him.[32] In this communion a dialogue of love takes place; a dialogue that for man is both equally clear and dark. And that is so because, this being a dialogue about love whose first origin is always God, the bride *knows* and *feels* that the Bridegroom is there; but, at the same time, because the love the Bridegroom feels towards the bride is something beyond any human concept or feelings, she cannot explain it even to herself. This is the way in which, within the deepest darkness, the brightest light is imparted through feelings and ideas, inexpressible even by those who receive them. More yet, it is a gift of a Life and a Love which rule out any attempt at depiction, not only of their essence, but of their more remote effects also. In the communication of this Love, man, upon receiving it, may feel he has reached the limit of his endurance and is in need of special help from God. For this Love is overwhelming, devouring, encompassing; it wounds without killing, and burns without consuming. Yet, in its tenderness, it never modifies the particularity of the human I. The Apostle explicitly tells

---

[32] The theme of the divine darkness ranks with great importance in the history of Christian Mysticism, in a line which runs principally from Saint Gregory of Nyssa, through Pseudo-Dionysius, to Saint John of the Cross. Cf. for instance, J. Danielou, *Platonisme et Théologie Mystique*, (Paris, 1953), p. 190 ff.

about this divine love for man, and does it using the same terms: overwhelming, consuming, constraining (2 Cor 5:14).³³

* * *

The arrival of the Bridegroom is forcefully expressed. There was a cry. It is something which precedes and heralds the arrival of the Bridegroom. It will be a clamor which will drown out all other noises, usually many in the life of each person, that will fade away before the great clamor caused by the Bridegroom's coming. For man it will be the moment to understand that things did not matter that much, and were not worthy of the excessive attention they had monopolized (Lk 10:41; Mt 16:26).

At midnight there was a cry announcing the Bridegroom's coming. We have already said the Bridegroom speaks from the darkness, and in the darkness of faith, but each time in a louder voice, with more love and a clearer message. A voice which is hidden, secret, intimate, not capable of being rendered into words, dim and bright at the same time, revealing as well as concealing. A voice that both cures and wounds with love, but causing a deeper wound along with the curing; which nourishes and quenches, at the same time causing more hunger; which extinguishes nostalgia, even as it kills with the lack we experience in not having completely overtaken the Beloved. And because it is as much secret and unutterable as it is radiant and clear, it makes one forget all other voices and teachings, rendering them empty (Mt 23:8; Jn 14:26).

---

[33]"Charitas Christi urget nos." The Greek verb συνέχω means in latin *continere*, *constringere*, *impellere*. Cf. Zerwick, *Analysis Philologica Novi Testamenti Græci*, (Rome, 1966). The Latin *urgere* of the Vulgate means to push, to press, to urge, to beset.

Clamor is a term which indicates intensity of degree: whisper, murmur, voice, yelling, clamor. The Bridegroom's voice becomes stronger each time in intensity and clearness; that is to say, in offering love and in requesting reciprocity. In reference to which the psalm says: "Yahweh's voice carves out lightning–shafts... Yahweh's voice convulses the desert... Yahweh's voice is power... Yahweh's voice shatters cedars."[34]

"Then all those wedding attendants woke up... The foolish ones said to the sensible ones, 'Give us some of your oil'... There may be not enough for us and for you"

In view of the Bridegroom's arrival, the virgins got up and trimmed their lamps. It was then that the foolish ones saw, with dismay, they did not have enough oil, and turned to the sensible ones in a desperate plea. It was a heartbreaking plea, but impossible to meet. The answer of the sensible virgins, courteous yet negative, though it may seem selfish, was the only possible one within reasonable limits: we should not forget that the gospel calls them sensible. For, though there is much that we can do for others, Christian life ought to be assumed personally by each of us; in this sense the oil of the lamps is not transferable.

We can, for instance, pray and suffer for others. Prayer of supplication and suffering have an extraordinary importance in the circulation of the supernatural life which takes place in the Mystical Body. All the sin of the world will have to pass through the heart of the Christian, just as through those filters that constantly purify

---

[34] Ps 29.

the water of a container without changing it: it is the compassion in Christ and the shared sense of the horror of sin. Only God knows what a just man can accomplish by doing so. As a matter of fact, the Bible tells us about the dialogue between God and Abraham, in which the Patriarch progressively lowers the number of just people that would be necessary for the forgiveness of Sodom.[35] Abraham stopped at ten, but even for their sake, and surely for the sake of fewer just people had they existed, would God have forgiven the city. The weakness of God, before the love of one righteous person, is as great as His own love. There were no ten just ones in Sodom, nor does it seem that there are many in our world willing to carry on a real plea for others. We talk about an authentic pleading; that which, because it springs from the love and compassion in Christ, is as far from routine and formal as it is close to the prayer of intercession of the Lord (Heb 5:7; cf. Rom 8:26).

Nevertheless, the road of Christian life has to be trodden by each one. Each one should keep his own lamp burning and obtain enough oil to do it. Our personal path cannot be walked by the others. One's own lamp and oil cannot be passed on, least of all when others have willingly disdained any effort to get them. Were one to do it, the attempt would be useless and in vain: "there may not be enough for us and for you," said the sensible virgins to the foolish ones.

It is not a matter of hindering others from suffering, but of teaching them how to suffer. Not even the Lord prevented people who were His own from suffering: for that was not the point. Moreover, taking away suffering, in this world, would be equal to preventing the possibility of sharing it with the Beloved. This would amount not only to ruling out love, for love always wishes to share everything

---

[35] Gen 18:23 seq.

with the beloved person, but also it would end by ruling out happiness, for there is no other font of happiness than Love. Suffering did not disappear with Christ; it has acquired a new sense: suffering is not only compatible with happiness, but an essential ingredient of it as long as we live in this world: "Blessed are those who mourn."[36]

The same thing could be said about parents who do not know how to love their children and try to save them from any sort of hardship. The question is not how to save anyone from hardship, but to teach everyone to find its Christian meaning. On the other hand, hardships have always accompanied human life (Jb 5:7). Solving all the problems for children is not so important as to teach them how to do it.

But, above all, the decision to give oneself up to the Lord should be personal, and no one else can make it for us. The oil of the lamps here is absolutely untransferable. That is why it would be useless to create a Christian environment, no matter how authentic, in which people were raised, but within which the making of personal decisions was not fostered. The whole of Christian education, in whatever area it is developed (family life, parish community, colleges, novitiates, seminaries, associations of the faithful, religious communities, etc.), is exposed to this danger. A collective environment, of fervor more or less deep, could become deceptive were educators to forget that Christian life is, in all truth, something that may only be established upon personal decisions.

---

[36] Mt 5:5; Lk 6: 21–23.

They had gone off to buy it when the bridegroom arrived. Those who were ready went in with him to the wedding hall and the door was closed"

This passage harbors three ideas: the Bridegroom comes at an inopportune moment; the door was closed for the virgins who were not ready, and they could not enter into the wedding; and, finally, the virgins who were prepared went in with the Bridegroom to the wedding hall.

It is true that the Bridegroom always arrives at an unforeseen moment. There is here a warning that is, perhaps, the most important message the parable wants to convey, at least from a certain practical standpoint. The fact that the arrival of the Bridegroom is unforeseen renders it inopportune, which happens when those who should be waiting have not done it properly.

One ought to note, nevertheless, that in this case the inopportuneness cannot be attributed to the one who comes, but to those who were waiting; because they waited in the wrong way; or worse, because they did not wait at all and, therefore, were not ready. And they did not wait because they did not love, and perhaps because they were not yet entirely convinced that the Bridegroom would arrive, or at least forgot about it. For the wise virgins, the arrival of the Bridegroom was not inopportune; dreadfully delayed perhaps, because they were longing for His coming.

The arrival of the Bridegroom was inopportune for the foolish ones. First, because, when He came, they were not in the place they were supposed to be: they went off to the shop looking for oil. We should remember here how important it is that when the Bridegroom comes, He finds each of us where we ought to be; in other words, in the state, condition or even place He wants us, and in which He expects to find us upon His coming. Secondly, the arrival of the Bridegroom was inopportune for these virgins because, at that precise moment, He did not find them doing what they were supposed to be doing. They were doing some *other thing*, undoubtedly good, but not the proper thing for them, or at least it was something that should have been done at another time. His inopportune arrival caused these virgins to try to recover lost time, but without success.

For those not ready the door is closed, for it is not possible to enter with the Bridegroom into the intimacy of the wedding banquet if one is not prepared, that is to say, if one has not died unto himself, since love ends up in the loss of one's own life in order to live the Beloved's life (Gal 2:20). The intimacy of the mutual nuptial surrender cannot exist without a communion of lives, or if the lives of those who should have been, reciprocally, lover and beloved are estranged. That is why, the two following verses, which close the parable, contain the unappealing judgement of the one who should have been the groom, 'I do not know you.'[37]

* * *

And the virgins who were ready went in with the Bridegroom to the wedding. We have already emphasized the fact that this parable told us a love story. It is now that the mutual surrender of the Bridegroom and the bride is consummated. The book of The Song of Songs puts it like this:

---

[37] Cf. Mt 7:23; Lk 13:25.

> *I belong to my love,*
> *and his desire is for me.*
> *Come, my love,*
> *let us go to the fields.*
> *We will spend the night in the villages,*
> *and in the early morning we will go to the vineyards.*
> *We will see if the vines are budding,*
> *if their blossoms are opening,*
> *if the pomegranate trees are in flower.*
> *Then I shall give you*
> *the gift of my love.*
> *The mandrakes yield their fragrance,*
> *the more exquisite fruits are at our doors;*
> *the new as well as the old,*
> *I have stored them for you, my love.*[38]

The bride speaks in these verses, and, in the first lines, makes two statements, as passionate as incredible. The first is,

> *I belong to my love.*

It is a confession of the complete surrender and belonging to the Bridegroom. Surrender which encompasses all that the person of the bride is, body and soul, and the latter with all its faculties: thoughts, imaginations, memories and volitions, everything. For how could anything else be left in us which does not belong to the Bridegroom? Many times, during the day, our thoughts, our imagination and our wishes wander about, busy with many things, when not all of them

---

[38] Sg 7: 11–14.

are about the Bridegroom and for the Bridegroom. We are missing our perfect joy right now, so long as we are pilgrims. To live occupied all day long with the Bridegroom — our mind as well as our heart— is to live all day long in Love (1 Jn 4:16), which means to live all day long in Joy. To think all that as impossible for man, would be to assume that we know how far extends the love of that ocean without shores, which we call God.

But the self-giving of the bride to the Beloved implies the self-giving of the Beloved to the bride in return. Twice it has already been said by the bride in the Song, and both times so as to indicate a perfect reciprocity, "I belong to my love, and my love to me,"[39] and above, "My love is mine and I am his,"[40] perfect possession, mutual surrender. It is the Love of the Father toward the Son and of the Son for His Father, which has been extended to the creature, and now dwells and is consummated there: God in the heart of His creature, the creature in the heart of his God (Jn 17: 21.23.26; 14:20; 2 Pet 1:4).[41] That is why the bride, referring to the Bridegroom, adds in the second verse,

And his desire is for me.

The love of God for man, and more for those who give themselves to God, is extremely different from an abstract and impersonal love regardless how great we affirm this latter to be. It is a particular one, addressed to me, of endless tenderness and intensity, with all its desire. It is a love in which I am wholly desired, that is to say, my complete person, as it is, with a love which comprehends all of

---

[39] Sg 6:3.
[40] Sg 2:16.
[41] Cf. P. Aubin, *Dieu: Père, Fils, Esprit*, (Paris, 1975), p. 57ff.

me; I am loved and desired by God as a whole, infinitely, to the end (Jn 13:1).

To say that all the desires of the Bridegroom are for me is to say something hard to believe: that God has fallen in love with me. And let us note that the expression must be used in all its senses of beauty, goodness, grandeur, and joy: everything implied in that expression when it refers to human love. We should keep in mind, at the same time, that if words are always insufficient, here they are more so than ever: for human love is but a participation, although from a distance, in the divine love.

The assertion that God has fallen in love with me is so hard to believe that it has to be an object of faith: "We have put our faith in the love God has for us," said Saint John.[42] And this is so, not only in the general sense of that fact, but also, and more properly, in the personal and experiential domain: God, being Who He is, is in love with me, being what I am and how I am. God loves me, desires me, longs for me, needs me, looks for me, waits for me, gives Himself to me, belongs to me and I belong to Him; and He tells it to me, and wants to hear it from my lips. But, above all, He wishes my belief in all this, in His love, so that when I experience it I accept it to be true, for He can make it possible, although I, with my faith, may have to make up for what seems incredible and unspeakable, thus opening myself totally to His love.

"We have put our faith in the love God has for us..." Perhaps this is the real sin of men, that they have not believed in His love. For there will be many ready to believe the mysteries of faith, but only the saints will put their faith in God loving us in that way.

---

[42] 1 Jn 4:16.

Come, my love,
let us go to the fields.
We will spend the night in the villages.

When the bride has experienced the love of the Bridegroom and finally believed in it, she feels the happiness of the absolute Love, the one which flows from the endless Love Who is solely and all Love. She understands the contingency of the things that are not God. She wants to be alone with her Beloved; far from any noise, far from the city, far from everything. To be there, where only love remains.

The city represents here all those things that are not God. In those moments in which the mutual giving of love occurs —giving of the Bridegroom to the bride and of the bride to the Bridegroom— the bride forgets about time and place, the where, the when. There is nothing left but love,

En tanto que de rosas
hacemos una piña,
y no parezca nadie en la montiña,[43]

said Saint John of the Cross. Let nobody appear on the hill, so that nothing disturbs the exchange of love between the Bridegroom and the bride.

But alas! One who goes to the fields must come back to the city, to pass the night at home, to continue again with ordinary life. Even in those moments of mutual giving in love, the bride realizes

---

[43] Saint John of the Cross, *The Spiritual Canticle*, stanza 16: While we fashion a cone of roses / Intricate as the pine's; / And let no one appear on the hill.

that she must go back again to the city: again to things, to people, to problems; again to suffer the departure from the Beloved. She is perfectly aware that her heart cannot yet break, as she would wish, into the love of the Beloved, and that the possession is not complete, for it is going to be perturbed. She knows the Beloved belongs wholly to her and she completely to Him, but as a pledge, as a token, in a self–giving which is not total yet because only in the Homeland can it be consummated. She knows that she will have to leave the quietness of the country to go back to the city. She knows it, but is longing for the moment when she will not have to return to it, nor look to the night for some rest at home, for she will have already found that rest, and this time for ever, by the Beloved, in heaven:

We will spend the night in the villages.

Maybe that is the yearning the Bride wants to express, the craving for that moment to become real; that moment in which she will not have to go back, nor depart from the Beloved. It will be that moment in which the night will be spent in the villages because there will be night no more: "And night is as clear as the day."[44]

> *And in the early morning we will go to the vineyards.*
> *We will see if the vines are budding,*
> *if their blossoms are opening,*
> *if the pomegranate trees are in flower.*
> *Then I shall give you*
> *the gift of my love.*

---

[44] Ps 139:12. Cf. Rev 21:23.

The bride wishes to go with the Bridegroom to see if the vines are budding, if the pomegranate trees are in flower, if the blossoms are opening. Perhaps those flowers and the perfume they exhale refer to a life in continually increasing intimacy with the Bridegroom. They are the blossoms of the Christian virtues, which, when authentic, give off a charming and captivating fragrance that is impossible not to recognize. That is what reveals the saints; not a glowing halo, but rather the charming simplicity, the enamoring goodness, the clean gaze which makes you muse, the seductive humility which conveys happiness, all that which speaks about superabundance of life (Jn 10:10) and about the nearness of God. Because holiness is naturalness without craftiness, spontaneous and virginal simplicity, love which flows like a mountain spring: clear, easy and overflowing. Holiness is strong and childlike at the same time; terrible as well as seductive; stern, but constantly overflowing with joy; rooted in reality and beaconing the truth, but also evoking dreams and nostalgias; capable of placing within the human horizon, in a clear way and as in a fresh morning without haze, all that is good, beautiful and grand. Holiness returns us to what we ourselves really are, and at the same time causes us to forget about ourselves, taking us to God. Holiness displays before us the peace and joy of our childhood, that peace and joy we thought lost for good. Holiness and beauty are the same thing.

The fragrance of true holiness is what inebriates the Bridegroom and intoxicates men. And only in this fragrance, exhaled by Christian virtues, is the mutual giving of love possible, as the bride says,

> *Then I shall give you*
> *the gift of my love.*

It finally is the consummated union, the same which takes place in the giving of human love, except that here it is supernaturalized, made divine, transcendent and purified. Nothing of what human love possesses as good and beautiful is strange, in itself, to the divine or divine–human love. For human love, to the extent that it is love —we ought to repeat it— is but a participation and figure of the true Love (Eph 5: 25.32).

This consummated love, which already takes place in this life though it will become total only in our Homeland, remains unknown, in its essence as well as in its existence, if Christian virtues are not seriously lived. The foolish virgins could not enter into the wedding feast because they had no oil for their lamps.

> *The most exquisite fruits are at our doors;*
> *the new as well as the old,*
> *I have stored them for you, my love.*

The bride has spoken above about flowers, now she speaks about fruit, which comes after the flowers. In Christian life, the flowers of the virtues are also followed by the fruit. Divine–human love yields, as exquisite fruit, an efficient apostleship: children and grandchildren; just as in human love the self–giving of love between spouses, once consummated, is followed by the fruit of children as a result of their love. However, in the divine–human love the outcomes are more abundant the more the supernatural surpasses the natural: one hundred times more (Mt 19:29), and even more since the reality is greater. Here we are contemplating the endless generosity of divine love answering to the total self–giving of human love; an authentic priestly life, for instance, or any human love wholly consecrated to God, will leave behind a trail of children that will last for ever, as long as the world exists (Jn 15:16; cf. 15: 5.8). The priesthood is everlasting, as well as love of which it is a fruit.

The bride talks about fruit that is new and mature. For the fruit can be new, not ripe yet, almost bittersweet, or ripe. Perhaps the latter is that mature fruit which is kept a long time wrapped in hay or something similar, and which later on becomes sweet to the palate. A life given to God out of love contemplates the sprouts steadily growing around it: those who are mature and ripe with an exquisite taste given by time and perseverance for years, the elder children; the others are new, the children of the children, with the bittersweet inexperience of the primeval self–giving, not ripe yet, but filled with promise. In the same manner, the life of each one of us, when it is about to reach its end, will be a ripened fruit, a mature fruit.

All of them, the new as well as the old, are offered by the bride to the Bridegroom, making them too, by so doing, part of the loving self–giving. For love consumes and feeds by and in itself. It could not be otherwise, for at the very end nothing is left except love.

But until that final consummation occurs, in which all is love and there is nothing save love, the bride has to long for it impatiently. The final cry which closes the book of the Song of Songs is,

> *Haste away, my love,*
> *be like a gazelle,*
> *a young stag,*
> *on the spice–laden mountains.*[45]

There is the final shout of the Apocalypse, with which the whole Bible closes,

"Come, Lord Jesus."[46]

---

[45] Sg 8:14.
[46] Rev 22:20.

Rare coincidence, since both express the same impatience and yearning. It seems as if the Bible wanted to say that it is, in reality, nothing except the impatience and the craving for the consummation of love between the Beloved and the lover, or between the lover and the Beloved. That is, indeed, the Bible: the love of Love and the yearning waiting of the enamored soul. This is precisely what the virgins of the parable were doing: waiting and waiting. And although they fell asleep —including, indeed, the wise ones— at the end, when they heard the voice of the Bridegroom, some got ready to go to meet Him. They were truly in love, those who came to understand that one has life when it is laid down (Mt 10:39), that there is more happiness in giving than in receiving (Acts 20:35), and that the greatest happiness, the only true one, abides in forgetting and overcoming everything, in order to enter, some day, into the wedding banquet, to enjoy that banquet with the Beloved:

> *Quedéme y olvidéme*
> *el rostro recliné sobre el Amado;*
> *cesó todo y dejéme,*
> *dejando mi cuidado*
> *entre las azucenas olvidado.*[47]

---

[47]Saint John of the Cross, *Ascent to Mount Carmel*, stanza 8: I abandoned and forgot myself, / Laying my face on my Beloved; / All things ceased; I went out of myself, / Leaving my cares / Forgotten among the lilies.

VIII

THE DISCIPLES ON THE ROAD TO EMMAUS

Now that very same day, two of them were on their way to a village called Emmaus, seven miles from Jerusalem, and they were talking together about all that had happened. And it happened that as they were talking together and discussing it, Jesus himself came up and walked by their side; but their eyes were prevented from recognizing him. He said to them, "What are all these things that you are discussing as you walk along?" They stopped, their faces downcast. Then one of them, called Cleopas, answered him, "You must be the only person staying in Jerusalem who does not know the things that have been happening there these last few days." He asked, "What things?" They answered, "All about Jesus of Nazareth, who showed himself a prophet powerful in action and speech before God and the whole people; and how our priests and our leaders handed him over to be sentenced to death, and had him crucified. Our own hope had been that he would be the one to set Israel free. And this is not all: two whole days have now gone by since it all happened; and some women from our group have astounded us: they went to the tomb in the early morning, and when they could not find the body, they carne back to tell us they had seen a vision of angels who declared he was alive. Some of our friends went to the tomb and found everything exactly as the women had reported, but of him they saw nothing."

Then he said to them, "You foolish men! So slow to believe all that the prophets have said! Was it not necessary that the Christ should suffer before entering into his glory?" Then starting with Moses and going through all the prophets, he explained to them the passages throughout the scriptures that were about himself.

When they drew near to the village to which they were going, he made as if to go on, but they pressed him to stay with them saying, "It is nearly evening, and the day is almost over." So he went to stay with them. Now while he was with them at table, he took the bread and said the blessing; then he broke it and handed it to them. And their eyes were opened and they recognised him; but he was vanished from their sight. Then they said to each other, "Did not our hearts burn within us as he talked to us on the road and explained the scriptures to us?"

They set out that instant and returned to Jerusalem. There they found the Eleven assembled together with their companions, who said to them, "The Lord has indeed risen and appeared to Simón." Then they told their story of what had happened on the road and how they had recognised him at the breaking of bread.

(Lk 24: 13–35)

"Their eyes were prevented from recognizing him"

According to the evangelist the disciples are to be blamed for their failing to recognize the Lord: "Their eyes could not recognize Him."

The Lord wants to give us His love and intimate friendship as a gift. But for Him to do that, He must first reveal Himself to us (Jn 14:21), because there is no love if the beloved is not present. Hence the revelation of His presence and love is impossible if our life is estranged from His; our eyes will fail to recognize Him, and we will not be able to see or hear Him, even though He may be present and call us (Jn 11:28). For it is imperative to be led by the Spirit of Love if one wants to recognize Him.

Perhaps that is why the disciple whom Jesus loved was the first to recognize Him at His appearance by the Sea of Tiberias:

> Simon Peter, Thomas, called the Twin, Nathanael from Cana in Galilee, the Sons of Zebedee and two more of his disciples were together. Simon Peter said, "I am going fishing."
>
> "We'll come with you," they replied.
>
> They went out and got into the boat but caught nothing that night. When it was already light, there stood Jesus on the shore, though the disciples did not realize

that it was Jesus. Jesus called out, "Haven't you caught anything, friends?"

"No," they answered.

"Throw the net to the starboard and you'll find something," he said.

So they threw the net out and could not haul it in because of the quantity of fish. The disciple whom Jesus loved said to Peter, "It is the Lord!"[1]

Nevertheless, we need not be incapable of seeing; grace can help us and give us a certain knowledge and love of the Lord. The Lord is then foreseen and foretold, although in a very obscure way (1 Cor 13:12), in a knowledge which is only beginning, but which leads us toward His love, a knowledge and love that grow together and depend on each other. And as they grow, they sweetly torment the soul, arousing in it the hunger and yearning for God.

This yearning is also a torment, because man is aware that the insufficiency abides in himself, and he cannot but suffer as he understands that God's absence is due to his own fault. But, above all things, love itself is a torment, so long as it does not fully possess the beloved. Love is like a fire which does not rest until everything is consumed, "Fire which never says, 'Enough!'"[2] Deuteronomy says that God is "a consuming fire,"[3] and the Letter to the Hebrews also calls God a "consuming fire."[4]

But if man, who, after all, has been created for love, does not possess it, then he has to look for substitutes. That is the reason for

---

[1] Jn 21: 1–7.
[2] Prov 30:16.
[3] Deut 4:24.
[4] Heb 12:29.

things like sex, drugs, or the mad search for power. These caricatures of love also bring torment to man, but of a completely different sort than the one produced by the love of God. Sex or drugs torment by causing a huge emptiness in man, whereas true love torments by leading man to his plenitude. Sex or drugs torment by destroying, but love torments by edifying, constructing, and giving life: 'I have come so that they may have life and have it to the full.'[5]

Sex and drugs lead to death, but love gets us closer to life: for, as time passes, when one is in love with God one lives life more and more intently every day. That is so because the feeling, as time goes by, that we are closer to true Life gradually grows stronger, and true love, indeed, ends by introducing us to the fountain of all life, the divine life.

Saint Paul speaks with excitement about the torment that the love of God causes when God is not yet fully possessed: 'Life to me, of course, is Christ, but then death would be a positive gain. On the other hand again, if to be alive in the body gives me an opportunity for fruitful work, I do not know which I should choose. I am caught in this dilemma: I want to be gone and to be with Christ, and this is by far the strongest desire...'[6]

An old book recounted in the following way the farewell of Saint Francis of Assisi, after he had been praying on Mount Alverna. It is a beautiful page, which tells us about the love of God and for God:

> 'Live in peace, little brothers. And goodbye! My body is leaving you, but my heart will stay here. Goodbye to all of you. And to you too, beautiful Mount Alverna, good and holy mountain, mount of angels. Goodbye! Good-

---

[5] Jn 10:10.
[6] Phil 1: 21–23.

bye, trees, plants, rocks, and birds, especially Brother Falcon, my awakener and companion. Goodbye! Goodbye to the rock before which I prayed! Goodbye to the little chapel! O Mother of God, I entrust the Brothers to you! I will never see you again!"

Francis was sitting on a small donkey, with his hands and feet wrapped in bandages through which seeped blood from the nails that pierced his feet and hands. What heavenly joy and pure bliss those wounds brought him. And what inhuman torture!

He gave his blessing to his Brothers. Then Leo led the donkey forward. But instead of going down, they went up higher, from one summit to another. It was as though Francis could not tear himself away from those sacred heights. And the Brothers who had to stay up there seemed to be drawn after him, for they followed him at a distance.

When the travelers finally came down into the valley that evening, Francis tried to get off the donkey, despite all his pain. He had to be extremely careful, with the bent nails projecting from his hands and feet. Dropping onto his knees and turning his face toward Mount Alverna, he cried, 'God bless you, Holy Mountain where God revealed Himself! God bless you!"[7]

Those who have felt, to any extent, the Presence of God, suffer a longing produced by His absence, and experience the desire of fuller

---

[7] F. Timmermans, *La harpe de saint François*, (Gante, 1933), p. 227. (Eng. tr.: *The Perfect Joy of St. Francis*, (New York, 1952), p. 307).

possession. The only sorrow of the saints is that God is not loved, either by them or by the world, as they wished He were. The biggest punishment for the world's evil is that the world should be without God, yet not even aware of its own tragedy.

If we do not see God, it is because our eyes are defective or weak, as was the case with the disciples on the road to Emmaus. And this trouble of our eyes may render darkness all around us: "If your eye is diseased your whole body will be darkness," said the Lord. Thus it is with a heart that has no love of God, it is all pitch darkness, such a terrible darkness that those who suffer it are not aware they dwell in it, a darkness so gloomy that it hides itself. That is why the Lord added,

> "If then, the light inside you is darkened, what darkness that will be!"[8]

But when our eyes come to know the Lord through faith, when grace stirs and enhances human generosity, things are quite different. Then the Spirit of the Lord makes patent His presence in man, even through his body, "If your eye is clear, your whole body will be filled with light."[9] Only this radiant brightness can bare witness to Jesus; it flows from the knowledge of the Lord, Who reveals Himself to those who love Him: "We speak only about what we know and witness only to what we have seen."[10] Thus, authentic witness to Jesus is given by the saints, that is to say, those who, because their heart is cleansed, have seen God (Mt 5:8) and are entitled to talk

---

[8] Mt 6:23.
[9] Mt 6:22
[10] Jn 3:11. Cf. 1 Jn 1: 1–3.

about Him: they are persuasive, since they talk about what they know and witness to what they have seen.[11]

"They stopped, their faces downcast"

Questioned by that stranger, the travelers to Emmaus stopped, filled with sadness. They were discouraged, only because things did not come out the way they had thought—

> "...All about Jesus of Nazareth, who showed himself as a prophet powerful in action and in speech before God and the whole people; and how our chief priests and our leaders handed him over to be sentenced to death, and had him crucified. Our own hope had been that..."

In short, they did not understand the meaning of the cross.

They had not understood the only way which Happiness uses to come to humans. Happiness goes arm in arm with Love, which always supposes the giving of oneself to the beloved. Now, in Christ that self-giving is crowned by His perfect obedience to the Father and by His total love for His Father and for men. Love and obedience are consummated on the cross. In the present condition there is no

---

[11] Such a vision in this world is only achieved through faith. The Apostle, Saint Thomas, deserved a serious warning from the Lord, because he looked for knowledge of Him through a merely tangible and human vision (Jn 20: 24–29). We ought to take into account the text of Heb 11:1, noting, however, that knowledge through faith does not mean an insecure or indistinct knowledge, but quite the opposite. Von Balthasar says that "We cannot just consider the definition of faith of Heb 11:1, as it is usually explained, as the only true one in an univocal sense," in *La Glorie et la Croix*, Vol. I, (Paris, 1965), p. 261.

other way for man (Jn 14:6), who will never find Happiness except by the giving of his very self, consisting of self-abnegation and self-renunciation by means of participation in the Lord's cross.

Happiness is departed from men when they seek after themselves instead of striding the road of true love. The absence of Happiness is called Sadness. The two disciples on their way to Emmaus did not yet know the way to true Happiness, so their sadness and feeling of failure overtook them, which is what has happened with so many people who have thought and still think like them.

And so Sadness is also, in fact, a lack of love.

But there are two different kinds of sadness, though it would be more appropriate to talk about two different causes for sadness. The first embraces those facts and situations which bring with them the unpleasant events of life: failure, hardships, illness, loss of beloved ones... Though it ought to be said that this sadness, in itself, can be overcome by faith; Christian suffering is compatible with Happiness (Mt 5:5). The second is the true and only sadness, the one that should always be written with capital letters, that which springs from the feeling that we are not saints, which is brought about in the soul by the absence of God and by the refusal to accept His will.

It is very difficult to tell what that kind of sadness is. Because it is a negative concept, we have first to understand what the joy of the Presence of God is, and therefore what its lack means. Something similar happens with blindness, which can only be properly understood as misfortune by those who enjoy sight. The worst thing about sadness is that it never reveals all its content to those who suffer it; only the saints comprehend it, for they have freed themselves of it. Thus the best way to know it is to look closely at their happiness; only then, once we understand that we do not have that happiness, do we catch a glimpse of what sadness consists of.

Sadness has a parasitic existence in people, eating at them like a ringworm. It sucks the sap of Happiness from them, and it even leads them to believe that anguish is the normal state of man. When Saint Paul speaks about the fruits of the Holy Spirit, he places charity first and happiness second.[12] It seems that for him love and happiness are intimately linked, as if the latter were a consequence of the former. Thus his urging, "Always be joyful."[13]

Christian testimony, and above all preaching, should always take into account the text of Is 52:7, 'How beautiful on the mountains are the feet of the messenger announcing peace, of the messenger of good news, who proclaims salvation!"[14] Christian preaching is the announcement of Good News: "Do not be afraid. Look, I bring you news of great joy, a joy to be shared by the whole people."[15] The apostle must always take care that all and every one of the truths which make up the Message of Salvation are preached. But the apostle ought to be aware also that ours is an anguished and fearful world, which perhaps does not need so much to be threatened with punishment as it needs someone to point it to the ways of salvation, and at the same time to disclose before it the Happiness contained in the Christian Message (Mt 12: 20–21). The apostle will also have to preach in a style of denunciation, as the Lord did sometimes, but considering always that the main content of his preaching should be the essence of the Message: a Message of salvation (Lk 4: 18–21). And never should denunciation manipulate the content of the Revelation, bringing out, for instance, some of its demands while others are silenced or falsified. That is how Marxism acts when pretend-

---

[12] Gal 5:22.

[13] 1 Thess 5:16. Cf. Phil 4:4, etc.

[14] Saint Paul quotes it partially in Rom 10:15.

[15] Lk 2:10.

ing to base social justice on the gospel, while it fosters hatred and class conflict, placing itself thus at the antipodes of Christianity. Von Balthasar said in one of his last books: "Christians will change nothing in human relationships by embroidering in their banners 'Social Justice' instead of 'Imitation of Christ,' as many a religious order is doing today; they should convert themselves in order to be able to change the hearts of those who can change the social conditions."[16] But it is easier, surely, to utter *prophetic denouncements* than to present the content of the Christian Message in an authentically joyful manner. For *prophetic denouncement* only requires a zeal which easily enough may be mingled with resentment or the venting of its own failure, and which is susceptible of manipulation by dark ideologies. No, it is impossible to present the gospel in a joyful manner if it is not lived. If it is done through effort, everything will look false, theatrical, and merely hollow, when not altogether self-defeating. For it is impossible to talk in a convincing manner about Happiness if one is not happy; and it is not possible to be happy if one is not in love; which, in turn, demands being ready to die to oneself, following the Lord's teachings, Who clearly stated,

> 'If you keep my commandments you will remain in my love, just as I have kept my Father's commandments and remain in his love. I have told you this so that my own joy may be in you and your joy be completed."[17]

As we can see, the Lord makes happiness depend upon love, and this in its turn depends on the keeping of His teachings.

In the same way, the Lord wants the pilgrims to Emmaus to understand the cause of their melancholy, cause which pertains to

---

[16] Hans U. Von Balthasar, *Catholique*, (Paris, 1976), p. 126.
[17] Jn 15: 10–11.

the intelligence and to the heart; to intelligence, because it did not know the ways of God; to the heart, because it did not open to love, thus banning the coming of Happiness. That is why He says,

> "You foolish men! So slow to believe what the prophets have said!"

"Was it not necessary that the Christ should suffer before entering into his glory?" The Priesthood of Christ and our participation in it.

The key for wholly understanding this beautiful passage of Saint Luke's gospel upon which we are commenting is in this verse.[18] The Word took a human nature, and became priest, to show His obedience and love to the Father (Phil 2: 7–8) and His love toward us. But one characteristic of the priesthood is to offer sacrifices to God (Heb 5:1), and the Lord offered and fulfilled this sacrifice through His own death, thus becoming priest and victim at the same time. All the sacrifices of the Old and New Covenants are figures of or refer to the Lord's sacrifice, from which they draw their value. Christ redeems us through His priestly offering on the cross, not that He dies, but that He shows, through His death, His perfect love and total obedience to His Father, as well as His love for us. For what redeems is not the terrible things the cross and death are, but that

---

[18] Sister Jeane d'Arc, "Un grand jeu d'inclusions dans les pèlerins d'Emmaüs," *Nouvelle Revue Thèologique*, 99 (1977), pp. 62ff. This verse contains, for her, the key of the whole narration.

love which is not afraid to go to such an extent in revealing and offering itself.[19]

We have been called to partake in all Christ is, and thus in His priesthood too, which is the same as saying in His sacrifice and death (Rom 6: 3–5). Having a share, since our baptism, in the Priesthood of Jesus Christ (1 Pet 2: 5.9; Rev 1:6; 5:10; 20:6) we are called to make of our existence, out of love, a sacrificial oblation or sweet–smelling offering, following the pattern of Jesus, Who also did the same out of love (Eph 5:2). Indeed, Jesus' death as well as our calling to participate in His Priesthood are acts of divine Love. Saint Paul, talking about Christ's love, which led Him to offer Himself for us till death, exhorts us to make our own the mind of Christ Jesus (Phil 2:5), which means we should offer ourselves as well in a priestly offering: 'I urge you, then, brothers, remembering the mercies of God, to offer your bodies as a living sacrifice, dedicated and acceptable to God; that is the kind of worship for you, as sensible people."[20]

In another text, he also exhorts us to die to things in order to live only for God, so that we may make that sacrifice a reality, 'For none of us lives for himself and none of us dies for himself; while we are alive, we are living for the Lord, and when we die, we die for the Lord: and so, alive or dead, we belong to the Lord."[21]

What has been said is valid for the ministerial priesthood as well as for the common priesthood of all the faithful. For, although the ministerial priesthood —different from the common priesthood, in

---

[19]Saint Thomas, *In Romanos*, c. V, lect. II. Cf. the book by P. Nau, *Le mystère du Corps et du Sang du Seigneur*, (Solesmes, 1976), p. 40.

[20]Rom 12:1.

[21]Rom 14: 7–8. Cf. also, regarding this same meaning of living priesthood as sharing the Priesthood of Jesus by offering ourselves and dying along with Him to things and to ourselves: Rom 6: 3.8.11; 2 Cor 5:15; Col 2:20; 3:3.

degree as well as in essence—[22] connotes a more intimate and special sharing in the Priesthood of Jesus Christ, nevertheless the invitation to the sacrificial offering is meant for all.[23]

This is what is so specific to the priesthood, as is the sharing in the Eucharistic Sacrifice, which is the same sacrifice of the cross, which in turn is the fulfillment of the Priesthood of Jesus Christ. The priestly victimization should make real in our lives what was said in the passages from Saint Paul quoted above,[24] as well as the teachings of the Lord Himself: "Unless a wheat grain falls into the earth and dies, it remains only a single grain; but if it dies it yields

---

[22]Cf., for instance, Second Vatican Council, *Lumen Gentium*, 10, 2.

[23]It is not true that theology about the ministerial priesthood is yet to be done —at least in its fundamental outlines— and that, due to this lack of adequate theology, the so called *crisis of identity* of the priest, about which so much has been said, is well founded. The priest has more than enough ingredients within the Doctrine of the Church —arrived at from both Scripture and the Tradition— as to live his vocation with full enthusiasm, knowing perfectly what its essence is. But it is certainly true that there is still a long way to go in the deepening of the theology of the priesthood. One of the points in which this deepening ought to be done is precisely the difference of degree and essence between the ministerial and the common priesthood. Perhaps the clarification of this question brings us to this: that the ministerial priesthood is a special participation in the priestly offices proper to the Christ Head; that is to say, that the ministerial priesthood incorporates him who possesses it into the hierarchy, something that the common priesthood cannot do. The ministerial priesthood, in consequence, confers a participation in the offices of teaching, sanctifying and governing that is very particular and which is not given by the common priesthood; it gives a special power over the Sacramental Body of Christ, and so over His Mystical Body (each is related to the other), which is proper to this priesthood. Laymen may, for instance, teach, but not *ex officio*, which means that they can be theologians —and good ones— but not preachers. On the other hand, the sacrificial offering we are dealing with is proper to both manners of priesthood, though the ministerial priesthood is called to live it in a particularly intensive way (and there is the difference of degree).

[24]In particular Rom 12:1.

a rich harvest. Anyone who loves his life loses it; anyone who hates his life in this world will keep it for eternal life."[25]

Unfortunately many mistake the personal experience of priesthood and the participation in the Eucharistic Sacrifice with things like partaking in the readings at Mass. Now, an external participation at Mass that does not include the sacrificial offering of one's own life means barely nothing. There has been little success from certain modern attempts which, through the introduction of elements alien to the liturgy, including many liberties and even oddities, are intended to bring Mass closer to the faithful. Perhaps the greatest danger of this attitude consists in the confusion brought among the faithful, snatching from them the real ideal of what the realization of their priesthood and their participation in the Priesthood of Christ are. Such realization and participation consist of nothing but a sacrificial offering, fragrant, made all life long and in union with the Lord, that takes shape in the steadfast implementation of His will at any moment; all that is expressed, fulfilled, and made possible, precisely through the Holy Mass, which, in turn, is the actualization or real presence of the only Sacrifice of Christ, Who died for us once and for all (Heb 7:27).

But there is no doubt that organizing popular or *folk* events is easier than teaching to live the priesthood as a sharing in the Sacrifice of Christ, because the latter demands necessarily that the teachers live it too. Von Balthasar, talking about the "kenotic" character of the Church, said: "As the man Jesus remained concealed among men, so what is *Catholic* lives among the forms of history. Flesh conceals. It is necessary to possess eyes illuminated by grace ('it was not flesh and blood that revealed this to you') in order to discover the splendor through the form of the servant (through the

---

[25] Jn 12: 24–25.

form of sin as well). Simple people perceive this better, even if they happen to do it through their popular and not too bright customs, and with art which may not reflect the finest taste. The wise can also discover it, so long as they are purified by humiliations and denials. On the other hand, it is not seen by those more than sensible people, the television theologians, the vicars of social concern and, in general, all those who believe they can manipulate Catholicism to make it more appealing, or more to their convenience."[26]

It was necessary that the Christ should suffer before entering into his glory. For sin is an act of lack of love, and God wished it to be atoned by love. It should be made clear that love, which is being, is infinitely stronger than the lack of love, which is no-being. There is the reason why the Father wanted the Priesthood and Sacrifice of His Son. And that is why participation in the Priesthood of Christ and in His work of redemption is not possible for us without participation in His sacrificial death (Heb 9:22). To live our priesthood —ministerial or common priesthood— is to experience the sacrificial offering, thus showing also our love to the end.

For all that, Priesthood and its consequence, the personal offering as victim, are an epiphany of love. The Priesthood of Christ has its origin in the love of the Father, Who wanted that priesthood for us as well, 'For this is how God loved the world: he gave his only Son, so that everyone who believes in him may not perish but may have eternal life'[27]; and elsewhere it is said, 'This is the revelation of God's love for us, that God sent his only Son into the world for us that we may have life through him'[28]; and again, 'But when the completion of the time came, God sent his only Son, borne of a

---

[26] Hans U. von Balthasar, *op. cit.*, p. 128.
[27] Jn 3:16.
[28] 1 Jn 4:9.

woman, borne a subject to the Law, to redeem the subjects to the Law, so that we could receive adoption as sons."[29] In the same way Christ, with His priestly offering, showed His love to the Father and to us, for "No one can have greater love than to lay down his life for his friends."[30]

The pilgrims to Emmaus had not understood that when the priestly victimization is taken away, then love is suppressed, having no form for revealing or realizing itself. Nor did the Jews understand, in general, that if the characteristics of the Suffering Servant of Yahweh were not applied to the Messiah,[31] then the latter, as He was conceived in the Father's plans, would be annihilated: atoner for sin and revealer of His love. That is why the Lord had to say to those two disciples, "Was it not necessary that the Christ should suffer...?"[32] It is also difficult for us to understand that to live the

---

[29] Gal 4: 4–5.

[30] Jn 15:13.

[31] Most of the authors agree in considering the following as the passages of Isaiah dealing with the Suffering Servant of Yahweh: 42: 1–4; 49: 1–6; 50: 4–9; 52: 13–53: 12.

[32] The man who enjoys the ministerial priesthood is neither a community representative, nor is he, nor can he be elected by the community; for, in this sense, the community is not in need of representatives, since it is a kingdom of priests (1 Pet 2:9). As the one which shares in the offices of the Christ Head, the ministerial priesthood cannot be, at any rate, a representation of the community, which, though integrated in Christ, does not share in His capital functions (those functions in which the rest of the Body is set over against his Head: cf. Eph 4: 15–16; Col 1:18; Eph 1:22). For the same reason, the ministerial priesthood can only receive its hierarchical function from the very Head. Cf. the Declaration of the Sacred Congregation for the Doctrine and Faith, about the question of the Admittance of Women to the Priesthood 15 October 1976, par. 5, and also the quotations from Vatican II and the Encyclical *Mediator Dei* made in note 21 of the same Declaration. There it is said that 'If the priest represents the Church it is because, above all, he represents Christ Himself, Head and Shepherd of the Church."

priesthood —the sacrifice and the offering of life— is the other side of love; should we take away one (sacrifice) we will have taken the other away too (the possibility for love to be unfolded): "Anyone who finds his life will lose it; anyone who loses his life for my sake will find it."[33] Hence it is easily deduced that one who for lack of love feeds his selfishness "will have lost his own life"; and it is advisable to notice the profound meaning these words carry.

It ought to be stressed that the theology of priesthood becomes impoverished if catechesis is limited to presenting it as a mere participation in liturgical ceremonies. And there is still another risk: the clericalism of laymen. For their reading at Mass and distributing communion are not absolutely necessary for them to live out their priesthood, whereas it is of fundamental importance that they live the priesthood in accord with their specific vocation as laymen. They should live the victimization and participation in the Sacrifice of Jesus Christ through their ordinary life, in the exercise of their own duties and tasks, and in fidelity to the will of the Lord. In this sense, the catechesis to the Christian people has a long way to go. For a mere participation in liturgical ceremonies, as legitimate as that may be, which does not go along with the offering of one's own life, soon becomes empty of any content and frustrating. Besides, not all can take part in those liturgical ceremonies. It becomes a more serious matter when we come to deal with ceremonies performed under the umbrella of a pretended *freedom of the Spirit*, but they are only oddities trying to make up, through fantasy and imagination, for the lack of spirit or the absence of the Spirit. This Spirit, though He blows wherever He wants, never does it outside the Church (nor outside the Church as institution) nor the sacrificial mystery of the cross of Christ. The theology of real priesthood can-

---

[33] Mt 10:39 and refs.

not be but the theology of the mystery of the cross (and the latter implies, among other things, obedience to the Church as institution and the acceptance of the whole content of the faith). It is true that the cross always has been shocking (1 Cor 1: 17–18.23), so it is not so strange that some endeavor to devise a new priesthood, less tragic and more reasonable for a world which never was very fond of the frightening. In very early times, the Gnostics attempted to develop a more understandable Christianity, and since then this temptation has been tirelessly haunting the Church; the Neo–modernism we are now suffering is but the last, to date, of those attempts. And because heresies always are gloomy, though they disguise themselves as *rationalism*, should modern Gnosticism be successful —in turning the mystery of the cross into nothing— then it will also suppress love, and with it the possibility of Happiness. Hegel pretended to have made Reason divine, thus eliminating God, Who, according to Nietzsche, had died; Feuerbach and Marx, disciples of Hegel, ended up by suppressing religion because it was irrational, and in doing so brought the postulates of the French Revolution to their climax. Now Marxism presented itself for decades as the only scientific and rational system. But the truth is that Marxist countries have been forced to live within the system —which we have recently seen crumbling in Eastern Europe— with walls, barbed wire and policemen to prevent people from fleeing, people whose faces reflected sorrow, a lack of freedom and fear of the Gulag. Yet sadness has always been the mark of heresy; it might be enough always to be merry to make oneself immune to its influence (Phil 3:1).

Intimacy with the Lord is not possible without participation in His Sacrifice. Two men who thought they could be seated with Him in the Kingdom, one to His right and the other to His left, were first questioned by the Lord, "Can you drink the cup that I am going to drink?"[34]

A wonderful fruit of the Sacrifice of the Lord is the Eucharist, remembrance and perpetual actualization of that Sacrifice. The Eucharist, in which the Lord gives Himself to us, is a fruit of love. It is also given to us in order that we may love: it entails reciprocity on our part, it is a gift for us to love our brothers and sisters, and we really experience love in it. But it was the Sacrifice that made this donation possible (donation as both the gift we are given and the self–giving of God to us), thus accomplishing in all truth the co–penetration, the being–in–the other, and the common–union (with God as well as with our brothers and sisters).

Hence fleeing from or becoming sad in the face of sacrifice makes no sense at all. For without the Sacrifice of Christ, and our participation in it, Love should never come down to us. The Lord clearly said it,

> "Yet you are sad at heart because I have told you this. Still I am telling you the truth: it is for your own good that I am going, because unless I go, the Paraclete will not come to you; but if I go, I will send him to you."[35]

'Unless I go, the Paraclete will not come to you..." Always sacrifice is of the essence that love may come. For that reason, whoever flees from surrendering his life runs away from Love, as it happens with the grain of wheat that does not fall to the ground and die: it stays for ever alone; because there is no fruitfulness without self–giving and without love.

---

[34] Mt 20:22.
[35] Jn 16: 6–7.

'It is for your own good that I am going... Was it not necessary that the Christ should suffer before entering his glory...?" The pilgrims on the way to Emmaus had forgotten it.

We also forget it whenever we run away to avoid the self-giving of our own life, not considering that we have been called to participate in the Priesthood of Christ, and thus in His offering as a victim.

And the Lord adds,

> "And when he comes, he will show the world how wrong it was, about sin, and about who was in the right, and about judgment: about sin: in that they refused to believe in me..."

The Paraclete, then, will prove the world wrong about sin. Because by rejecting Christ, in Whom it has not believed, the world is left without His Spirit, and consequently it has no more Love. That is why the lack of love reigns in our world.

The Lord goes on,

> "About who was right: in that I am going to the Father and you will see me no more..."

The Paraclete will also admonish the world about justice, and about who or what was right. That is to say, by giving the world what it has chosen: to see the Lord no more. And even the disciples themselves will see Him exclusively through the veil and trials that faith involves, in that way sharing Christ's sufferings and His rejection by the world.

And lastly,

> "About judgment: in that the prince of this world is already condemned."

So the Paraclete will accuse the world with a judgment. Because the prince of this world has already been judge at a trial in which Love has overcome evil.

That is why the world hates Love, the Spirit, Who accuses it and shows it for what it is.

"Then, starting with Moses and going through all the prophets, he explained to them the passages throughout the scriptures that were about himself." Prayer.

As the Lord Himself was explaining to them the meaning of the Scriptures, their minds were filled with wonder and their hearts with love. Prayer is like that: a loving dialogue with God in which He keeps the initiative.

It has been often said that prayer is talking with God. It is true. But, in fact, prayer has more to do with listening to God than with talking to Him.

We had better say, from the start, that prayer cannot be made up of a mere string of petitions brought to somebody to be answered. Prayer is not an almost impersonal relationship concerned with soliciting favors or claiming rights: "When you do pray and do not receive, it is because you prayed wrongly, wanting to indulge your passions."[36]

Prayer is not an examination of conscience, either. Some turn it into a tedious list of faults and sins which most of the time are the same, and where it seems more a desire to justify themselves than to meet God.

---

[36] Jas 4:3.

Prayer is not just simple conversation as in ordinary life, where two or more people discuss any theme whatsoever.

Prayer is the mutual donation of hearts that occurs between two lovers. It is mostly a mutual giving of love in which both lovers are consumed by the flame. So it was felt by the two travellers to Emmaus, for then they said to each other: "Did not our hearts burn within us as he talked to us on the road?"

It is true that all the other things may appear in prayer, and, in fact, they almost always do: petitions, thanksgiving, repentance and conversation. But, above all, prayer is a self-giving in love.

And God always takes the initiative in this loving self-giving and conversation: "Look, I am standing at the door, knocking. If any of you hears me calling and opens the door, I will enter his house and have supper with him, and he with me."[37]

"If one of you hears my voice..." It is a matter of listening to the voice of the Lord. He is both the One Who stands at the door and the One Who knocks. It is up to us to hear His voice, to listen to Him and also "to open the door," that is to say, generously to open our hearts so that He can "come into us" (the more active part of this self-giving of love belongs to Him, since He is the Bridegroom) and give us the intimacy of His love. That intimacy is expressed in the symbol of a supper, which encloses another important teaching: love means reciprocity; for the text does not say, "we shall have supper together," but rather, "I will have supper with him, and he with me."[38] It follows that our attitude in prayer is not merely passive, something always to be considered.

The same idea is conveyed in the allegory of the Good Shepherd in the tenth chapter of Saint John's gospel: first of all, prayer is a

---

[37] Rev 3:20.

[38] Some modern translations, wishing to modernize the text, actually distort it.

matter of listening to the voice of the Bridegroom.[39] There we can find a number of ideas very similar to those in the text we have just examined.

It is said, for instance, that the gatekeeper let the Shepherd in. It is also said that the sheep hear the voice of the Shepherd, and even know it, which leads us to think that they are used to hearing that voice, because they hear it frequently. Still more: it is said not only that the Shepherd calls the sheep, but that He calls them each by name, thus evoking the intimacy and tenderness used by God toward the human being in prayer. There is another lesson not less important, for the sheep are said to follow the Shepherd because they know His voice, wherein it seems that the very hearing of the voice of the Shepherd, and their knowing it, are presented as the causes of the sheep's determination to follow Him. That is to say, the sheep find courage to follow the Shepherd, though the way may be harsh (meaning the cross), precisely because they have grown accustomed to hearing His voice, and listening to Him in the intimacy of that self-giving of love which is prayer. There they find wings to fly after Him. Finally, according to the text, the one whose voice the sheep do not recognize becomes a stranger to them, and they will not follow him; rather, they will run away from him. From this we may conclude that the Lord Himself will become a stranger, and that following Him will be impossible unless we make it our custom to listen frequently to the Good Shepherd's voice, or, to put it another way, without the frequent and loving listening of which prayer consists.

As we can see, we are very far from that prayer which is reduced to doing one's duty, or is confined to a mere listing of requests, or is just a report of faults and sins. On the contrary, the prayer we

---

[39] Jn 10: 2–5.

are dealing with cannot be understood without taking into account the Lord's words, "I shall no longer call you servants, I call you friends,"[40] that is, if we do not understand that God has called us to His friendship and wants to bestow upon us the endless tenderness of His heart. No wonder that the pilgrims to Emmaus realized how they felt their hearts burning after having spent a long time with the Lord, listening to Him.

Many are those, nevertheless, who have spent their lives not knowing that the only thing God wanted from them was their friendship. They did not understand that they had been born to enjoy the intimacy of Love Itself, and, because of that, to be happy now in this life. For man comes from Love and was born to find happiness in loving, that is, in consuming himself in the fire of self-giving and self-surrender which Divine life itself is about. The Lord once said that the purpose of His coming was that: "I have come to bring fire to the earth."[41] Now one understands better some mysterious words of the Baptist,

> "I baptise you with water, but someone is coming, who is more powerful than me, and I am not fit to undo the straps of his sandals; he will baptise you with the Holy Spirit and fire."[42]

The Baptist compares his humble baptism in water with baptism in the Holy Spirit and fire. There also is a total immersion in the latter, but now in the infinite abyss of a fire of love: in the Person of the Holy Spirit. That is why, to leave no room for doubt, the Baptist speaks of a baptism in fire too, an expression in which "baptism" and

---

[40] Jn 15:15.
[41] Lk 12:49.
[42] Lk 3:16 and refs.

"fire" must be seen to be in apposition with each other, for baptism in fire can be only an utter immersion into that infinite Fire Who seals the mutual self–giving of the Father and the Son. This same infinite Fire, the Spirit of Love, is also given to us:

> "I have come to bring fire to the earth."[43]

And elsewhere:

> "When the Paraclite comes, whom I shall send to you from the Father, the Spirit of truth who issues from the Father..."[44]

Also:

> "So that the love with which you loved me, Father, may be in them, and so that I may be in them."[45]

That is why we read in one of the Psalms, in an expression which we should apply to ourselves, that Yahweh appoints flames of fire His servants.[46]

* * *

We have said that prayer is a conversation of love between God and man, a mutual self–giving of love, in which God carries on the initiative, our part being to adopt a docile attitude in order to be able to listen to His voice.

---

[43] Lk 12:49.
[44] Jn 15:26; cf. Jn 14: 16–17; 16: 6–7; 16: 13–14.
[45] Jn 17:26.
[46] Ps 104:4.

We feel too often alone in prayer, not hearing anybody; moreover, we have to struggle against our imagination, absentmindedness, temptations, physical and moral tiredness, and even against our sleep. If prayer is as we have said above, why does it frequently become so difficult and why do we so often feel lonely in it?

To answer that question, we may start by saying that, in general, the reasons why we do not hear God are the same as those which prevent us from hearing a friend and enjoying friendship. Saint John has handed down to us these words of the Lord,

> "Whoever holds to my commandments and keeps them is the one who loves me; and whoever loves me will be loved by my Father, and I shall love him and reveal myself to him."[47]

Those words tell us that the Lord is willing to reveal Himself to us, if we love Him, indicating as well that those who love Him hold to His teachings. A life strange to His, alien to His Spirit, makes the hearing of His voice impossible.[48] It is the first and fundamental condition that we hear Him.

Let us go back to the disciples on the road to Emmaus, and examine the conditions in which their dialogue with the Lord took place. They talk first, but soon enough they keep totally silent, and devote themselves to listening to the Lord. There are also other circumstances which facilitate the dialogue: they are within the solitude of a roadway, far from any noise, and the tranquil peace of night is falling...

Truly enough, when we go to pray, we must forget about our noisy affairs, and just start listening. Our spirit is besieged by too

---

[47] Jn 14:21.
[48] Also cf. Jn 18:37.

many noises and preoccupations. It is imperative that the Lord be more important than anything else, so that we may be able to quiet the endless uproar of problems when prayer time comes. If we also recall that prayer should be a constant habit (1 Thess 5:17; Lk 18:1), until it becomes a spirit of prayer, then the intent of keeping the imagination in check must also be constant; otherwise, the change into the time of prayer will be too sudden and we will fail in the attempt.

It is also important in prayer not to attempt to impose subjects of conversation on the Lord. This should be understood as not ruling out a previous preparation, in some manner, of certain themes for prayer; prudence and humility seem to advise it, particularly to beginners; and nobody must hurriedly think he is not a beginner. But apart from this, to give freedom to the Spirit, the true spiritual Master and Guide, is needed. The Lord said it in His talk with Nicodemus,

> 'The Spirit blows where it pleases; you can hear his sound, but you cannot tell where it comes from or where it is going.'[49]

The Spirit is the supremely free and efficient cause of all freedom (2 Cor 3:17; 1 Cor 12:11; cf. Rom 8:15). He blows where, how and when He pleases, and nothing is left but to let Him guide us. His voice is heard (here again a mention of the fact that prayer is a listening to God), but where He comes from or where He goes is unknown. For humans, as limited beings, cannot embrace the thoughts and ways of God (Is 55: 8–9) Who, for that reason, is always unforeseeable to them. What God may say or ask, what He may give, or how far He is going to go, cannot be divined in advance, for He is immeasurable for us (*si intelligis non est Deus*). That

---

[49] Jn 3:8.

is why prayer cannot be *planned* in advance, because you cannot channel infinite Love; neither can the how much, nor the how, nor the manner of that Love be foretold.

It is even less possible to burden God with answers and solutions to our problems, no matter how reasonable, logical, or inevitable those solutions seem to us. There is no room here for the answer of naturalistic philosophy, proper to the Ancient oracles, grounded upon *know yourself*, for the wisdom Who speaks here does not come from man's innermost, but from outside him, transcending him completely.

In the passage from Saint Luke we have been commenting on, the theme of the dialogue was furnished by the Lord, "What are these things that you are discussing as you walk along?"

Later on, the answer to the anxieties and perplexities of the disciples will be wholly unexpected and, of course, impossible to have been anticipated.

* * *

An important obstacle in prayer —actually the only one— is the fear of the cross. But were mortification to be absent, there would not be progress towards intimacy with God. Saint Peter recommended being sober of mind for prayer (1 Pet 4:7), and it is a well known anecdote of the Curé of Ars that when questioned by another priest, who complained about the indifference of his community, and asked what sort of action should be taken, the Curé of Ars answered him,

> "Let us see. Have you prayed and preached? Have you fasted? Have you slept on the floor? Have you whipped yourself?"

Love for the cross is as important to prayer as it is necessary for a fruitful apostleship. Prayer and mortification are essential to apostleship. Without them, demons, according to the Lord, cannot be expelled (Mt 17:21). And He added that unless the grain of wheat falls into the earth and dies, it cannot yield fruit (Jn 12:24). We ought to mortify ourselves lavishly, though always under the control provided by good spiritual direction; that is the only way we can *force* the Lord, when He does not seem willing to show Himself, or He wants, as it were, to pass us without stopping: "When he made as if to go on, they pressed him to stay with them saying..."

A mortification which has been shrunk to a minimum, perhaps a tacit pact with oneself not to make one's life too difficult, are enough to render all progress in the friendship with the Lord impossible. That attitude shows a scant love, and we have already said that love is a fire which needs to be fueled with love itself: there is no love without love. Love is always a mutual self–giving and self–donation, and it always expects to be reciprocated. It is true that God loved us first (1 Jn 4:19), even when we were still sinners (Rom 5:8), but it was undoubtedly a love which ever looked forward to being requited (1 Jn 4:19).

Another danger, all too often present in prayer life, is that of looking for oneself instead of looking for God. It happens so when we seek perceptible and warm feelings. Feeling happy in the presence of our Beloved is good and inevitable —how could it be otherwise?— but one cannot set his affection —or his appetite as it is called in the Spanish spiritual classics— on those feelings, for then God is not sought for His own sake. God, were such the case, would go away, at least until our prayer becomes purified.

This defect requires a struggle if it is to be uprooted. It demands patience and readiness to accept darkness along with the apparent absence of the Lord. That is why we ought to exercise ourselves in the pleasurable acceptance of God's will, and to look only for

Him, no matter how He may come to us. In this way, the happiness that His presence arouses, which is good, is overcome by a humble patience and a constant fight against darkness, temptation or tiredness, and this is the safest way.

* * *

A proof that in prayer the initiative belongs to God, as well as the more active part, is found in the Song of Songs, a dialogue of love between God and the enamored soul, a dialogue whose more extensive part and whose more beautiful and caressing remarks pertain to the Bridegroom. Let us look at some verses:

> *You are fair as Tirzah, my Beloved,*
> *enchanting as Jerusalem,*
> *formidable as an army!*
> *Turn your eyes away from me,*
> *they take me by assault!*
> *Your hair is like a flock of goats*
> *surging down the slopes of Gilead.*
> *Your teeth are like a flock of ewes*
> *as they come up from being washed.*
> *Each one has its twin,*
> *no one unpaired with the other.*
> *Your cheeks, behind your veil,*
> *are halves of pomegranate.*
>
> *There are sixty queens*
> *and eighty concubines*
> *(and countless girls).*
> *My dove is the only one,*
> *perfect and mine...*[50]

---

[50] Sg 6: 4–9.

For He is the primeval fountain of love, the Master, the Guide and the Voice we yearn to listen to. A Voice we are always waiting for,

> *I sleep, but my heart is awake.*
> *I hear my Love knocking.*[51]

We do not have to worry too much about talking, as the Lord reminded us,

> 'In your prayers do not babble as the gentiles do, for they think that by using many words they will make themselves heard."[52]

On the other hand, talking is not the only way to communicate oneself, and sometimes not even the best; a glance is, quite often, more expressive, as it is between lovers: The Apocalypse, for instance, says that the eyes of the Lord are like burning flames,[53] or that His voice is like the sound of the ocean.[54] But the sound of the many waters of the ocean could resemble either tranquil, murmuring waves on a peaceful summer morning or the frightening and fierce roaring of the wild sea, or perhaps the soft monotone evoking a waterfall heard through the thicket. As the sounds of those many waters can be so different, and awake such a diversity of feelings within us, so the voice of the Lord can talk to us in many ways. But His voice, though it may seem to be in a rage, or even silent, always speaks to us about the same thing: it tells us about His love.

---

[51] Sg 5:2.
[52] Mt 6:7.
[53] Rev 2:18.
[54] Rev 1:15.

The Lord can also speak to us in His silence, since His voice can be a silent one. For when we are before Him and our will and effort seem to no avail; when, even then, He tells us nothing and we are listening only to silence, or to ourselves; when all that happens, it is not a time to quit or to despair: it is He talking to us about patience, humility and steadfastness, for that is what we undoubtedly need at that moment.

"It is nearly evening, and the day is almost over." Prayer, (continued).

The disciples on the way to Emmaus uttered this phrase, one of the most beautiful of the gospel, after they heard the Lord talking. They felt merry, different and wholly transformed. Before that they were sad, demoralized, with their merely human way of thinking, and with eyes incapable of recognizing the Lord. But now, the fire burnt within their hearts has changed them —'Did not our hearts burn within us as he talked to us on the road?"— and they feel happy, filled with enthusiasm, open to the new horizons unfolding before them, with a better and truer comprehension of things.

It is always like that in prayer, once we have been in contact with the Lord. For, in spite of the fact that we think ourselves loaded with evil, disheartened, tempted or overwhelmed by an unfavorable environment, we always feel transformed whenever we get in touch with holiness, even the holiness of a mere man. What would occur if we got nearer to the One Who is Goodness, Beauty, and Love? Certainly we would end by being different persons.

The gospel tells us about the transformation worked in some men who got in touch with the Lord and talked to Him. Saint John recounts one of them:[55]

> As he went along, he saw a man who had been blind from birth. His disciples asked him, "Rabbi, who sinned, this man or his parents?"
>
> "Neither he nor his parents sinned," Jesus answered, "he was born blind so that the works of God might be revealed in him."
>
> Having said this, he spat on the ground, made a paste with the spittle, put this over the eyes of the blind man, and said to him, "Go and wash in the Pool of Siloam."

So the blind man did, and came back able to see. This caused a great stir among the people, who asked him whether he was the same man or not, and how he recovered his sight. He said,

> "The man called Jesus made a paste, daubed my eyes with it and said to me, 'Go off and wash at Siloam'; so I went, and when I washed I gained my sight."

But it was the Sabbath and the day's rest had been broken; that did not seem sufficiently orthodox, and someone thought it necessary to take the former blind man to the Pharisees. A judicial inquiry was begun. But the former blind man always answered the same,

> "He put paste on my eyes, and I washed, and I can see."

Something shocking had happened, and the Pharisees discussed it among themselves. They all agreed on something:

---

[55] Jn 9: 1–38.

> "That man cannot be from God: he does not keep the Sabbath."

Or perhaps there was no such miracle, and the unfortunate man present here was not blind from birth. The inquiry went on and the parents were summoned to testify whether or not that man was really their son. Two poor, aged and frightened people arrived, and evaded the question as best they could,

> "We know he is our son and we know he was born blind, but how he can see, we do not know. Ask him. He is old enough."

Then a new interrogation of the former blind man, though now in a peremptory tone, and with questions only answerable in one way:

> "Give glory to God! We are satisfied that this man is a sinner. Admit he could not cure you!"

But the poor beggar, the former blind man, felt himself now another man. He was transformed, feeling assured and courageous; nothing mattered except that he should not betray the unknown man to whom he was so grateful. His answers had, then, the simplicity and force of common sense:

> "Whether he is a sinner I don't know; all I know is that I was blind and now I can see."

And the Pharisees charged again:

> "What did he do to you? How did he open your eyes?"

The beggar got impatient,

'How many times should I say it? Do you want to become his disciples yourselves?"

Indignation, shouting and insults followed. They told him,

'It is you who are his disciple, we are disciples of Moses: we know that God spoke to Moses, but as for this man, we don't know where he comes from."

But the man was changed. He did not care where his thought might bring him, and the rage he felt pressed him to speak bluntly:

'That is what is just so amazing! You don't know where he comes from and he has opened my eyes! We know that God does not listen to sinners, but God does listen to men who are devout and do his will. Ever since the world began it is unheard of for anyone to open the eyes of a man who was born blind; if this man were not from God, he wouldn't have been able to do anything."

The Pharisees' indignation reached its hottest point:

"Are you trying to teach us, and you are a sinner through and through ever since you were born!"

And they sent him away.
Jesus found him and asked him,

'Do you believe in the Son of man?"

That was a thrilling moment. That man had recovered his external sight and was grateful and brave; now it was a matter of acquiring interior sight as well. The title of Son of man was the one, among all the others with which the Messiah was known, which more clearly entailed His divine character.[56] This question carried, therefore, a direct challenge to his faith. But the beggar, already touched in his heart, gave in and surrendered himself:

"Lord, I believe," and worshiped him.

* * *

The two disciples were so happy after having listened to the Lord, that they did not want the experience to end. That is why "they pressed him to stay saying, 'It is nearly evening, and the day is almost over.'" They gently compelled Him. Their remark that it was becoming late was a mere pretext; something had to be said to make that man stay.

The same ought normally to happen in prayer. The Spirit uncovers in prayer a world of divine secrets, which is inaccessible to people, but given by God to those who love Him: "To us, though, God has given revelation through the Spirit, for the Spirit explores the depths of everything, even the depths of God. After all, is there anyone who knows the qualities of anyone except his own spirit, within him; and in the same way, nobody knows the qualities of God except the Spirit of God. Now, the Spirit we have received is not a spirit of the world but God's own Spirit, so that we may understand the lavish gifts God has given us."[57] Thanks to the Spirit who lives within us, we are able to know the gifts of God; the most important of which and the one that contains all the others is His

---

[56] According to the prophecy of Daniel: 7: 13–14.
[57] 1 Cor 2: 10–12.

love. Should God Himself not reveal it to us nor make us feel it, that Love would be unknown to us. But if He does, then our joy is complete (Jn 15:11; 16:24; 17:13). Whenever one prays with good will, joy and peace are already obtained. It does not matter that prayer has been difficult and under trial: it is God's own voice, which talks to us from the silence of His seeming absence. He was there, more hidden than absent, giving us serenity in the midst of suffering, injecting peace and happiness despite our tears and, perhaps, our lack of understanding of His ways.

It is clear, from the narrative, that the Lord wanted to remain, even more than the disciples wished to detain Him. The text suggests that by saying "he made as if to go on." He wanted them to ask Him for it, for in fact love can operate in no other way: it needs a door to be open to it voluntarily. That is why God humbly requests our love and yearningly hopes that we let Him love us. The only reason why He does not turn Himself upon us with caresses of love is that we impede Him from doing so, either because we openly reject Him, or perhaps because our madness leads us to believe we are worthy of His gifts, focusing our delight on them rather than on Him Himself.

Conclusion

The two pilgrims to Emmaus recognized the Lord at the breaking of the bread. Such breaking of bread is our Mass. We also achieve that recognition by our living the Mass, partaking in the sacrifice of the Lord as victim. To know Jesus requires a long journey, through which there is performed our Mass, which is the same as saying the offering of our life. That journey begins with our baptism, when we are buried together with Him to share in His death; reaches its epitome with our own death, which is a perfect participation in His; and it becomes fruitful in eternity, when we will be glorified by sharing His resurrection. But recognizing Him in this life means that we must really live the Mass and all that it entails: the Sacrifice of the Head, always being made actual so that the members may participate in it. He who shuns the cross never gets to meet the Lord. Many books and articles of lofty theological speculation are written today, but, as always, poor and humble people are the ones who attain a much better knowledge of the Lord. For by itself knowledge only puffs up, while love is what really builds something. It can be no other way, for since God is love, who will come to know Him if not those who love, those who came out of their egotism to give up everything? And these are usually the poor and the little ones, never the wise nor those who hold the power of this world.

There was a poor woman, who forgot herself entirely and gave everything to God. She called herself the slave, the handmaid of the Lord, and she gave God such a full and utter yes that it became the archetype of the yes of the whole Church. Nobody has ever pronounced it as she did. Thus she is the Master of all affirmative and generous answers given to God. When we may try to give our yes, nothing is better than to seek her help. For she, besides being Master, is also our Mother.

IX

WITH TRIMMED LAMPS

Then the kingdom of heaven will be like this: Ten bridesmaids took their lamps and went to meet the bridegroom. Five of them were foolish and five were sensible: the foolish ones did take their lamps, but they brought no oil, whereas the sensible ones took flasks of oil as well as their lamps. The bridegroom was late, and they all grew drowsy and fell asleep. But at midnight there was a cry, "The bridegroom is here! Go out and meet him." At this, all those bridesmaids woke up and trimmed their lamps, and the foolish ones said to the sensible ones, "Give us some of your oil: our lamps are going out". But they replied, "There may not be enough for us and for you; you had better go to those who sell it and buy some for yourselves". They had gone off to buy it when the bridegroom arrived. Those who were ready went in with him to the wedding hall and the door was closed. The other bridesmaids arrived later. "Lord, Lord," they said "open the door for us." But he replied, "I tell you solemnly, I do not know you". So stay awake, because you do not know either the day or the hour.

(Mt 25: 1–13)

The Lord often talks to us in parables. A parable is what we call an example. It shows us events and customs from simple and ordinary life, and through them we are invited to discover one or several lessons of capital importance to us. Sometimes the Master adds a detailed explanation; at other times, He closes with a sentence in which is to be found the main key to understanding the parable. At any rate, the parable always bears a wonderful world of possibilities and suggestions for people of all times and circumstances. That is why a parable always challenges our intelligence and our imagination. In it we come to feel, in a very special way, something that ceaselessly happens with the gospel: if we are to understand it we need, on the one hand, to love the people of our own time, those we are living with, so that we can know their problems; on the other hand, we must be open to the light of the Spirit, the only One Who can guide us in the interpretation of those words. When one proceeds in that fashion, one sees how everything fits together: human beings, their problems, their sufferings and their joys; and there is the Word to help with all those things, Who is Spirit and Life, as the Master said (Jn 6:63), for everyone who wants to listen.

The more important lesson that today's parable wants to convey to us is perhaps this: the lamps must always be well-supplied and trimmed. And no excuses, no matter how right they may seem, shall be of any avail: neither the Groom's tardiness, nor the uncertainty about the moment of His arrival, nor our sleep or tiredness, nor the hardship of obtaining oil, nor the confidence that we can get it at a later time... Lamps were made to shed light and they must be ready at all times. Nobody puts a lamp under a bushel basket, but on a stand where it gives light to all in the house (Mt 5:15). Besides, we being, according to the Master's saying, not only the salt of the earth, but also the light of the world, are to have our lamps burning at all times (Lk 12: 35–36).

We are, as the Apostle put it (Eph 5:8) light in the Lord. But we also need to know that such a task was never easy for the Christian, and nowadays is less easy than ever. Today it is certainly not easy to be a trimmed and lit lamp which shines before the world with steady and ardent flame as testimony to Jesus Christ. And I consider it important to have a clear conscience about this.

The Spirit of Evil, or Demon, is a spirit of confusion and absurdity. Since his power is now greater than ever, he has consequently been successful in spreading confusion all over. You know, of course, that I am referring to the Church Itself. Therefore, when you are setting out to bear your witness to Jesus Christ, a distinct, vibrating and audacious witness, you are going to face such tremendous chaos of minds that your work is going to turn out to be very hard to accomplish. It is true that such a state of chaos has been made possible because it was accompanied by a number of complicities which we shall talk about later. But the fact is there: huge as a rampart against which your voice will crash and return to you wholly hollow; or in the form of an icy north wind with power to blow out the light of your lamp, leaving you, too, in darkness.

Surely, the Christian lives on Hope. But nobody said that such virtue may excuse us from the task of being realists and knowing the world around us. Those real facts will not provide us with an alibi: our lamps must be trimmed and burning; no matter how, but they must be shining.

For instance: when facing Marxism, that problem of our time, you want to shine out with clear–cut criteria, you are going to meet immediately the sad reality of people's disorientation. Your clear vision, your telling them about the atheism of that ideology, the destruction of man it brings about and its deceiving tactics —all that will be useless. It will be of no avail either to make them see the facts so obviously before them with all their reality and monstrosity: countries entirely enslaved, oppression of minds and bodies, and even the oppression of a class (the working class) to which, and in a very particular way, liberation had been promised. When you wish to show all these things, you always will find somebody telling you that ours are times for dialogue; that Vatican Council II did not want to condemn anybody; that you should not be reactionary; that a common base can be found, upon which a spectrum of just social claims may be built; that, for the time being, we may lay our principles aside (in reality Marxism never relinquishes its own) and fight together. You will even be told that Marxism is the only true realization of Christianity. Not long ago, a certain character, calling himself, no less, a *Catholic–Marxist philosopher*, appeared on a TV colloquy as the representative of Catholicism. If you manage to recover from your astonishment, and dare to display your shock, they will tell you not only about the silence of the Hierarchy, but also about the active militant role of certain shepherds within Marxism.

When alarmed by the wave of Naturalism and widespread absence of supernatural values among Catholics, when you want to stress supernatural realities, they immediately will forestall you. They will tell you that religion was meant *for people* and their real needs (just as if true religion were not for people), it being well understood that people have no other needs except earthly ones (all others are ruled out). You will be accused of enclosing yourself within an egocentric piety which separates you from others. They will tell you, for instance, that authentic prayer is nothing but working for the sake of others.

When you choose to be steadfast to the Church, to celebrate and to live the most important event of Christian worship, the Holy Sacrifice of the Mass, according to the norms and teachings of Catholic liturgy and dogma, they will confront you with their thousands of eccentric Eucharistic ceremonies which claim to be an authentic and *living religion* for modern Catholics. Those celebrations damage, on many occasions, the content of our faith. But should you attempt any reaction, they will come back with other arguments we will deal with later.

Now, you can always turn to the teachings of the Magisterium to unmask the liars, though it is not going to be easy; that recourse has also been foreseen: many are the famous theologians who, roaming freely within the Catholic sheepfold, are intent on questioning the binding force of the doctrinal teaching of the Magisterium, constantly stressing among the faithful that it is personal conscience that decides.

We could go on with the list of examples, but it is not worth while. I did not really set out to enumerate, nor even to skim through the gravest problems that injure the Church. My intention was to show you, through some concrete illustrations, what I have said above: there is a rampant confusion within the Church, and thus it is not easy to shine, like lamps, in a world determined to remain in darkness. Neither do I pretend to refute those errors well known to you, for this is not the place to do it. But I certainly want to call your attention to something much more serious which has made those errors possible.

Those errors, and many others, could be easily refuted. The problem, for Christians called to burn like lamps in the midst of the world, is more complex. I hinted at it before, and it could be expounded like this:

Confusion would not have flourished without the complicity and silence of many. In your work of apostleship you ought to take that into account. A clear, transparent, coherent, simple presentation of the Message of the gospel is not well looked upon. Some preachers tend to present it as what modern dialectic philosophers would probably call *mediated*. The presentation of the gospel is certainly mediated today by many things. What I mean is that today the gospel is, in a number of cases, made dependent on political, social, economic and even religious (!?) interests, which are to be protected and to which the honest preaching of the gospel is deemed to be possibly harmful. Do not ask me how anybody could possibly think that evangelical truths and mankind's interest may be incompatible. The fact is there, and cannot be denied.

Much is said today about dialogue and reaching out one's hands; and a policy of so-called compromise is often practiced. But dialogues, when misguided, and more often the attitude of compromise are fitting soil for thoughtless people's naive attitudes, and for yielding up one's principles when one is not firmly rooted in them. Some Conference of Bishops may not declare itself against a secular and atheist Constitution which disintegrates the family, because the political moment advises so. As for the religious policy carried out in certain countries, the thinking of their governments has been taken into consideration, but in such a way that perhaps what seemed to be clear lessons of the gospel have been too much interfered with, and decisions have been made which have not always proved themselves right. Many a theologian is allowed to freely spread the most outrageous heresies, undoubtedly with the good intention of avoiding giving the world the impression that freedom is persecuted. Today nobody doubts that some decisions or manners of speaking (correct in themselves) on the part of the Hierarchy have given cause for a number of people to look easily after their own interests. Think, for instance, of what happened in the Conference at Medellín, and how theologies of revolution and liberation managed to take advantage of it, when it would have perhaps been sufficient to have presented a bold exposition of the true content of the gospel and of the real mission of the Church.

We ought to remember that we are not called to judge someone else's intentions, and that we may well be wrong when pointing at any particular fact as an example, for, among other reasons, we do not know with certainty all the information that went into consideration of the problem. But it does not prevent us, simple Christians, from resenting so many problems hampering the clear and pure preaching of the truth. Are the use of tactics and the wielding of human prudence really better than a plain and consistent presentation of the Word? It is true that a long time has elapsed since, for instance, Saint John the Evangelist disdained to talk to the heretic Marcion, and avoided him at the public baths, refusing to deal with him. Nevertheless, the time for martyrs, those who bravely give up their lives for the gospel with all its demands, is never over.

Moreover, we witness today a toleration of placing authentic faith in disrepute. For those who have wanted to keep themselves steadfast to their faith, to their Church and to the Magisterium, have been labeled as reactionary and old-fashioned people. How could it not hurt us in our innermost soul to see the Word of God in chains? (cf. 2 Tim 2:9).

Behind these attitudes there may be very serious matters at work, but we are not the ones called to examine them. We refer to the problem, mixed up as it is with a kind of tolerance, of choosing what is thought to be the lesser of two evils; and to the problem of how such a choice may be reconciled with the demands of Revelation and with wisdom and prudence, not only human but supernatural. That is the same as asking whether or not the preaching of the gospel and the needs of men allow tactics, delays, silences and opportunistic shadings. Or else: does it make sense to put on hold, even as Cartesian method, a number of uncontestable truths of the Revelation because they are not convenient to the present socio–political moment?

What I want you to realize is that when you want to be a light among men, your task is not going to be easy, since you are facing up to an attitude of total rejection. That means that the results of your testimony will undergo difficult trials when you attempt to teach doctrine. It will be time then to look for other means, for one way or the other, your lamps must remain burning.

Do not think, after all that has been said above, that speaking out will be useless. You will have to speak, more so than ever: what are we doing now but teaching doctrine? What I am trying to convey is this: it is essential at the present moment to hang on, above all, to those means which have always turned out effective. The Master Himself has clearly told us about them: ''In the same way your light must shine in people's sight, so that, seeing your good works, they may give praise to your Father in heaven" (Mt 5:16).

Accordingly, the light of your lamps will be effective when it illuminates more than anything else your good works. Your good works, your very life, will be what people will have to acknowledge, and confusion will be powerless against them. We arrive at a conclusion already known, though it now gains special relevance: you shall have to enlighten with your deeds more than with your words. To the devaluation of language, to the lack of support you will often encounter, and to the distortion which nowadays assails truth, you will have to reply with something irrefutable: the testimony of your life.

That is the oil which keeps the lamps of the wise Christian virgins burning despite everything. The irreplaceable worth of holiness is, again, self–evident. Against it nothing can prevail, neither ramparts, nor the freezing winds of the wintry world.

Do not forget that according to today's parable the foolish virgins also had their lamps, but those lamps never had a chance to burn, for they never got oil, thereby becoming useless. It has always been thus in the Church, where each one holds his or her office: some are shepherds and others sheep; each one receives his or her proper charisma; some are given a particular vocation, and others receive yet other callings. But there is neither vocation, nor charisma nor office that is worth much without holiness. A moment came at which the foolish virgins, still in possession of their lamps, but with no oil, had to hear those sad words the Bridegroom addressed to them, 'In truth I tell you, I do not know you."

Another suggestion implied by the parable may be pointed out. There is a hint of concealed confrontation between the foolish and the wise virgins. At first there is just a discrepancy in their attitudes, which turns, later on, into an anguished plea from the foolish to the wise ones: too late had they understood the necessity of oil. Nevertheless, the wise ones told the foolish, in a polite but firm way, that they could not provide them with oil. Let us notice a change of terminology: the virgins were called wise and foolish, but at the very end. Most likely, in the eyes of the world, the foolish ones were first considered wise, and vice versa. From this it follows, among other things, that the foolish virgins (or wise according to the world) were regarded as the ones who really knew what they had to do; on the other hand, the wise ones (wise according to God) were thought by the world to be fools and to have gone astray.

This confrontation between the foolish and wise virgins is the same, after all, as that between God and the Demon, charity and hatred, holiness and mediocrity. In that confrontation, the wise virgins must tread the same path as the Master, and no choice will be left them but to offer their own lives, for 'He was the light of men; and light shines in darkness, and darkness could not overpower it" (Jn 1: 4–5). To shine and yield warmth: that is the task given to the virgins of the parable. And the end is already known: the wick of the lamp, because it has been burning, wears itself out.

The parable of the ten virgins is perhaps one of the most beautiful in the gospel. In it we are told about virgins who were unable to carry out their commitment, about times of waiting and of delay, and toward what human folly can lead us. But it also speaks about diligent virgins, wedding banquets, Grooms who come at unexpected moments, and, above all, about the love between the Bridegroom and the bride that the Song evokes. At the end the wise virgins entered with the Bridegroom into the wedding: they truly are the bride, the woman the Lamb has married (Rev 21:9). They had accepted, given and fulfilled a promise, and now enter with Him into the eternal feast offered by that Love that was before anything was created.

X

CHRISTIAN WORK

It is like a man about to go abroad who summoned his servants and entrusted his property to them. To one he gave five talents, to another two, to a third one, each in proportion to his ability. Then he set out on his journey. The man who had received the five talents promptly went and traded with them and made five more. The man who had received two made two more in the same way. But the man who had received one went off and dug a hole in the ground and hid his master's money. Now a long time afterwards, the master of those servants came back and went through his account with them. The man who had received the five talents came forward bringing five more. "Sir," he said, "you entrusted me with five talents; here are five more that I have made." His master said to him, "Well done, good and trustworthy servant; you have shown you are trustworthy in small things; I will trust you with greater; come and join in your master's happiness." Next the man with the two talents came forward. "Sir," he said, "you entrusted me with two talents; here are two more that I have made." His master said to him, "Well done, good and trustworthy servant; you have shown you are trustworthy in small things; I will trust you with greater; come and join in your master's happiness." Last came forward the man who had the single talent. "Sir" he said, "I had heard that you were a hard man, reaping where you have not sown and gathering where you have not scattered; so I was afraid, and I went off and hid my talent in the ground. Here it is; it was yours, you have it back." But his master answered him, "You wicked and lazy servant! So you knew that I reap where I have not sown and gather where I have not scattered? Well then, you should have deposited my money with the bankers, and on my return I would have got my money back with interest. So now, take the talent and give it to the man who has the ten talents. For to everyone who has will be given more, and he will have more than enough; but anyone who has not, will be deprived even of what he has. As for this good–for–nothing servant, throw him into the darkness outside, where there will be weeping and grinding, of teeth."

(Mt 25: 14–30)

This parable, like all others, contains several lessons, one being the principal lesson. Now the main lesson this parable gives us seems to me this: one must work.

Work is one of the topics people talk much about today, and which, in one way or another, they are most worried about. Hence, since we live in a confusing world, it is not rare that work has become a concept surrounded by conflicting ideas. It would seem that things should not be that way, for work is a simple matter, and simple things are not intricate, but that is the way people are.

On one hand work is overemphasized. For Marxism, for instance, it is work that generates man; no need for me to remind you of such commonplace phrases such as *the world of work*, or *the working class*, or *the forging of man through work*, and many others. At the same time, while they talk about all that, people want to work less and less all the time; to work less and earn more: that is what everyone demands. The claims seem contradictory: on the one hand, the right to work; on the other hand, the right not to work, or to work less, or to work little.

Inconsistencies aside, the fact is that people are working less and less; at least that is what we see in our country. I am not referring here to the phenomenon of unemployment, which is also driven by poor performance at work (although that is not the only cause). I am referring to the fact that people do not want to work. Add to this the problem of early retirement, the problem of free time, and, related to the latter, that phenomenon, which seems so strange to me, of forty eight hour weekends.

So we find ourselves with the social problem of lack of work and the seemingly contradictory social problem of the lack of desire to work. In reality, there are no inconsistencies, and anyone with a modicum knowledge could give us a simple explanation for all this: it would suffice to talk about political tactics to sink a country's economy; although, above all, we would have to talk about the loss of a sense of morality. People allow themselves to be fooled and do not want to work because, having lost the idea of transcendence, they think work is a misfortune or at least a lesser evil.

To us, work is a gift from the Lord, and we have already said that the main lesson given by today's parable is that we have to work. Work was envisioned by God as something beautiful and good for mankind. Work draws man nearer to Jesus Christ, making him a fairer image of God —'My father still goes on working, and I am at work, too" (Jn 5:17)— for it is through work that man becomes associated with God in the activity of creation. God settled man in the garden of Eden "to cultivate and take care of it" (Gen 2:15), in other words so that with his work he might transform it into a still better paradise. That is why to refuse working is, after all, to reject the work of creation, to turn one's back on God's love revealed in creation, to desire non–being rather than being. Deep down, the refusal to work means hatred of God.

Now, do not think that work itself is beautiful only because through it man becomes the partner of God in natural creation. There is something more important. For God also wanted man to work along with Him in the building of His supernatural kingdom. Thus we realize this wonderful fact: the construction of the Kingdom of God —that starts here on earth, and is perfected in heaven— also depends on us. The parable clearly states it: "It is like a man... who entrusted his property to them"; and in the parallel passage from

Saint Luke, in an imperative manner: "Trade with this until I get back" (Lk 19:13); and also in another passage from Saint Matthew, with pressing urgency: "Why are you standing here idle all day?... You go into my vineyard too" (Mt 20: 6–7). All this reminds me of the passage in the Song of Songs (Sg 8:11):

> *Solomon had a vineyard at Baal–Hamon.*
> *He entrusted it to the overseers,*
> *and each one had to pay him the value of its produce,*
> *a thousand shekels of silver.*

As the divine work, which is creation, is one of love, so our work is also a product of love. Therefore, work becomes corrupted if severed from love. And that is why tiredness as a result of work is a sign of love. Thus only those who become truly tired can find God: "Come to me, all you who labor and are overwhelmed, and I will give you rest" (Mt 11:28). Tiredness is a very special attribute which enables us to approach the Lord; in such a condition we should reach the evening of our life: with all our energies burned. The energies we have received certainly cannot remain unspent, or else we would be punished as it happened in the parable to the servant who received one talent and hid it to give it back to his Lord. Things being so, our death will be meaningful if caused by exhaustion, or, if you prefer, in action, but never after an honorable retirement. We will have time enough to rest, although later on, of course, when we reach our permanent Home (Phil 3:20; 2 Cor 5:2).

Great things cannot be understood or achieved but through work, tiredness and suffering, and Love is the greatest thing. And here is the tragedy of modern youth: they have been distracted both from work and from weariness, and now it has become very difficult for them to find God. For without tiredness nothing can be understood, and one cannot come to love others; without it tedium and inner emptiness settle into one's life. Jesus started His dialogue with the Samaritan woman when "tired by the journey" (Jn 4:6), and His whole life was a tiredness which grew deeper along the dusty roads of Palestine and in the midst of cramming crowds who did not even let Him have a meal (Mk 3:20).

Weariness is a kind of defenselessness, the condition of those who have consumed all their strength and given up all possessions, the penury of one who cannot live any longer because he has given away all he had to live on (Mk 12:44). It is the situation of one who has tried all his life, apparently unfruitfully, and then finally makes the last attempt with a supreme effort, trusting in God (Lk 5:5). Tiredness is the essential condition of the prize. It barely matters that, seemingly, little has been gathered, if "you have shown you are trustworthy in small things..."

When people think about working less, Christ does not promise to remove our burden, just the opposite (Mt 11: 28–30). What He does promise is to make it light and easy. For rest does not consist in working less, but working more, so long as it is done out of love. Be very attentive to the Lord's words: He calls all who labor and are overwhelmed. He does not tell them to abandon their task, but to shoulder His yoke, so that they learn that the work is easy and light, and may find true rest for their souls.

Weariness brought about by working out of love yields love; and love is the only joy. This is the way in which tiredness, as corollary of one's efforts, leads to happiness (Jn 4:36). Now we can see how fatigue is a fruit of love, and love is the result of fatigue. That is why we have said before that the young people in our society of consumerism, easy work and free time, since they do not experience true tiredness, are in a difficult position to experience love (it is well known to you that their concept of love is a mere caricature). Materialistic society, by depriving them of the cross, has played a dirty trick on them; for the truth is that in this world real love always carries the mark of the cross. Young people who go for the easy life become consumers of drugs, erotic song–lyrics, literature and films, for they cannot do without love, since they have been created for it.

Weariness out of love brings us to particular situations. This for instance: when time passes and the body crumbles, happiness is more deeply felt. It is not a nostalgia that looks back with sorrow toward years and things lost for good, but a nostalgia that looks forward, toward the Beloved now close at hand, toward happiness, whose first fruits have already been savored. Weariness out of love stirs in us a sense of marvel and wonder for an old age felt as the plenitude of one's life, matured through love. It is this weariness only that preserves genuine youthfulness, preventing us from glancing at the past with nostalgia; it makes us, at the same time, feel the happiness of the love we are presently enjoying and the desire for that which we sense is about to come as a plenitude of a future already near.

When you proselytize, do not insist on much from the lazy. In this parable, the lord deals in very severe terms with the servant who refused to use his talent to yield profits, calling him wicked, lazy and good–for–nothing: very grave words. Experience also advises us that it is very difficult to change those people; so I believe you can start thinking, when you meet them, that nothing is lost if you turn your apostolic zeal toward other directions. Do it as soon as possible.

There are those who might consider as little the fruit reaped with the weariness of a life consecrated to Love: the one who received five talents brought five more, and the man with two talents brought two more. But this thinking would suppose that the talents received amounted to little, when the truth is that God became almost wild in His generosity with us. And notice this: if it is true that God pours Himself out to us, it is also true, according to the lesson of the parable, that we give Him back as much as we have received: five talents in return for five talents; two for two. No, to say that is not accurate. We really return more, as we give the interest along with the capital: ten talents returned when just five were received; four when two were initially entrusted. We give exactly double. Such a wonder has, I believe, this significance: we have received His Love and now we give Him back ours as well; we have received His Happiness and now we bring Him back ours as well; He gave us His life and now we hand it over to Him, but adding ours too as a gift and manifestation of our love. Thus we are now sharing the divine Love, we are now love responding and loving that Love. The madness of God, out of His love for us, moved Him to give us the capability of rendering to Him more than what He gave us. He gave us His love, and precisely because of that, He has found ours in response (Sg 8:12):

> *But I tend my own vineyard myself.*
> *You, Solomon, have your thousand shekels,*
> *and those who oversee its produce their two hundred.*

XI

SAINT JOHN THE BAPTIST

The beginning of the gospel about Jesus Christ, the Son of God. It is written in the prophet Isaiah, "Look, I am going to send my messenger in front of you to prepare your way before you. A voice of one who cries in the desert: Prepare a way for the Lord, make his paths straight."

John the Baptist was in the desert, proclaiming a baptism of repentance for the forgiveness of sins. All Judea and all the people of Jerusalem made their way to him, and as they were baptized by him in the river Jordan they confessed their sins. John wore a garment of camel-skin, and he lived on locusts and wild honey. In the course of his preaching he said, "After me is coming someone who is more powerful than me, and I am not fit to kneel down and undo the straps of his sandals. I have baptized you with water, but he will baptise you with the Holy Spirit."

(Mk 1: 1–8)

Today's gospel shows us the character of John the Baptist, the Precursor. His appearance is impressive: clad with a garment of camel-skin and girded with a leather belt; he also lives on locusts and wild honey, and comes from the desert crying with dreadful voice for conversion and repentance.

Nonetheless, you should not pay much attention to his appearance; it might lead you to misjudge him. John the Baptist was a saint —the greatest among all the children born to women, said Jesus— and it is well known that saints are always like children. This is more real than the harshness of his shouts, his reproaches and his garments. I can imagine his eyes, as always the saints' eyes are, those of a child who never learned how to lie: very transparent, revealing in their depth the beauty of blue seas without shores, the formidable beauty of God. Now and then he is bewildered, trembles and does not know what to do: "It is I who need baptism from you, and yet you come to me!"; and he tried to dissuade Jesus (Mt 3:14). Sometimes his doubts and fears were great, as when he was imprisoned and despatched some of his disciples to ask Jesus, "Are you the one who is to come, or are we to expect someone else?" The same happens to us: sometimes we see things clearly enough, whereas at other times we just see shadows; at times we feel very assured and, like the Baptist, we signal to the people that Jesus is passing by; at other times, even though we live in the certitude of faith, we are in anguish and have to come into Jesus' presence and cry to Him with our mouth and heart, asking whether He is the real One or should we await someone else. Therefore, do not let the authoritative shouts of the Baptist deceive you, for at times his shouts were also uttered in anguish, just as happens with us. But for all of that, it is good that the gospel tells us how the fabric of true holiness is knitted; in that way we do not get discouraged and, by the same token, we rejoice upon seeing the humanity of the saints. How could they be holy if they were not human?

But there is something else that speaks more clearly about the humanity of the Baptist. You ought to know that the Baptist is the saint of perfect happiness. He did not even have the patience to wait until he was born to start being happy; he leaped out of joy, though still in his mother's womb, upon hearing the Virgin's voice. That is why we can think of him as a lucky acrobat eager for happiness. We were born crying, but before he was born he was already acquainted with joyful jumping and laughter. Later on, when he was grown up, he himself plainly spoke about his joy, "The bridegroom's friend, who stands there and listens to him, is filled with joy at the bridegroom's voice. This is the joy I feel, and it is complete." Nor does this contradict what we have said before; you are familiar with that paradox of the interior life: suffering, bottomless peace, and happiness of soul are joined together in those who love God.

The Baptist is the man of perfect happiness because all the essential conditions to possess it are found in him. He spent his life in the desert, away from people, in an uninterrupted dialogue with God. He is also the saint of penance, as the gospel suggests when describing his character and way of life. He was truly humble, which is fundamental to Joy. Let us insist on this latter point: John the Baptist accepted his mission of being just a voice crying in the desert; he deemed he must grow less for Christ to grow greater, emphasizing, in front of everyone, that he was not fit to undo the straps of the Lord's sandals. He was placed on the dividing line between the Old and the New Testaments. His mission was to signal Jesus' presence to the people, but from afar, heralding His passing by, and bringing Him to his disciples' notice, who abandoned John to follow the Messiah. He knew how to fade away in the nick of time, contenting himself with meeting Jesus only from a distance and after many absences which only too seldom became a brief presence.

A dialogue with God, a life of penance and a great humility, those are the ingredients for that wonder that is Happiness. I should like to dwell further on humility. The willingness to vanish, just as the Baptist did, is so important because, by so acting, we offer all we have to Love. He who is in love gives up everything in a freely embraced poverty which abandons all that is not the Beloved. Now we see how humility leads toward poverty, poverty to love, and love to Happiness. The acceptance of our own disappearance, or of death to our own self, deprives us of nothing; it also brings us to Happiness. Truly speaking, dying to one's own self is not as much a detachment, or a sacrifice, as setting oneself on the road leading to Love, and consequently to perfect Happiness. Yes, I know that somebody may consider all that as mere words. Nevertheless, I should say, if you want me to talk from the bottom of my heart, that I feel happy upon realizing that God, in His kindness, has allowed me to be nobody. It is not a happiness founded upon the acceptance of resignation; it is, on the contrary, the joy born from what I deem to be a wonderful present of unbelievable worth, and one which I would not renounce at all. You are aware that because of certain circumstances I cannot preach; that has been my situation for most of the year and even for much of my priestly life. There were times when I have asked myself about the motives there could possibly be to ban a priest from preaching, though I do confess that the matter does not much trouble my mind. What is really significant is the possibility that

God has presented us with something, and we, on our part, have offered it back to Him. It would be all too wonderful that God had given us something with the sole idea that we keep it for Him alone. After all, God does not want our word but our love. He wants to see our self-denial for love's sake rather than our triumphs. I think He likes it so much that He does not wait till we get to heaven before He gives us His Love along with perfect Happiness.

I have tried to introduce you to the Baptist as a person extremely human who enjoyed Happiness; and I have told you about the requisites for it to be granted to us. But do you realize that we have been circling around the same theme without ever describing what that Happiness consists of? We have actually not described it, because it is not possible. It is first necessary to feel Happiness in order to talk about it; that is to say, one must first be in love. A deaf man, for instance, will not be able to talk about music since he never heard it; neither could a blind man tell us about colors, nor could he describe the beauty of a starry summer night. Furthermore, it would be impossible for me to speak about Happiness, even though I had felt it, if you have not experienced it as well. And we cannot explain to a deaf man what music is, nor can we get a blind man to understand the beauty of the starry nights or of a dawn in spring. Only the one who is in love is entitled to talk about love, and only he can experience the joy of being in love and being requited.

Here is the reason why most of the time we have to approach this theme in a roundabout way. That is also why we priests find it so difficult to say anything about God, or about the love of God (which is the same, for God is love), that subject being, nonetheless, the only matter we should really be talking about. But because we do not know how to do it, our preaching is frequently debased. We do not talk about God any more, nor about the means that lead us to Him, and even less about the obstacles which lead us away from Him. Once we have lost His Love, all is reduced to a mere talking about this world, and to a simple taking of sides in some trivial human affair. But when one no longer talks about the uncreated Love, Happiness is gone forever; the only thing left then is our share in the work of deepening mankind's emptiness. At the same time, we lead people to believe they are doomed to incurable sadness.

Once again you can see that we have digressed from our theme: the attempt to explain the Happiness of the Baptist. From what depths did this Happiness flow? I believe he himself pointed to the key of his secret when he said, "It is the bridegroom who has the bride; and yet the bridegroom's friend, who stands there and listens to him, is filled with joy at the bridegroom's voice. This is the joy I feel, and it is complete." So his joy is complete because he listens to the bridegroom's voice, goes where the bridegroom goes, and enjoys his friendship. Therefore, it is a matter of listening to the voice of the bridegroom, talking to him, remaining in his company and being his friend. In other words, we are dealing here with the intimacy of love, with a mutual listening, talking, and being together in àn interchange of lives. It is, after all, a total self-giving of love and for love (that is why the simile of the nuptial self-surrender is used), a total donation to the bridegroom ("It is the bridegroom who has the bride"), reciprocally to accept and possess him. That is the secret of the Happiness of the Baptist: He fell in love with Love, fully aware that that love was returned by Him.

But the love of the Baptist may be sensed as something yet closer to us. All it takes is to realize that it bears a resemblance, in a certain way, to the story of our love for God. His, indeed, is a love which flows among intimacies and meetings, as any love does ("The bridegroom's friend, who stands there and listens to him..."), but also through absences and distances. The Baptist had to confine himself to pointing at Jesus from afar, meeting Him face to face on only a few occasions. Their hearts were always present to one another from the day of their first meeting when both dwelt in their mothers' wombs; but later their encounters became rather fleeting. At times the Precursor did not seem to be very sure of the presence or identity of the Beloved (Mt 11: 2–6). Do not be bewildered at it; the cross and personal misery, which are always our companions in this world, often succeed in making God elusive, inapprehensible, as if we could only see Him through a veil or in fragmentary and incomplete features as if through a lattice (Sg 2:9):

> *My love is like a gazelle,*
> *like a young stag.*
> *See where he stands*
> *behind our wall.*
> *He looks in at the window,*
> *he peers through the opening.*

It is true that for us God is evasive, intangible, fragmentary and veiled in the darkness of faith, all that and much more. But, at the same time, that suffices to bring us to perfect Happiness. For He stands there, behind the wall, window or lattice. And that, being the first fruits of love (more than first fruits we would venture to say) is, for the time being, enough for anyone who is in love. For the lover is not so much seeking the joy of feeling himself satisfied, but he rather seeks the Beloved's presence, that presence being the Happiness which fills him to the point of overflowing. Besides, it is not relevant for the lover if that presence is complete or incomplete, bright or in darkness, still or fugitive; he is well conscious that before the self–giving may take place, he must have a share in the Beloved's cross and walk in His footsteps. In that way, the self–giving of love will become more real: the bridegroom surrenders himself, but he also receives everything from the bride. That is so because there is no love where mutual giving, from one to the other and vice versa, and self–giving are absent, since that is precisely what love is. Even more, the partial possession of the Beloved is not a barrier to Happiness, because we are fully aware that the self–giving we are talking about, now only made as a pledge or first fruits, causes the Beloved more impatience and hunger for love than it does to us. He desires us much more than we want Him. It is He Who seeks, whereas we are those looked for. Did you notice that it is He Who restlessly peers through the windows and lattice? He is not approaching with a tranquil pace, but running and leaping over the mountains and the hills. No, we are not the ones who sigh more deeply when consumed in a longing for love (Sg 2: 8–9):

> *I hear my love.*
> *See how he comes*
> *leaping on the mountains,*
> *bounding over the hills.*
> *My love is like a gazelle*
> *like a young stag.*
> *See where he stands*
> *behind our wall.*
> *He looks in at the window,*
> *he peers through the opening.*

How then are we not going to experience perfect Happiness when we know (experience) that we are zealously desired, impatiently and frantically sought, yearningly awaited by Love?

As you see, it is impossible, after all, to talk about the secret of the Baptist's Happiness. In order to do that, one has to be a child, a poet and a saint; although it would perhaps be enough if we were really in love, since to be in love would most likely entail already having become precisely saints, poets and children. It is not an easy task, for even though we feel at times our love for Him, it is close to impossible to be convinced of His love toward us. At prayer we often make the mistake of talking at length about ourselves: we are overwhelmed with our problems and trifles, persuaded of their importance. But the truth is that there is little to say about ourselves, whereas a dialogue with God Himself as its theme would never end. We would be better off if we asked Him to tell us about Himself. We would learn many things. For instance: that He is not good or very good, but Goodness Itself; and the same could be said regarding beauty, for we would understand that He is Beauty Itself. And I am not saying that we would just learn it in a speculative manner, but that we would *see it* and *sense it*, although through the lattices and walls of faith. As I told you before, it is not a vision or complete possession, but it certainly is a pledge and first fruits, enough for us to achieve Happiness. That is so because to see and feel Beauty in Itself, though it may be through the veil of faith, amounts to much more than to possess all the riches of the world.

Therefore, in spite of my inability to talk to you of the secret of the Baptist's Happiness, I have indicated the way: dialogue with God in solitude, a life of penance, and, finally, humility. That was all I could do. I, like him, will have to be content with pointing Jesus out to you, only to watch how you are taking after the Master. My mission as priest is similar to the Baptist's: to show ways and to smooth them. Yours is to tread them, together with Him, of course, who is the way, and end up, finally, finding Him completely. That will occur in the evening of your life, once you have felt your heart burning with love for Him, and after having pleaded with Him, as the disciples did on the road to Emmaus, that He stay with you for ever, "Master, stay with us. It is nearly evening, and the day is practically over."

XII

WITNESSES TO THE LOVE OF GOD

A man came, sent by God. His name was John. He came as a witness, to bear witness to the light, so that everyone might believe through him. He was not the light, he was to bear witness to the light.

This was the witness of John, when the Jews sent to him priests and Levites from Jerusalem to ask him, "Who are you?" He declared, he did not deny but declared, "I am not the Christ." So they asked, "Then are you Elijah?" He replied, "I am not." "Are you the Prophet?" He answered, "No." So they said to him, "Who are you? We must take back an answer to those who sent us. What have you to say about yourself?" So he said, "I am, as Isaiah prophesied: 'A voice of one that cries in the desert: Prepare a way for the Lord. Make his path straight!' " Now those who had been sent were Pharisees, and they put this question to him, "Why are you baptizing if you are not the Christ, and not Elijah, and not the Prophet?" John answered them, "I baptize with water; but standing among you — unknown to you— is the one who is coming after me; and I am not fit to undo the straps of his sandals." This happened at Bethany, on the far side of the Jordan, where John was baptizing.

(Jn 1: 6–8.19–28)

John the Baptist came to bear witness to the light. To be a witness to the light means to show it to the people, mainly through one's own life, so that they may see it and believe in it. That requires a witness completely filled and overflowing with light. In the case of John the Baptist, to be witness to the light meant to show it to the people in a way that they would understand that he was not the light ("he was not the light"), yet at the same time and thanks to his life, understand what the light was ("he came as a witness, to bear witness to the light"). The light is meant to be seen and so it happened that the people, upon seeing the Baptist, came to believe ("so that everyone might believe through him").

All this is important, not as praise of the Baptist but because his role in regard to Jesus is, in a sense, the same as ours. We have also been called to bear witness to Jesus through our life. It is true that faith comes from hearing (Rom 10:17), but faith must also come through our eyes. People should hear the word in order to receive faith (Rom 10:14), but later that word must become flesh, become alive within the apostle if its truth is to appear. The perfect union is given in Christ, the Word made flesh (Jn 1:14), Who simultaneously worked and taught (Acts 1:1; cf. Mt 5:19; 11:4). At any rate, the text we are commenting on stresses the fact that our life must be an enlightening witness. Indeed, the apostle is called to be, simply through the example of his life, a champion of the light and a witness to it. Jesus Christ should be manifest through the performance of His apostle.

Undoubtedly the Baptist fulfilled his mission very well as witness to the light and leader of people towards faith. Today's gospel tells us that his presence made an impression on the crowds and moved them, to the point that the leaders of the Jews sent somebody to ask him whether or not he was the Messiah. In the same way, the example of our own life should be more than enough to show the true light to the people, as Saint Francis is said to have preached sometimes: walking through the streets or the squares of this or that town without uttering a word. At times it has been thought possible to bring people to the faith using well elaborated, and often complicated, *techniques* of apostleship, but that is naive, and has grave consequences, since most of the time it ends in emptiness and deception. Truly speaking, the matter is both more simple and more difficult: our life must be more luminous, so that people may see Jesus in it.

Someone may think that we cannot be witness to the light when we really are darkness; but the truth is that, though weak and sinful, with grace we are able to struggle and follow the Lord. Let us remember His words, "Anyone who follows me will not be walking in the dark" (Jn 8:12); as we can see, it is not true that we are nothing but darkness. He went even further, "You are light for the world" (Mt 5:14), adding, as if to insist that we must be witness to the light: "No one lights a lamp to put it under the tub; they put it on a lamp-stand where it shines for everyone in the house. In the same way your light must shine in people's sight, so that, seeing your good works, they may give praise to your Father in heaven" (Mt 5: 15–16).

To say that we must be witnesses to the light is to say that the life of Jesus must shine through ours to the point of our being utterly possessed by Him (Gal 2:20). We might try to state that idea more explicitly, and ask ourselves how we are supposed to show Christ through our life; in which particular manner we are to be

His witnesses; and what exactly is it that people must see in us. It was, we should not forget, the love of God and that God is love that has been particularly shown through Jesus. Therefore, we can think of the love of God as that which people must see in us, a love they do not know and in which they do not believe (Jn 14:17). We may still go deeper into detail and say that people must see this in us: that we are in love with God and God is in love with us. And we should not dismiss this matter as trivial in the belief that one is merely speaking flowery phrases. What I want to convey is that our relationships with God must be far from mediocrity and tepidity, and in general from what could be called conventional relationships. What God wanted was to be able to write a beautiful story, in which He would relate the adventure of His love affair with each of us.

Before moving ahead, it is convenient to clarify a question which is very real today, and which probably contains a serious error. Today, when talking about the duties of a Christian, much emphasis is laid on what is called temporal commitment. The Christian, it is usually said, must appear committed to people, which would be true had this formula not hidden within it a secret intention of filling faith with a purely human and earthly content. It is true that the Christian must be committed to his fellow men and women; but what is really important is that one sees him committed to God. Besides, it is a fact that temporal commitment, considered by itself, is nothing but a word–game, if not the codified expression of Marxist doctrine. The truth is that what people need to see in our life is that we have truly believed in the love of God; that such love is a reality in our life because we let God love us uniquely, as only He does, and that we requite Him in the proper manner. This is all the more important in the case of a priest. The figure of the *committed* or involved–in–politics priest, exclusively concerned with temporal problems of people, no matter what he or others may say, is the figure of the frustrated priest who has failed in true love. His anguished worries exclusively centered upon the injustices mankind undergoes are, quite often, nothing but his desire of concealing and appeasing the yearnings of a heart that had been expressly called by Love and now is totally empty; and what makes things worse: one will never be able to love people when turning one's back on Love, and never shall injustices be mended when, from the outset, one falls into the injustice of rejecting Love. Those who have trodden these ways naturally set up an ample array of arguments against what has been said. I know them all, but I would persist in reminding them that we all are going to be judged precisely in terms of Love. Were they to retort that there is no true love but that of committing oneself to people, I would answer only, for the time being, that it is dangerous to contrive an alibi in order to hide the fact that one did not want to fall in love with Love.

We, on our part, will keep on thinking it important that the Love of God may shine in our life; that it may be seen that God is in love with us and we are in love with God. That love must certainly be seen, because, if one does not possess it, to talk about it is of no use; and, if it is possessed, then there is no need to talk about it since it becomes something obvious. But you should not forget that man, in order to fall in love with God, first needs to believe in God's love for him, because love, when perfect, always exists between two persons who requite each other, between an *I* and a *you* who declare to each other their mutual love. Love always looks to be answered, and tends to the mutual and utter surrender of both lover and beloved.

Unfortunately, it is difficult for us to believe that God is in love with us; but if we do, we come to believe that God loves us, in the sense that we become convinced that we are, in a general and abstract manner, included in God's affection for mankind, which was shown in the creation and in the redemption. Nevertheless, that is at a great distance from the experience of feeling that God has fallen in love with our particular *I*. Should you look for an explanation, it will be found in the condition of misery our fallen nature and our personal sins have placed us in. The fact is that God loves us in the way only He knows and can do. It is therefore necessary that we believe in that love and return it, so that it can be shown through our life. For it is a unique, passionate, tender, trustful, and immensely joyful love, which gives itself totally, without retaining anything for itself, in the hope only of being returned. This love which has always existed, freely became childlike and vulnerable so that he could feel the need of us, and finally became one like us in order to live the indescribable dialogue in which an *I* and a *you* mutually give to each other. It shall suffice to think of the incarnation of the Word, the death of Jesus on the cross, and the Eucharist, to believe in that love God professes toward each one of us. We could also read the whole Song of Songs and linger at the verse (Sg 4:9):

> *You ravish my heart,*
> *my sister, my promised bride,*
> *you ravished my heart*
> *with a single one of your glances,*
> *with a single link of your necklace.*

Or at this, in which the Bridegroom says (Sg 6:5):

> *Take your eyes away from me,*
> *they take me by assault!*

I believe that such a love of God for me demands that I love Him unreservedly. But to love unreservedly means something more than just a total surrender to Him. That surrender was already accepted and accomplished long ago: indeed, lover and Beloved have already given each other all they possessed as their own. We are talking about something different here. I ought to love that Love in the real belief that He loves me in that particular way expressed in the Song of Songs: to the point that I have ravished His heart and He, consequently, must take away His eyes from mine because my glances are killing Him with love.

I am certainly convinced that, if I do not believe that Love is able to love me in such a manner, regardless of what I am, I do not believe then in Love. God does not love me because of my merits, but out of Love. It is not my merits that move God to love me with that love, but my yes to His love. A yes that is yielded like a fruit by His Love, but which is also truly mine because that Love made it so. Only in this way could I become a *you* for the Divine *I*, and He become a *you* for my human *I*. It is a yes which brings forth nothing, but to which it has been granted that it may be freely uttered. That is sufficient, really it is everything. That yes impassions God, because through it I tell Him I have believed in His love and that, even though I had the power of keeping my heart, which was truly given to me, nevertheless I have donated it to Him instead, because I have loved Him more than myself. Consequently, a time should arrive in our life when all that matters will be not whether we are bad or good, but just that we are in love with God. Moreover, you will discover that you will always be bad; but that will not hamper Love from loving you, nor will it deter you from loving Love; that will be the only thing you will be concerned with. You will understand that there is nothing you can give except your yes to Love, letting Him pervade you. And then, once you are aware that Love desires and woos you, you will realize, for the first time in your life, that you are infinitely worthy. This shall happen when you clearly see the awesome power you have been given: to open yourselves to Love and answer Him; to love Him and allow Him to love you, to give up everything and to receive everything. Your love story with God, as any love story, is written in personal you–to–you terms. Your nothing will have become something immensely great and beautiful, because God will have granted you His own heart so that you may be able to love Him with His very own Love. Do not be surprised at this; if God wants to give Himself completely to you, it is precisely His heart that He yearns to give you. Better: because God is all heart, since He is all Love, it will be His heart that He will grant us when giving Himself totally to us.

You will never be able to describe your innermost love for Love. It would be, to make a comparison, as if you try to talk about a dawn in spring: you may describe it, but never your feelings about it. Your relationship of love with Love will be kept just between you and Love. The people around you will observe, as we have already said, that you are in love and that your love is returned; but, because perfect love occurs only and exclusively between two persons, the content of that mutual Love will not be perceived by them (Rev 2:17). Thus it happens with the Holy Trinity, where the Person of the Holy Spirit is the mutual Love between the Father and the Son; and thus it happens in the divine–human love, in which each person is a single person for God. Later on, indeed, since Love is like a consuming fire, He will burn everything within His range; but that will be as a consequence and an extension of a love given and consummated between lover and Beloved. The flames of that love will be spread, setting other people afire, so that other similar love stories may be written between God and humans. This is the way in which that devouring fire, like the burning bush Moses saw, burns without destroying, being at once sweet and dreadful, for it stirs in man the desire of being consumed by it and so dying for it (Sg 2:5):

> *Feed me with raisin cakes,*
> *restore me with apples,*
> *for I am sick with love.*

Saint Teresa said that she was dying because she was not dying. The bride of the Song looks for some kind of comfort, for she realizes she is dying with love; she knows that such comfort can only be provided by Love Himself if she does not want to be burned and crushed under the magnitude of that same Love. The bride of the Song is dying with love precisely because she possesses Love and feels burned by Him, but also because she does not utterly possess Him and, in consequence, cannot be thoroughly consumed by Him. That is the way Love kills and burns: because He is possessed by us, but at the same time that possession is not yet complete. The truth is that Love surrenders Himself completely, but for the time being we are incapable of proceeding in the same way, thus our union is not total. Therefore, as long as this life endures, the unfolding love story between God and us is a story of presences and absences at the same time. Presences are provided by Him; absences are furnished by us, since we are the motive why that presence of our mutual love, being constant for Him, is not constant for us. Saint John of the Cross would tell us here that a log must crackle and lose all its impurities before becoming thoroughly one with fire. Nevertheless, these absences render presences possible later on, since the former arouse our longings and desires for the Beloved; and you already know how ardently Love delights in being desired, awaited (this is why the foolish virgins of the parable never came in with the Groom), and even called. Although He rather takes pleasure when it is He Who knocks (after being sought and expected), and we promptly open the door (Rev 3:20; Lk 12:36; cf Sg 5: 2–8).

In brief, the mission you have been called to is not one of denouncing injustices, nor being successful in making a better world and an improved mankind. All that will follow afterwards, if you understand the meaning of your life and are faithful to it. The Baptist came to bear witness to the light, so that through him all came to believe. You have come to be witness to the Love of God, so that men believe in that Love. Injustices —rather, sin— are but the consequences of the lack of love and of the fact that men have turned their backs on God and rejected Him. You must show that Love again, and since men took seriously their lack of love and their *no* to God has been too categorical, you will have to take Love very seriously and give Him an equally firm *yes*. Do not be foolish. In our time the apostles of compromise have nothing to do except make fools of themselves. Almost nothing will be accomplished by that large army made up of clergymen involved in politics (the term taken in all its senses), priests and religious unwilling to appear as if severed from the world, lay people who conceive apostleship as a mere putting into effect some techniques, or as a social and political compromise; their only contribution will be to deepen and widely scatter sensations of emptiness. Many of them are false witnesses, for they testify to a God they never knew because they never loved Him ("Whoever fails to love does not know God, because God is love" 1 Jn 4:8); consequently, their witness is fruitless. But you have been entrusted with a mission: to show to a world which does not believe in Love (since it only loves itself, which is precisely the opposite of love), that you have indeed believed in that Love and are in love with Him (1 Jn 4:16). Your quest is to show that you are in love with God, that you took Love seriously. And you, who have felt a vocation to the priesthood, if you think that your mission is to be committed apostles, diligent, full of zeal, correct, dependable, and anguished for mankind, be aware that you never touched the bottom of what God wanted for you. He freely called you to give Him the utmost inner part of your heart, which people usually keep for themselves; to give Him your whole life which all too often you persistently live as if your own; to write, together with Him, a wonderful love story. Therefore, when your life flows through correct and normal ways —I would rather say through ways of sanity— it is because you are not on the right path. Your ways must be ones of madness: first, because people, in their stinginess, will consider you mad; and then, because most likely you will be really mad, crazy for Love and out of love. And this will be true in the sense that Love conflicts with what people ordinarily understand as lucidity of judgment: "God's folly is wiser than human wisdom, and God's weakness is stronger than human strength" (1 Cor 1:25).

XIII

HOPE, THE VIRTUE OF OVERFLOWING JOY

It is New Year's Day. A year is gone and another one has just begun. This feast brings back to our minds the problem of the time through which our life is flowing. Although, for us, to talk about time as a sequence of things and the passing of our existence is to talk about waiting; did you realize that our life is but a long wait, a craving, looking forward to somebody who is coming, who is Jesus? This is what I think the meaning of hope is; therefore, we might call it the virtue of Waiting. Because that waiting for Jesus arouses great longings for Him in the enamored soul, and because those longings kill with love and cause an incredible joy at the same time, we can refer to the virtue of Waiting as the virtue of Overflowing Joy. For the absence of the Beloved brings about the desire for His presence, which is also love (although it is an imperfect and non-consummated love which naturally tends to its perfection); and you already know that love always entails Happiness. Waiting is yearning to be loved, and more a waiting, more a longing, the more it is done in love; otherwise there is neither yearning nor waiting, for he can neither wait nor hope for anything, who does not desire that which can in fact become the object of his love. That is why Waiting as a virtue demands that we be in love with God; that is to say, this virtue, which is one of the three great theological virtues, is always escorted by the other two, particularly by charity. Therefore, to talk about the virtue of Waiting is to talk about unrestrainable and unchecked yearnings, as well as fiery longings and unspeakable joys; things that refer to a Whole which one desires and knows he is going to possess and Whom one has already met as well as partially enjoyed in the form of first fruits. In reality, the joy given by our partial possession, and the longing of that Whole we know we are going to possess, are the same thing and both make up that Overflowing Joy of which the virtue of Waiting consists. Therefore, that virtue has nothing, or little, to do with a vague confidence in reaching some future prize which is thoroughly unknown to most of the people who reason in this fashion. A virtue of hope lived and presented as uncertain confidence appeals to nobody. On the contrary, the authentic virtue of Waiting belongs to people in love (that is why it depends so much on the virtue of charity, to the point of disappearing when charity is gone); they are impatient (because they hope to possess the Whole), and also joyful (because they have met Love, and understood, ever since, that nothing has sense in itself unless it is within an affirmative answer to that Love). Thus the virtue of Waiting is both possession and want, joy for what one already has and happiness in the certainty of one day possessing what is lacking. In that certainty, the uncheckable yearnings for the Beloved Who is coming yield, in their turn, more yearnings and more happiness because they stir and enkindle love to a higher degree, preparing, by so doing, the way later to make possible a more perfect surrender. Thus the virtue of Waiting moves you to look toward the future, and prevents you from looking to the past, rendering those who enjoy it eternally young; and, when it is not there, the senility of spirit appears immediately; then there is nothing to wait for, unless it be the nostalgic memories of a meaningless past that exists no more and shall never come back. Emptiness and boredom also make their presence felt here, for life is meaningless when one does not hope anything from it except a more or less disguised ending in nothingness. It is true, as you know, that some ideologies preach a kind of perpetuity of the individual through his integration into the perpetuity of the species or humanity, or through a future paradise of a society without classes, without a State, to be enjoyed by others, and for which cause to die now is worthy. But it is doubtful that all this may deceive anyone honest with himself; an Existentialism faithful to its principles will have been more authentic. Therefore, a society that waits for nothing, since it convinced itself that God is dead and is not ever going to return, has become a society of anguish and escape. This is how an earthly Catholicism (getting closer to Marxism) which has pretended to forget the divinity of Jesus Christ (getting closer to a Liberal and Rationalist Protestantism) has become a cold, unhappy Catholicism, which harbors neither expectancies nor desires of Love, but only human hopes.

The virtue of Waiting thus understood, as a yearning and joyful waiting because it is done in love, should be the normal attitude of the Christian. It was said so by the Lord in the parable of the ten virgins who were waiting for the Bridegroom's coming. And He uttered a stronger statement elsewhere, "Be like people waiting for their master to return from the wedding feast, ready to open the door as soon as he comes and knocks" (Lk 12:36). I ought to warn you here against a quick and superficial reading of any passage of the Holy Scripture; in this particular one, for instance, we lean towards stressing the advice that we should open the door soon, overlooking that attitude of craving, of waiting. Therefore, according to the Lord, our normal attitude should be a yearning and an impatient one, caused by the absence of the One our heart thirsts for; in the same fashion as the thirsty is dying for a glass of water, the hungry for eating, the sick for getting well, and the one in love dying for what his heart loves, "Be like people waiting..."

Now waiting suggests absence, or, if you like, desire. For we wait for somebody who has not arrived yet, or we desire something we are lacking. The same thing happens with the virtue of Waiting. It makes us conscious of Jesus' absence, and stirs within us the desire for His coming, thus arousing in us longings for the Beloved and yearning for His Love. And since today we are celebrating one of the feasts dedicated to the Virgin Mary, Mother of God, there is nothing better than coming before her so that she may tell us about all this. Nobody ever felt more intense longings for Jesus than she did. Her longings must have been particularly vivid, for instance, after the Annunciation: expectancy, silence, and attention to God, were the characteristic notes of those longings. Hers were restrained longings, for, in her prudence, she hid the mystery from Saint Joseph's knowledge; and uncontrollable longings as well, that is why she revealed it to her cousin Elizabeth. This makes us understand that the wonderful mysteries of God, when revealed to men, carry along with them a discrete modesty —as a sign of both unspeakable and authentic things— being unrestrainable at the same time, for God takes pleasure in showing His own glory when and how He wishes. On the other hand, I deem that the longings of the Virgin Mary looking for her twelve year old Son who was lost were of a different kind; they must have been anguished longings. In all truth, the anguish for the Beloved's absence, increased even by the feeling of our own guilt, can be dreadful and unbearable. Also think about the longings of the Virgin Mary looking for her Son, now grown-up, through streets and squares while He fulfilled His mission, that sometimes provoked a seemingly unpleasant answer from Jesus (Mk 3: 31–35). I think that these longings will have been serene although eager, and perplexity was likely their peculiar note: Why did Jesus absent Himself? Why did He hide? What odd plans took Him away from her heart, depriving her of the joy of His presence...? And, finally, the longings of the Virgin Mary for becoming definitively reunited with her Son, after the Ascension, were of another sort, for these were of plenitude: all things were understood here and nothing was left but waiting; everything was now accepted, even the Beloved's will to delay the waiting. Now the virtue of Waiting, due to the fire of charity, was hardly such a wait, because it had almost been transformed into charity and complete possession (1 Cor 13: 8.13). Waiting full of expectation and withdrawal; tireless waiting in anguish and perplexity; waiting in plenitude that has almost become love... But the virtue of Waiting, as long as we are in this world, is always there, forming part of our life. It is curious to observe that the different stages of that virtue in the Virgin Mary resemble, somehow, what happens to us as well. Therefore, when we find the impetus and anguish brought about by our wait for Jesus burdensome, we can come before Mary to talk to her, for nobody has ever experienced the anguish of a heart badly injured with a wound of love waiting for the Lord's presence as she did.

But be alert to avoid any confusion. We have, indeed, talked about longings, anguish, tireless searches, and perplexities as things proper, undoubtedly, to the virtue of Waiting. Nevertheless, they are not essential to it. The Waiting we are dealing with is one carried out in love. Hence, what is essential to it is the Overflowing Joy produced by the enamored longings for the possession of the Beloved. Thus we are facing again the mysterious paradoxes of the supernatural life, for those longings caused by Overflowing Joy are at the same time longings that kill, because they kill with love brought about by the desire of the Beloved's presence and by the desire of looking forward to His presence with even greater yearnings: longings for the Beloved, longings of love, longings for greater longings, longings for dying with love. The virtue of Waiting kills in a twofold manner: by making unbearable the craving for what remains in the possession of the Beloved, and by making unbearable the Joy for what we already have of His possession. Both things kill with love, the yearning for the utter union, which has not been reached, and the Happiness because of the first fruits of Love that the Groom has already given. Therefore the state of death, though we are still alive, is characteristic to Christians. This is the sense in which expressions like the following must be understood: "Unless a wheat grain falls into the earth and dies, it remains only a grain; but if it dies it yields a rich harvest" (Jn 12:24). So the only meaningful life, the real life, is that spent dying with love. And consider that if you think we are just using metaphors when we talk about these realities, then you believe these words of the Apostle to be neither real nor true: "For the love of Christ overwhelms us when we consider that if one man died for all, then all have died; his purpose in dying for all humanity was that those who live should live not any more for themselves, but for him who died and was raised to life" (2 Cor 5: 14–15). None of us lives for himself (Rom 14:7), since it is no longer we who live (Gal 2:20), which means that we have died, or rather, that we live dying with love. We are at the antipodes of Existentialism's saying that man is a being–for–death. The death we are talking about here is life, in fact the only life, which was given to us by Jesus (Jn 10:10). The choice for Love is the choice of coming out of oneself and surrendering to the Beloved, renouncing one's own life and living henceforth only His, thus understanding that life is not such a life unless it is a dying of love and for love. On the contrary, he who has chosen to love himself tries to please himself by his self possession and contemplation, and this is nothing but lack of love. The Overflowing Joy of Love always abides in the contemplation of the other and in the self–giving to the other —only God is able to love Himself as *other* in the depth of the trinitarian mystery. But he who prefers himself is left without love, for love is essentially a dialogue and an enamored surrender which always demands an *I* and a *you*. The Overflowing Joy must be for us a self–giving, a coming out of ourselves (Acts 20:35), for that Joy is but the unrestrainable impetus towards the Good in Itself; and we are not that Good. Joy is the contemplation of the other as other, which is a contemplation in love, and becomes a total Joy when the other is the Wholly Other. Something of this kind is hinted at when the supreme happiness in heaven is said to be vision. It is, indeed, the absorbing contemplation of the Other, shrouded in the bliss of a face which gazes at the other face in a loving glance that meets the other loving glance and mingles with it. Certainly, the contemplation of the other as other is of the essence of love; and this reality is properly signified when we say that a contemplation of the face must take place, for, according to our human way of talking, when we use that expression it is well understood that the whole being of the Beloved is contained there. That is why the Groom says to the bride in the Song (4:9):

> *Show me your face,*

and particularly the eyes, since our looking is the best way we have to show our love. That is why the Groom also tells the bride (4:1; 1:15):

> *Your eyes are doves,*
> *behind your veil,*

and elsewhere (4:9),

> *You ravish my heart*
> *with a single one of your glances,*

and in another passage (6:5):

> *Turn your eyes away from me,*
> *they take me by assault!*

It is plainly clear that, according to the language of love, He does not want her to turn her eyes away, but, quite the contrary, to look at Him more intently, so that He can feel better the torment of love. And be advised that this contemplation of the Beloved's eyes is of the uttermost importance; for the sole contemplation of the other's face is not enough, it must be a contemplation of a face turned to me, and which in its turn is also contemplating me. What I am trying to tell you is that if we want it to be a contemplation of love, then the face must be contemplated not only as beauty and as kindness, but as beauty and kindness *which give themselves to me*; and the other must contemplate me in exactly the same manner, for we already know that love is the joy caused by mutual surrender. Therefore, we should stress that narcissism is anti–love since it rules out the contemplation of the face and eyes of the other as other, as beloved, as a being who gives himself to me. Here lies the reason why the contemplative prayer demands the contemplation (or, if you prefer, the knowledge) of Jesus' face; we will attempt to deal with this now.

According to what we have been saying, love requires the contemplation of the Beloved's eyes, in order to make the dialogue of love not only possible but also more perfect. We must admit this, if we want to talk with precision and to see things as they are, rather than to think that the Love of God remains at the level of ideas, abstractions, and generalities. Should we accept this latter line of thought, it would lead us to the absurd corollary that love has its own ways and demands except when one deals with Love Himself. Therefore, the contemplation of Jesus' face, from now on, can be included within the ways of the Love of God, although we ought to hasten to note that it is a vision in faith (1 Cor 13:12), and not through the senses, which does not diminish a bit what we have said above. An important passage pertaining to this matter seems to me the one of 2 Cor 4:6: "It is God who said, 'Let light shine out of darkness,' that has shone into our hearts to enlighten them with the knowledge of God's glory, the glory on the face of Christ."[1] According to this, God may give us light (he has done it, and is still doing it; notice that the future is not used), so that we may achieve a certain knowledge of Christ's face and of the glory of God that shines upon it. We should make it clear that precisely because of what we have just said, talking about a corporal vision of Christ's face by us in this world would have no sense. As the Apostle said, the divinity shines on His face (cf. Col 2:9) and, as it were, *comes out* on His human countenance, rendering it thus impossible for us to see His real face (that is to say, in its full glory, or simply in its fullness. The vision of the divinity is not possible for us in this state of earthly life, for even in Heaven, the elevation by the "lumen gloriæ" will be required). It is a face that becomes unimaginable to us (we would always envisage it in a mere human fashion when, in reality, Jesus' face also radiates the glory of His divinity). Nevertheless, we can have access to His face when elevated by grace, although, as long as we live on this earth, that access takes place within the light and shade of faith, our indispensable purity of heart (Mt 5:8) and our conformation to the life and death of Jesus. It is then when, through the absolute dark of the veil of faith, we would *feel* Jesus'

---

[1] The text is from *The New Jerusalem Bible*, (New York: Doubleday & Company, 1985), which seems to be the best translation.

presence; in the *blindness* of the night of our faith we should *see* His eyes looking upon ours, and we would certainly know that He was behind that veil, uniting His glance to ours, giving Himself to us and accepting our love. For faith's veil is an obstacle for the eyes of the flesh, but not for our understanding when elevated by grace; it is then that our eyes, actually unable to see, are capable, nevertheless, of searching for the presence of the Beloved, turning beautiful because of that presence. The veil only works on us, not on God, Who perceives the beauty of our absorbed eyes gazing on Him, eyes that He Himself has made fair. Therefore, the Bridegroom says to the bride (Sg 4:1):

> *Your eyes are doves,*
> *behind your veil.*

This veil does not cover our heart either, for the latter can go through the former and impetuously soar to the Beloved, leaving behind the understanding and the imagination. The eyes of the Beloved's face are out of reach of human curiosity or pride of any kind, but they are there for the poor, the childlike and the pure in heart (Mt 11: 25–26), appearing to them not just as eyes filled with great kindness and great beauty, but as the eyes of Kindness and of Beauty; Kindness and Beauty Who are not only shown but offered to them as well. Besides, if the Groom asks the bride to let Him see her face (Sg 2:14), we ought to think, if we really believe in the Love of God for mankind, that this plea carries with it the reciprocal offer, as is always the case in the relationship of love, "Whoever loves me will be loved by my father, and I shall love him and reveal myself to him" (Jn 14:21).

"Desired eyes of the Beloved," Saint John of the Cross called them; for us, eyes that are longed for and awaited. We return to our theme, the virtue of hope, which we have agreed to call the virtue of Waiting, or, using another term, the virtue of overflowing Joy, for always hand in hand with charity and faith, it provides us with joyful yearnings for our meeting with the Lord. Sometimes, when I read certain things about hope, too scientific and dry in my opinion, I think about what would happen if we tried to describe the beauty of the human body by merely depicting the skeleton. The skeleton is, indeed, part of the human body, but it is not the whole body nor the beauty of the body. Hope is the virtue of longing and joy, and it can only be understood when it is lived, just as love is only understood by those in love. It is that joyful longing that brings about in us that tense attitude of yearning and waiting. It is an attitude referred to by Jesus when He said, "See that you have your belts done up and your lamps lit" (Lk 12:35), and also when He expounded the parable of the ten virgins.

This parable (Mt 25: 1-13) deals precisely with the virtue of Waiting. The virgins were waiting for the Beloved's coming, and the sin of the foolish ones was that they could not wait, perhaps because they were not sufficiently in love. That is why they had no oil ready, and then, on top of it, they fell asleep. The gospel calls them foolish in order to distinguish them from those who did get the oil ready, who are called sensible. But if you read the parable carefully, you will notice a singular detail: in reality the sensible virgins also fell asleep. What does it mean and where is the difference between them? It seems to me that the parable contains a reproach to all the virgins, though in a more serious way to the foolish ones. The sensible ones waited indeed, but in a fashion worthy of the title of sensible. In other words, if we consider that word in its deprecatory sense, we must say then that their sin was that they waited (one ought to concede that), but without longing or passion of any kind. Their love was not strong enough to prevent them from falling asleep. They must have been waiting and loving to the point of frenzy, which is the only manner of waiting and loving. The unrestrainable yearning and the frantic expectation for the meeting with the Beloved had kept them awake, for love, if authentic, is an unstoppable fire which nothing can quench nor put to sleep except the Beloved's presence.

The absence of the authentic virtue of Waiting deprives us of the Overflowing Joy. Here lies the reason for the sadness of so many Christians, who nevertheless had been called to Happiness. The lord clearly links Joy to the virtue of Waiting: "Blessed are those servants whom the master finds awake when he comes" (Lk 12:37). We see here that the Lord does not promise that happiness only for a future, but quite to the contrary, He asserts it for the actual moment, "Blessed are those servants..." The only condition to be met is that they be found awake, that is, waiting. That is precisely the essential thing: to stay awake while we wait and yearn, feeling the longing caused by the absence and craving for the Divine Presence. Then the moment —always unforeseen— of the Beloved's coming becomes indifferent, for what really counts is our love's unrestrainable yearnings: "It may be in the second watch that he comes, or in the third, but blessed are those servants if he finds them ready" (Lk 12:38).

Today we are celebrating the New Year's feast. Have you given any serious thought to the way in which people celebrate feasts like this? It could be a good opportunity for us to realize how we should love Jesus and how we ought to let Him love us. For we ought to love Him with all that intensity of people who are celebrating the New Year; and we ought to let Him love us with the whole of the Love He wanted to give to all men and women. In other words, it is a matter of loving with a thorough self-giving to Love, and to allow Him utterly to permeate us.

Somebody other than you might think, as usual, that all this is too lofty. But that would be as foolish as saying that God is too high: God is in His place, it is we who are too low. Have you ever been aware of what happens in real prayer with the unresolved problem of ever-annoying distractions? Very well, there is a passage in the Song, which I did not understand for many years, that goes as follows (Sg 2:7):

> *I charge you,*
> *daughters of Jerusalem,*
> *by all gazelles and wild does,*
> *do not rouse, do not wake my beloved*
> *before she pleases.*

If we approach the Lord laden with problems and besieged by thousands of little torments from our poor imagination, He can abate them and, at His conjuring, make everything be forgotten, only love being left. Saint John of the Cross paraphrased that:

> *A las aves ligeras*
> *leones, ciervos, gamos saltadores,*
> *montes, valles, riberas,*
> *aguas, aires, ardores*
> *y miedos de las noches veladores:*
> *por las amenas liras*
> *y canto de sirenas, os conjuro*
> *que cesen vuestras iras*
> *y no toqueis al muro,*
> *porque la esposa duerma más seguro.*[2]

---

[2]Saint John of the Cross, *The Spiritual Canticle*, stanzas 29–30: *Swift-winged birds, / Lions, stags, and leaping roes, / Mountains, lowlands, and riverbanks, / Waters, winds and ardors, / Watching fears of night: / By the pleasant lyres / And the siren's songs, I conjure you / To cease your anger / And not touch the wall, / That the bride may sleep in deeper peace.*

The virtue of Waiting is the virtue of Overflowing Joy, not because it is a waiting, but because it is waiting for Love. Longing for Love is already love, and makes that Love already present in some way, in the form of a pledge, which is the origin of Overflowing Joy as something already actual and real. Love with His total presence will come afterwards, and the other Joy along with Him; of It I cannot speak. I beg your pardon for daring to talk to you about the former, and I only stammer it out. For, as you know, if there were anything wrong with the Love of God, it would be precisely that: one cannot talk about it; and if, nevertheless, the attempt is made, then one comprehends better what the old theologians said about God: that which we keep silence about is truer than what we say. I wish I had the heart to love Him and lips to talk to you about that love. I have told you, nevertheless, that longing is part of the virtue of hope, and this nostalgia will accompany us all our life. But that does not prevent me from weeping like a child because I do not know how to talk to you about the Love of God, although I am sure that you will forgive me; in the meantime, I will continue thinking of that Love Whom I have never been able to return. Blessed are those who said yes. When you meet them, come and tell me immediately, so that I can also make my way to them, as a poor beggar, for them to teach me to do the same. We talk about many things, when the only theme of our conversation should be the Love of God; who will relieve our sadness for not having done it? Oh Truth, so old, yet so new —said Saint Augustine— too late have I known Thee, too late have I loved Thee...! Saint Augustine knew It late, but many people will never know It. Or perhaps they will! All it will take is that Truth and Love may be seen in your life. For that reason I would say that your mission is none other than this: to tread along the ways of the world as minstrels of Love; but one ought to do a fair job, in order to seduce people by the tune of your songs and the poetry of the feats you are going to sing, for you are going to sing the wonderful deeds of the Love of God. Words are meant for talking with human beings, and fiery words for talking about Love and with Love. All problems will disappear, being reduced to only one, whether or not we let Love permeate us. For that reason I want to address myself to you, who have received a childlike heart, who still believe in poetry, who never thought of yourselves, who have chosen poverty because you have known how to love and have given everything... You, wherever you may be, are those who kept the flame of Joy burning among mankind; those who have prevented God's abandoning us, for His Love abides with you forever. We have not been able to do it, but while learning it, we will call to our side the virtue of Waiting and also Her Who is our hope, The Blessed Virgin Mary, for they both help us and put on our lips the cry with which the Apocalypse ends, "Come, Lord Jesus..." (Rev 22:20).

XIV

WAYS TOWARD TRUE LOVE

At times, the gospel tells us about confrontations between Jesus and the demon. The Lord, by defeating him, gave us also the possibility of overpowering him, so that, whenever we are tempted, we can always come out victorious (1 Cor 10:13; Heb 2:18). Certainly, the demon tries to take us away from God in many ways; for instance, by making us cowards.

Cowardice as an obstacle to Love

You can be certain that we will have lost everything, if the demon can make that happen. Since God invites us to be holy, which is the same as to love Him earnestly, the demon will do everything in his power to scare us and foil our affirmative answer. I am sure you remember how often Jesus invites us to surrender our life and to die to ourselves. Now, the demon will make any possible effort so that we become frightened by those calls, and all too often he will succeed. When that call comes to take shape in, for instance, work well done, purity of heart, or detachment from this or that, then we will consider ourselves incapable of facing up to them. We will be afraid of our selfsurrender; for we will have let two subtle temptations creep into our hearts, only to yield to them later on: on one hand, all those things will seem to us very difficult, and at any rate only fitting for a select group of Christians to which we do not think we belong; on the other hand we are convinced that if we give up worldly things we will become miserable and sad, for it would mean doing violence to our nature and depriving ourselves of the happiness those things provide. By acting in this fashion, we are forgetting something important, that the demon is the father of lies and he always lies, as Jesus Himself warned us: "You are from your father, the devil, and you prefer to do what your father wants. He was a murderer from the start; he was never grounded in the truth;

there in no truth in him at all. When he lies he is speaking true to his nature, because he is a liar, and the father of lies" (Jn 8:44).

That is true. When we are made aware of the earnest demands of Christian life, or when we somehow become acquainted with the mortification of the saints, we are frightened, and such demands seem to us very difficult to accomplish. But this happens because we suffer an error of perspective. If we look at the problem from below, standing only on the level of difficulties, and with a merely human perspective, then that problem rightly frightens us, for we have powerful motives why it should do so. But if we look at it from above, from the view–point of divine love, then we comprehend the demands of christian life as something that is going to propel us towards the heart of God and, in consequence, as something that is going to provide us with perfect Happiness. Once we have experienced that Happiness, then dying to ourselves does not seem to us so difficult; then the opposite will frighten us, that is to say, the possibility that we could shun self–surrender. Therefore, to die to ourselves not only has no sense except for the Love of God, but it is something that only can be accomplished along with this same Love. But then, dying to ourselves is no longer a demand; it is something that takes us to Love and makes us joyful.

Cowardice makes us lukewarm. Tiberio, a character in José María Pérez Lozano's novel *Las campanas tocan solas*, said that the faith of tepid people is a cowardice, like shadow which wants to justify itself for its lack of sunlight. That is why the Apocalypse says: "I know about your activities: how you are neither cold nor hot. I wish you were one or the other, but since you are neither hot nor cold, but only lukewarm, I will spit you out of my mouth" (Rev 3: 15–16). The coward, indeed, is afraid of Love; scared before the magnitude of the sea, he chooses to remain in the stagnant pool.

He is afraid of great things, and had he been able to, he would have made a world enclosed in itself and within which each of us would think only about himself. The coward has learned to label as *exaggeration* anything that surpasses the measure he has established for things; and because the measure is always small, it becomes clear to him that there are no great things; in any case, things that appear great are only exaggerated or out of place. He is also afraid of being loved, for he is aware that then he will be called to self–surrender, when what he prefers is to keep to himself since he deems himself the greatest good; thus he never learns to love, nor consequently to know God (1 Jn 4:8). He never perceives the beauty of things either; he is too busy constantly looking at himself. Even more, since the coward is afraid of God, he eventually becomes afraid of everything: true happiness, others, he himself, and his own cowardice (hence he does not want to admit that it exists). Therefore, fear turns out to be characteristic of the coward: he feeds on it, breathes it, and lives on it, thus immunizing himself against Love: "In love there is no room for fear, but perfect love drives out fear, because fear implies punishment and whoever is afraid has not come to perfection in love" (1 Jn 4:18). And lack of faith always comes along with fear and lack of love: "Why are you so frightened, you who have so little faith?" (Mt 8:26; cf. Mk 4:40). We now see the truth in what we said before, that the faith of the lukewarm is nothing but cowardice.

You should be alert against some who consider themselves revolutionaries but are really cowards. Any kind of revolution is false which does not begin in the real conversion of those who promote it. And cowardice, in its accompanying fear, often disguises itself as virtue. For instance, sometimes it calls itself prudence, at other times zeal for the people; because the coward will never admit that he has no courage to look at Love face–to–face. Here is the explanation of the strange *updating* that many clergymen have carried out; they have rightly given cause for the saying, filled with bitter irony, that they have changed the contemplative life for the contemplation of life. For the shock of a world facing the giving up of the self seemed reasonable to them, and they thought a life completely dedicated to God would be taking things too far. We come back to what we said above: the attempt to bring measure and moderation to everything has been also tried with Love, Who, by definition, rules out any measure. Obviously this attitude tries to justify itself by saying that the goal undertaken is one of giving oneself more and in a better way to others; but the truth is that once Love, Who is the fountain of all love, is annihilated, a self-seeking search is all that remains. When, for instance, Saint John of the Cross's *universal mortification*, is considered an exaggerated expression, it is because one has decided to judge Love according to one's own measure, destroying Him by so doing. No wonder then that the Apocalypse placed cowards at the top of the list of those to be thrown into hell (Rev 21:8).

Simplicity as a way towards Love

But the demon not only labors to make us cowards. He also tries to make us complicated, stealing simplicity from our souls.

It is difficult for me to explain to you what simplicity is, but you will understand me better if I tell you that the demon succeeds in making us complicated when making us always look at ourselves. God is simplicity without limits, which is to say that He is Being; and although some of the ancient philosophers identified God with the One, the truth is that God is totally beyond any number, even the one. On the contrary, things are beings: with their composition, their radical finiteness or imperfection —mixture of being and nothing, or of being and deficiency— and with a being which has been received by participation. And since God is not compounded of act and potency, but is pure Act, sole Being, infinitely Simple, He Whose essence consists of existing, when we look at things as if they were self–sufficient —severed from their origin— we see them more as what they are not than as what they really are. By so doing, we abandon the natural attitude towards things and adopt an artificial standpoint when dealing with them. When we do not look at them as they are, we do not embrace a normal posture towards them. Besides, the more we turn to the complexity of things and move away from the infinitely simple Being, the more complicated we become.

Since God is infinitely simple, we can say that Simplicity is identified with Him, and, consequently, with beauty and kindness. That is why simplicity is irresistibly attractive, making it difficult to talk about: for to talk about simplicity is to talk about God. When we love God above everything —and accordingly all things and people within the heart of God— we do not mind what others think or say about us; which makes it possible for us to appear before others with a natural air, that is to say, as we are, without the malformed and deceitful layer of sin, without the artificial worries caused by our attachment to things. So, he who truly loves God is free from useless worries, and the beauty of simplicity shines in him; wonderful and enigmatic simplicity; he who possesses it carries with him the whole grandeur of pure Love.

That is the simplicity the demon tries to steal from us, the simplicity of living with just one thing in our mind and heart: God,

Who is the Only One, the infinitely Simple. The devil will endeavor to direct us towards a multitude of creatures in an attempt to make us complicated, so that we know neither what we are, nor where we are heading, nor what we want, and in order also to make us feel empty, unreliable, and insecure, with a darkened mind and a blurred heart. Simplicity being the opposite of complexity —and do not mistake complexity for profundity: simplicity is profound— it always settles our mind and heart in Him Who is also the Only One, as we have said. There is a unity or simplicity of end and desires that incites us to deem all other things as contingent. This does not mean to diminish them, but to place them in connection with God in order to know their full entity, subordination, and finitude. In this way simplicity tranquilizes and appeases our spirit, releases us from any dependence and calms us, at the same time directing our heart towards God Who is Love and leaving us in a state of spiritual poverty. For, indeed, simplicity and spiritual poverty are the same thing.

Let us stress this last thought. We are saying that spiritual poverty takes us to the Love of God, to true Love, to love God totally and to let Him love us totally too, to be all for the Whole and to accept the Whole as totally for us (Sg 2:16):

My love is mine and I am his.

It is not that we do not value things; now we truly love them, more than before; but now we love them in God and from God, Who fills our heart. Spiritual simplicity and poverty consist of this: the bride is only and totally for the Bridegroom, and the Bridegroom is entirely for the bride. In this union the words of the Apostle become real: "Yet it is no longer I, but Christ living in me" (Gal 2:20). Henceforth, the bride has nothing as her own, since she has given everything to the Beloved, including her thoughts and desires. They are not two lives any more, but a single heart and soul (Jn 17: 21–23.26; cf. Acts 4:32). For that reason the bride says to the Bridegroom:

> *Yo tu vida viviera*
> *si tú te me entregaras por entero,*
> *y la mía te diera*
> *si, en trueque verdadero,*
> *quisieras cambiarlas, cual yo quiero.*[1]

But we have already said that the relationship of love between God and ourselves is not without contention (Sg 2:4), at least until the consummation of love is achieved. In any relationship of love, each of the lovers struggles in order to be the one who gives more; further, each one wishes to become needy before the other and wholly at the other's mercy, in such a manner that the lovers possess themselves no longer, for they have given to each other in self–surrender (Sg 2:16):

My love is mine and I am his.

Accordingly, the bride's appeal, that the Bridegroom interchanges His life with her, will be answered by the Bridegroom in the same terms. And because the Bridegroom's words are always true and

---

[1] A. Gálvez: *Cantos del Final del Camino*, Shoreless Lake Press, New Jersey, USA, 2020, 68. From now on *CFC*. *I would live your life / If you utterly relinquished yourself to me / And I would give you mine / If, in true exchange, / You wanted to trade them as I wish to.*

bring about what they say, and because He has already utterly surrendered Himself to the bride, even as a eucharistic supper, He can also say to her:

> *Mi vida ya es tu vida*
> *y la tuya es para siempre ya la mía;*
> *mi vida es la comida*
> *que yo a ti te servía*
> *cuando tu amor me diste en aquel día.*[2]

Some of this full and mutual possession in intimacy of love, of the Bridegroom by the bride and of the bride by the Bridegroom, is expressed in that passage of the Song (2:6; 8:3) in which we see how both mutually give and surrender one to the other:

> *His left hand is under my head,*
> *his right embraces me.*

The prayers of saints are said to be always effective, for they only want what He wants since their will is entirely submitted to God's will. That is true, but do not think that the will of either one is made void; truly, any relationship, even more one of love, is always a matter between two persons. The truth is that the Bridegroom also yields to the bride's will, this being the reason for the power of the heart of the saints and of their intercession. And there is the reason for the Lord's absolute promise (Jn 14: 12–14; cf. Mt 21:22; Mk 11:24; Jn 16:24), which has only one condition: faith in Him; that is, a thorough confidence that moves somebody to give himself

---

[2] *CFC*, 69. *Already my life is your life / And already your life is forever mine; / My life is the meal / That I gave you / When you surrendered to me that day.*

to Him exclusively out of love. Only in this way may the promises of Christ be understood in all their strength. It is impossible to think about any relationship —least of all when we deal with a relationship of love— in which only one part counts. Obviously, the devil will try to make of our prayer life, and of our friendship with God in general, anything except a *you–to–you* relationship; he will see to it that we believe ourselves to be alone, and that our prayers cannot be anything but petitions, addressed to a distant God Who perhaps may listen to us, but Who has nothing to tell us. The next short step, obviously, is to think that He does not listen to us at all, which is contrary to Jesus' words, "I shall no longer call you servants, because a servant does not know his master's business; I call you friends, because I have made known to you everything I have learnt from my Father" (Jn 15:15; cf. 13:21), and equally contrary to what we have said a relationship of love is: dialogue between a *you* and an *I*, mutual self–giving between an *I* and a *you*, mutual possession of both, and complete joy in total giving.

But this mutual giving of love, in which God surrenders Himself to us and we to Him, would be desecrated should we think that all is reduced to a situation in which we are going to obtain from God a number of things. For, although the statement "my Beloved belongs to me" is true, there is more truth here than appears. We should inquire here about the possible meaning of the fact that God gives Himself to us and is ours, as well as about the sense in which certain expressions of the Song should be taken (6:3; 2:16; 7:11):

> *I belong to my love, and my love to me*
>
> *My love is mine and I am his*
>
> *I belong to my love,*
> *and his desire is for me.*

One can always say, of course, that all this is poetry, or fall back upon some simplistic interpretations of the Song of Songs, which are surely attempts to reduce the Love of God. Why could not God love us with that intensity when He is precisely Love itself? Why measure God with our human standards, believing that He can only do what looks reasonable to us? Surely, such expressions as those quoted above from the Song mean something much deeper, and the first thing to do with them is to believe them true. If we do so, then they will take on a truly ineffable meaning: that God gives us what is innermost and most delicate of Himself, His own heart, His Love. Indeed, what would it matter if God gave us things, but did not give us His Love? Could Jesus' words mean something different: "I have made your name known to them and will continue to make it known, so that the love with which you loved me may be in them, and so that I may be in them" (Jn 17:26)?

In God, too, we may call Love that mutual self-giving performed between the Father and the Son, that is, the Holy Spirit, Who is like the seal of their union and self-surrender. That is why Love essentially is a giving up or surrender, and why Jesus said that "there is more happiness in giving than in receiving" (Acts 20:35). Yet love also consists of receiving, because the lover receives the beloved's surrender, and the former, in his turn, receives the latter's gift; if each one of them surrenders himself to the other, then each one receives the other. At any rate, when dealing with love, the other is received, but as a gift, as something that springs and arrives from the innermost depths of freedom and will, from the most private part of the person who loves, from the innermost part of his heart. That makes love essentially free, and the Holy Spirit is thus also called the Gift, and His graces are called gifts. The Father and the Son simultaneously breathe together the Holy Spirit in a reciprocal giving (active expiration). Once He has been breathed, has received the infinite breath of love, the Holy Spirit remains essentially a Gift (passive expiration). Therefore, it makes no sense questioning whether or not the lover (the one who gives himself) expects to receive something from the beloved or to receive the beloved himself, since he is simultaneously giving and receiving in the very same act of loving; and all that through a giving which is also a receiving and a receiving which is also a giving, and where all is reduced to a mutual surrender or reciprocal donation of one to the other. We can say, therefore, that in love, although there are two who receive each other, there are very particularly two who give themselves; that is why Love is essentially Gift. Equally, he who loves can neither give himself without receiving the beloved, nor receive the beloved without giving himself, for love is a tender breath simultaneously breathed by two lovers. In this way love is the joy of giving oneself to the beloved: there is more happiness in giving than in receiving. All the expressions of the gospel inviting us to true love speak more about self–giving than about receiving: dying to oneself, losing our own life, renouncing our family or possessions, disappearing as the wheat grain in the earth, accepting our pruning, looking for the last place... And always trying to die to oneself in order to fall into the Beloved's arms, to give oneself in order to make possible the invasion of Him Who is Gift par excellence.

On the contrary, the devil will try to engross us in contemplation of our own selves, by means of which he can succeed in making us regard the surrender as something unbearable, preventing us from carrying it out: "Sir, I had heard you were a hard man, reaping where you had not sown and gathering where you had not scattered; so I was afraid, and went off and hid your talent in the ground" (Mt 25: 24–25).

Poverty as a way towards Love

We are no longer children when we think ourselves adults depending on no one; that is what has happened in the modern world: we believe we have discovered that we no longer need God. The devil spares no effort to foster in us feelings of self-sufficiency, thus robbing us of the happiness that springs from our feeling like children. But the truth is that the human being, in order really to be one, needs to be a child, to feel dependent on God as Father, for that is to be in the truth: "In truth I tell you, unless you change and become like children you will never enter the kingdom of Heaven" (Mt 18:3; cf. Mt 18:4; Mk 10:15; Mt 11:25; etc.).

Poverty goes with infancy. The child is an indigent who needs others, his parents above all. And indigence is poverty, to which Happiness has been promised: "Blessed are the poor" (Lk 6:20). To be sure, poverty is not a good thing in itself, but only to the extent it is paradoxically opposed to riches (2 Cor 8:9), and so long as, freely embraced, it creates a space for the Whole. Poverty, in consequence, consists of the First Commandment, since one who has chosen only God is left without anything else. We should say here that it is not a matter of feeling contempt for things, nor a renunciation as a kind of rejection which can be viewed as a minor evil.

There is no minor evil we must choose as a means to an end. There can be no evil, whether great or small, in renouncing all things for the sake of Love, though the devil will seek to make us believe the opposite. Those who are in love with God do not consider themselves less for having renounced all things, nor even perceive it as a denial. There is, indeed, a renunciation (Lk 14:33), but it is done in such a way that he who has God has everything, for even those things he had renounced are now found in another way. The lover of God does not feel the renunciation of things as an abnegation; he would wish to do it anyway, even if it was not necessary, because he finds everything in God, reckoning everything else as quite relative; but above all because, moved by the impetus of his love, he wishes with all his strength to give God all he has. In this way, complete self-denial is not only painless, but is transformed in the fountain of true Happiness, for we have already said many times that love is giving everything. The lover of God does not renounce things thinking that they are bad or may hamper him; his motives are different: delighted with the feeling that God is giving him everything, he wants to do likewise; both give birth, in so doing, to a relationship of love in which they utterly give each to the other. Here is the paradox of the happiness felt by the human being when he sees himself before God in fellowship with poverty, or rather, as a poor person. For that reason I believe the poverty of spirit (Mt 5:3) to be the most difficult and, at the same time, the most perfect, happy, and beautiful among all poverties.

Poverty in spirit leads us to perfect Happiness, because thanks to it we steal God's heart, that is Love. But Love is the Whole, and, consequently, He gives Himself thoroughly. And the lover of God is happy not because he possesses all, but because he has Him Who is the Whole; he is not happy because he is rich, but because he loves and is loved, and loved by the Whole, Whom he also loves entirely and completely, for being totally immersed in Love Himself, he possesses Him and is possessed by Him.

In this sense, human love, as wonderful and indescribable as it is, is something left far behind, for it is just a participation in divine Love. The part is less than the whole, but when we are dealing with the Whole then the distance is infinite (we are talking here of *part* in the sense in which it is understood in theology by the theory of participation). Therefore, human love, so long as it is participation and not totality, cannot ever be a perfect love. On the contrary, in divine–human love, although the created being never loses his nature, nor can he receive totally the Whole because He is infinite, he does indeed receive Him as Whole and gives himself totally to Him as the Whole. This is a thing that cannot occur in a purely human relationship of love, even though the lovers may be elevated by grace; creatures cannot be ends for other creatures, nor entirely satisfy their hearts either. On the contrary, self–giving to divine Love not only consists of a donation of body and soul —the whole person— but also of that which is most profound and particular in the person, that which cannot ever be given to another human being in spite of our wish to do so. And that is the limitation of the human love regardless of how perfect it may be; it will be able neither to give itself totally nor to be received in totality.

Poverty out of love implies no contempt for things. That would be absurd, since he who loves God also loves the works of His hands and sees them as what they are, vestiges of God. He who loves God loves things because they tell him about God, but does not linger in them, because they are not God; he looks at them with tenderness since all and each of them in its own way are a canticle to the Beloved, but he does not appropriate them, for they are not the Beloved, Who exclusively fills his heart; he wonders and is happy at them because the Beloved passed by leaving in them a token of His own beauty and kindness, but does not take possession of them, for it would be to keep the part once one has known the Whole. Thus only he who loves God is the one who looks at things without selfishness and with true love; only he who loves God is the one who truly loves people and does not take advantage of them. Just the opposite happens when a so–called love for mankind is not based in love for God: people end up being treated as instruments and finally destroyed. Because things are always telling us about the Beloved's passing through them, they are saying that He is not there and that we must go on searching. To be sure, he who lingers among things also ends in searching —since things cannot satisfy him— but a searching which is increasingly despairing, for it leads to the nothing and the void. Quite the contrary happens with him who searches for God; because he finds progressively clearer vestiges of Him and catches an increasingly better glimpse of the end of the road, he is more inflamed with love and yearning, and filled with Joy.

When, with the help of grace, one has renounced everything and fully opted for God, a passionate and unusual love story starts between God and man, the most beautiful story ever told, which never can be told. By then God and Man are already the Bridegroom and bride of the Song of Songs. It is then that the Bridegroom puts His Love in the bride's heart and kindles a burning Fire in her (Deut 4:24). This is impossible if we do not surrender everything and our love is not hard tested in fidelity. Even when we want to surrender our self completely, first we must die to anything that is not God, and since this is a self-giving of love, it must be ardently desired by us. It is Love Himself Who is at stake here. That is why God kindles in the bride's heart a fire which is infinite, to the point where it now can be borne by a creature elevated by grace.

This fire of love carries its own characteristics. It is unspeakably enjoyable and simultaneously painful, and both to the limit point the human can endure, who must be helped by God in that endeavor. This suffering plays several keys at the same time. The human being knows God in a new way, as the extremely desirable, although he also knows that He cannot be totally possessed. The human being is burning with that desire, and with such an intensity that he can experience the sensation of his heart and spirit abandoning the body, both drawn by the power of infinite Love, and the body is neither able to follow them nor to endure that pressing love. Love is soliciting by nature, for it gives everything; this earnest request is addressed to the innermost depth and freedom of the other person: it is expecting but not demanding, longing though not claiming, and wishing without forcing. But when dealing with infinite Love, that call is infinitely attractive; and we cannot adequately answer to it now, although we desire to do it with all our soul, and that is why we feel like dying. What is caused here is an enormous and ineffable strain between, on the one side, an invitation and a giving which are infinite, and, on the other, a capacity of receiving and answering which is very limited. Consequently, the bride says to the Bridegroom:

> *Los susurros del viento*
> *dijeron a los pinos del otero*
> *que yo por ti me siento*
> *de amores prisionero,*
> *y con ansias de verte yo me muero.*[3]

Here the bride feels herself truly dying with love. But it is a real death, since here all expressions of human love, which either signify little or are completely empty of meaning, are left behind. They are used in human love, for they are indeed beautiful, but usually have no real significance. Here, on the contrary, the bride feels that

---

[3] *CFC*, 112. *The whispers of the wind / Told the pines on the hill / That for your sake I am feeling / Trapped in love's nets, / And that I am dying with yearnings to gaze upon you.*

she is really dying. The Bridegroom is more than her life, and she no longer feels that life because He is absent; besides, her heart has abandoned searching after the Bridegroom, and one cannot live without a heart. But, above all, the bride experiences herself dying because of hunger or want; or from lack of air, for she is in need of that which is more necessary than air; or because of darkness, for she wants what is needed more than light. She now is aware of what dying signifies: lacking something that was her life. Even that is not exactly the case, for now we are dealing with a greater life, greater than the natural one and which, therefore, causes a greater death than natural death. In reality the bride dies for the sole reason that He is absent; or at least because she does not feel Him, which to her is the same. For though she has been deprived of her heart, of light for her eyes which see no longer, and of the breath which was her life, even then she could live without them. But she knows that she dies only because He is absent. Now she comprehends that nobody dies because his heart stops beating, but because, when that occurs, one stops loving, and it is impossible to live without Love. But she dies, and at the same time she does not want to cease her dying, because she is conscious that she would die if she did not die, and she would not live if she did live. She wants to die not because her death is going to take her to the Beloved, but because she wants to be consumed in Love and burn in a self-giving holocaust of her life to the Beloved. She understands that love is consummated by a death of love, and that nobody loves perfectly unless he dies for love of the beloved person (Jn 15:13). To be precise, we ought to say that she dies out of love because the death of love is not yet the consummation of love, but the prior and last step towards Love: that is why she is able to die. Like the swan, which sings its fairest song before dying, her death is a canticle of love and a last salute to Love. The Bridegroom already died with love, but now the bride dies because she realizes that is living without dying for the absence of the Beloved; and because she wants to share the Beloved's destiny, and wants to be with Him; but above all because she wants to die with love for the Beloved, and thus enjoy infinite happiness, already felt by Him, sprung from the utter, everlasting self-giving to the other.

> *Los dulces ruiseñores*
> *que cantan en los chopos del otero,*
> *al verme que, de amores,*
> *por causa tuya muero,*
> *han volado a decirte lo que quiero.*[4]

The consuming fire, which burns and wounds, still conceals the Beloved. Consequently, it kindles in the bride a larger love and stronger desire to be burnt and wounded more thoroughly by that very fire. They are a burning suffering and a wound which are more intense because they do not increase and, above all, because of the Bridegroom's concealment. Thus the bride says:

> *El cierzo sonrosado*
> *de las frescas mañanas en la aurora*
> *cantaba alborozado*
> *de Aquél que me enamora;*
> *mas no quiso decirme dónde mora.*[5]

---

[4] *CFC*, 14. *The sweet nightingales / Were singing on the poplars along the road, / And seeing that, out of love, / For your sake I am dying, / They flew to tell you what I want.*

[5] *CFC*, 121. *The rosy air / Of the fresh mornings at dawn / Was joyfully singing / About Him Whom I love / But it refused to tell me where He dwells.*

This concealment, as well as all that happens in this story, is quite singular. It is shrouded in the terrible darkness of faith, but the bride knows that He is there, with a kind of presence which cannot be explained: it is not simply knowing, but perceiving, as it were, the presence. Perhaps it is a perception —which is an overflowing reception— of His Love; perhaps it is a presence of the holy Spirit, Who, more than unveiling the Person of the Beloved, tells us about Him, overwhelming us with His breath. Thus the bride says:

> *Y al permitir los velos*
> *oscuros de la fe, en que te escondiste,*
> *enciendes más los celos*
> *del pecho que me diste*
> *y agrandas más la llaga que me hiciste.*[6]

But Love of the Beloved is not the Beloved yet, and what the bride desires with all her heart is the Beloved Himself. Love, indeed, demands the presence of the other, leads to a *confrontation* with the other, and if it talks about the other and kindles a desire for him, is because it aims to the lover's *ending* in the other. In this way, a personal Love talks about the Beloved and stirs the desire of the Beloved, but in an infinite manner, for what He says about the Beloved is infinitely attractive; and because the breath that he carries from the Person and presence of the Beloved is infinitely real and perfect; it is a breath that burns with love. That is why Love never speaks about Himself (Jn 16:13), but about the One Who exhales or begets Him, about Him Whose breath He is. Love, consequently, is

---

[6] *CFC*, 115. *And by allowing the obscure veils / Of the faith, where you have hidden, / You stir more my zeal / For the breast you gave me / And deepen more the wounds you inflicted on me.*

appeased only with the possession of the Beloved Himself, requesting, as we have said a number of times, the contemplation of the Beloved, of His face, of His eyes:

> *Pasando por el prado*
> *tus ojos con los míos se encontraron;*
> *y, en su mirar callado,*
> *tan encendidos dardos se cruzaron*
> *que dos llagas de amor ambos causaron.*[7]

The bride seeks the full possession of the Beloved, but in vain, since it is as yet impossible:

> *Al paso me miraste*
> *en silenciosa insinuación de amores,*
> *y luego me dejaste,*
> *buscando en los alcores*
> *por senderos de arbustos trepadores.*[8]

We said before that suffering with love for the Beloved plays several keys at the same time. One of them has a particular significance and extraordinary beauty. I am referring to *com–passion*, the fact of sharing the sufferings and death of our Lord. To be sure, the

---

[7] *CFC*, 110. *Walking along the meadows / Your eyes met with mine; / They looked at themselves in silence, / And they were wounded / With the wound of love they mutually inflicted.*

[8] *CFC*, 102. *In silence, you gazed at me / In a voiceless, insinuating love, / And you left me wounded / Running through the hills / And waiting for you in vain among the flowers.*

Fire of love brings a great sensitivity towards evil and sin, which also entails an exceptional comprehension of the Beloved's sufferings; after all, they are the consequence of sin. In the light of that Fire, the graveness of the problem of Evil is vividly understood, as well as the reality of the sufferings and death of Christ. If we unite to that an ardent love for the Lord, then we are already abiding in compassion as far as we can live it; a compassion which will be reflected in the weakening of our body to the extent willed by God, although the true martyrdom will take place in our hearts. There is something here which in beauty and grandeur surpasses by far the most dreadful element of sin. It is now understood that the Beloved has defeated the world (Jn 16:33): the whole malice of sin is seen there, but transformed and transfigured upon the face of crucified Love. In this way God has changed evil into the greatest beauty ever imagined, thus converting hatred into love; and where there was sin before, now only love stands. Here the bride is urged by two desires which are really one: on the one hand she willed to be already with the Bridegroom, on the other she would wish to suffer with Him and for Him:

> *Un beso yo le diera*
> *en la sangrante herida del costado;*
> *aunque entonces muriera*
> *de amores abrasado*
> *y no sufriera más por el Amado.*[9]

Let us remember, in relation to this, that the essence of Mass consists in making actual before us the same and only Sacrifice of

---

[9] *CFC*, 123. *I would give him a kiss / In the bleeding wound of his side / But then I would die / Burned with love / And I could suffer no longer for the Beloved.*

the cross. In it Christ, truly present, offers Himself to His Father as a victim; He is there, dead and risen for us and to us. Mass is meaningful for us when we are united with Christ, our Head, in the same feelings and reality of His victimization, for the members of the body must follow their Head. And that ought to be a reality; that is to say, it is essential that our day and our life are truly a Mass. To achieve that aim we must, once we have died to our own self, say yes to God in everything, with a yes that is real and said with a completeness that is a real totality. Thus, when we offer the Mass, all of us being in our proper roles and places, we are attending to the expression and epitome of our life and death. Therefore, Mass cannot be for us a mere ceremony that leaves us indifferent, for nobody is disinterestedly present at his own life, even less at his own death. When things are seen in this way, the way they really are, Mass appears as something majestic as it is impossible to speak of adequately. It is pitiful that at times stress has been laid upon what is secondary or accidental, and it has been thought necessary to *add* to the Mass certain dramatic trappings and innovations, as if the symbolic rite were insufficient. I perceive no worth at all in such innovations when they are not united with a true victimization, together with Jesus Christ's, of the priest and of those who also offer the Sacrifice.

We said that the suffering this Fire of love brings about is Happiness as well. It ought to be so, for it is a suffering of love and for love. The proof is in the fact that the bride ardently desires to suffer more, in the hope that Love widens the wound He has inflicted. Suffering with love filled with longings and desire for the Beloved, which, at the same time that it pains for it has nothing to give, is the most beautiful in this world since it is the love nearest to pure

Love. Tears of love for Love, the fairest ever, fairer than those tears which are like pearls of the morning dew:

> *Las perlas del rocío*
> *posadas en las flores del collado,*
> *al ver el llanto mío*
> *por causa del Amado,*
> *de envidia suspiraban a mi lado.*[10]

To weep with love is not to cry in sadness, but in Happinesss, for happiness is but the conscience of love. The truth is that this weeping expresses the desire for a totality which is not yet possessed, and for a totality which cannot yet be given, though one wants to. Many things are contained in the weeping of love for the Beloved. For instance, the craving for our voice —which is always the same— to be silenced in order to be able distinctly to hear His; the desire to talk no more so that we can be listening all the time: listening to Him, Who is the Word, and Who became man for my love; the longing to abandon the tiresome looking of eyes that were searching all over but never were satisfied, so that we may gaze only at Him, for we feel very vividly that only His loving gaze will soothe our hearts. In the weeping of love there is a desire of forgetting: the insufficiencies, defects, and wickedness of mankind, as well as the imperfection of things around us, so that we may finally find Kindness. The weeping of love for the Beloved and before Him pulls us closer to people: we see them there, in common cause with us and so needy of us; so small, so frequently unfortunate, and, above all, so loved by Him. On other occasions, the weeping of love makes us

---

[10] *CFC*, 3. The pearls of dew / Laying on the flowers of the hill, / Upon seeing my weeping / Caused by the Beloved / Sighed with envy by my side.

look at people as if in a distant memory, at so far a distance that they almost go out of sight, and in which we even look estranged to ourselves. Then we feel nothing but Him, filling and fully satisfying ourselves, in a moment that, because it is one of love, has gone beyond time, placing us, perhaps, on this side of the line closest to the borders of eternity.

Life as poetry is a way towards the Love of God

The worst trick the devil can play on us is to make us believe that life is not poetry but prose.

He achieves that goal by turning us into prosaic people, which here means ordinary or lukewarm. Nevertheless, the world and the things in it are exuberant with poetry, and to man is entrusted the mission of discovering and singing it. It could very well be said that things ought to be poetic, and men and women should be poets. For poetry perhaps is but the very beauty of things in so far as they are known and sung by man. For the world was made good, and things are fair —after all they are vestiges of God, the Utmost Beauty.—

Therefore, it is not possible to talk about God and not make poetry. For God is Beauty Itself, and since at the present moment we cannot know Him but through things, His vestiges, we cannot talk about Him without referring to the beauty of things. We must then be poets, if we want to talk about God, for by no means can one say anything about Beauty if he does not know or feel it; besides, what we say ought to be spoken beautifully, for the same reason that one cannot talk about love if he is not in love. It must be stressed that to talk about God in a beautiful way it is not necessary to produce works of literature or elegant compositions of oratory. Such are often the marks of poor preaching, for instance, while a mere murmuring may better correspond to fair speech about God. If sometimes preaching appears dull and causes a sensation of emptiness, it is because it is born from a prosaic heart that never knew Beauty and, consequently, is not in love. A miserable heart is an ugly heart, unable to talk about Beauty; it may talk beautifully and about the beauty of things; nevertheless, it will abandon the listeners in the middle of the road when they realize that Beauty is not that: as if being hungry we were given only crumbs, and remain hungry. Many have remained within the beauty of things, because they did not know Beauty, and many with the vocation of poets have lived a vulgar prosaic life: I wish they had paid attention to the cries of their non–satisfied hearts, and continued searching, for they would have ended by finding (Mt 7:8).

For that reason, I would allow only poets to talk about God. They are the real idealists, the enthusiasts, those who forget about themselves, who think of giving themselves with no concern for receiving; who do not worry about money, who do not appropriate things, though they love them; who believe that life was given to be given; who look beyond the horizon; who still think the world is good; who refuse to accept that love should consist of pleasure and egotism; who do not admit that hatred has written the history of mankind. I would permit to talk about God only those who delight in gazing at the blue of the sky and listening at night to the silence of the stars; who understand the singing of birds or the message of flowers in spring; who have cried many times with happiness; those whose hearts have been like a child's, allowing you to look into the depths of their eyes, only to see in them the glimmering of the vastness of a sea with no shores. How could anyone talk about infinite Love, if he never surrendered himself nor gave anything? To talk about God can only be done after experiencing the weariness of one who has given all, with a heart and life broken because they were offered for the sake of others. Talking of God is only possible once we have felt tears welling out of our eyes for mankind's suffering, which was also assumed by Christ on the cross. To talk about God in a conventional and routine way is a sort of profanation. We need to be cleansed if we want to make the attempt, in order to go back to the primeval purity of creation, finding anew the sense and beauty things had before they were stained by mankind; only through this path will we find an adequate language and be able to talk without restrictions: neither minding what people might say, nor thinking whether we do well or not; nor bringing up false or useless problems; nor lowering Love to the level of our stinginess; nor thinking that people are not going to comprehend a pure song addressed to pure Love.

Unfortunately, our prosaic world has also chosen a prosaic Christianity, one measured by worldly standards, thus defiling God's work. It has wanted to eliminate any element of risk and transcendency from faith, so that everything may remain this side of the horizon and within the miserable limits of a poor, human security. The results of this choice are clearly there: Liberation and Secularized theologies; Liberal and Modernist theologies, presenting a Christ stripped of His divinity; a revolutionary Christ in a mere human form; a Christ Whose message has no other content than that of teaching that we should all earn and eat the same. One might add to that list the priests who are concerned only–for–this–world; religious who exchanged an eternal bond for a temporal one, who are ashamed of talking about the Love of God, fearful opportunists who would betray God in exchange for lentil soup. The devil has contrived to let the world be seen under a different perspective, more prosaic, which is not more real, but much more fictitious, because in that way the world is more miserable, more selfish, more apart from its Creator. The devil has robbed our hearts and eyes of the sense of poetry, and consequently he has incapacitated us for recognizing and loving God. It was enough for his success that he, in his office as father of lies, crept into our ears with the hint that poetry is the unreal and prose is the truth.

Conclusion

In this meditation I have tried to tell you about the Love of God. After going around the theme it is time to abandon it. This commentary was not intended to be a doctrinal exposition, but only a testimony the value of which, if any, is that it has been given by us, who are living in these modern times saturated with politics and materialism, while hungering for the love of God.

We have already said that it takes a childlike heart to talk about the Love of God. Now, who has one? The lord tells us we must become like children, but, when we see that we cannot achieve that condition, we conclude that it must be He Who freely grants us the childlike heart. Children feel what they say and say what they feel; because their hearts and their eyes have no scales, nor have they been trapped by fear, they easily trust in their Father, Whose presence suffices rapidly to banish the fears of night. One must be a child to approach God, for He —for Whom time does not exist— is a permanently new-born baby, a Child eternally young and infinitely simple. Even human love is ineffable, but divine Love escapes any depiction. It is just not possible, for instance, to express all the desire for intimacy with Love that this verse of the Song (1:2) puts in the Bride's mouth:

Let him kiss me with the kisses of his mouth.

It is an intimacy with that Love Who, because it is perfect, is completely unselfish, and does not seek to receive any happiness from us: He has all. He comes to give Himself, but not because He needs anything from us; He does not come to give us things, but His very Self. He loves us to the point of dying with love; and He, being Life, did the unbelievable: to die for love for us. It is as if Love was gently whispering to us, asking our leave for Him to call us *you*. As if He was murmuring in our ear what He has always wanted to tell us: I love you. It is as if we, upon hearing it, felt that His way of saying it is different from all the others we know; as if He told us that He has had our name in His heart for ever, but now the time has come to utter it to us: into our ears, before our face, in the innermost hidden place of our being, as only Love knows how to pronounce it, while He awaits in longing silence our response (Sg 8:13):

> *You who dwell in the gardens,*
> *my companions listen for your voice;*
> *let me hear it.*

One does not know what produces a greater rapture; we did not even dream that we could be loved in that way, that Love was going to wish to listen to our voice, gaze at our face and receive our heart (Sg 2:14):

> *Show me your face,*
> *let me hear your voice;*
> *for your voice is sweet*
> *and your face is lovely.*

Until now we had loved ourselves, because, consciously or unconsciously, hungry for love, we believed that nobody could love us better than we; but now we have forgotten all about ourselves, for we have understood that we can be loved only by Love, and we are not that Love. We know that love does not exist in the solitude where one abides secluded with oneself, for Love is —in essence— coming out of oneself towards the other, looking one towards the other, a gentle and complete gift of each to the other granted by the lover and the beloved, a link that ties two persons. Love cannot exist in one person —as we have said— because it is a link, a self–abandonment, a looking, a kiss, the bridge that connects two persons, a speaking and hearing at the same time. Love is one sole heart that belongs to two who are joined together; It is conversation as well as silence, and contemplating oneself, but in the eyes of the Beloved.

> *De tu vergel un ave*
> *por tu ausencia cantaba en desconsuelo;*
> *y oyó tu voz suave,*
> *y alzándose del suelo,*
> *a buscarte emprendió su dulce vuelo.*[11]

Here the little bird, the bride, takes off in a flight of love towards the Beloved. Some day that flight will be definitive, the last one; it will take place after her death, when she will finally encounter Him, that is why she calls that flight sweet. But first it is necessary that she lifts herself from the ground and be detached from everything, which the little bird will not be able to do unless she hears the Beloved's voice. He is the only one that with His Love can move her to do it. Before that, and in order for her to hear the voice,

---

[11] *CFC*, 9. *From your orchard a bird / For your absence was singing unconsoled; / And she heard your gentle voice, / And taking off from the ground, / With sweet flight she soared to meet you.*

she must cry in great affliction, which represents the sufferings and labors that will truly prove her fidelity and love.

Here *mine* means the power to make space for the *I am yours* uttered by the other person. There is no *I* any longer between lover and beloved (and this happens with God in a remarkable and unique way), for it becomes a *you* at the very moment it is uttered. As a result, a stream of love flows between both, making of the three beings —lover, beloved, and love— one sole thing, and this for ever.

We finish here, well aware that we have barely started. Love can only be sung with love, but if we want to sing to the infinite Love, then we need an infinite song of infinite love. It is very likely that our best song to Love, for the time being, can only be intoned in silence. There, once we have forgotten everything about ourselves, silenced our murmuring voices, when nothing is left to be called our own, when we have become nothing but love, we will be able to listen and to sing. Think, for instance, of those early hours of the new day, when the world is not yet awake, and He urges us to love Him in solitude and abandonment:

> *Me requirió el Amado*
> *para que de las cosas me olvidara,*
> *y estándome a su lado,*
> *a solas lo mirara*
> *antes de que la aurora despertara.*[12]

Surely, if He wants to gaze at us in solitude, it is to tell us that He loves us. We can foretaste in some way how that *I love you* uttered by Love itself will be: it could kill us with love. Perhaps that is

---

[12] *CFC*, 34.61. *I was urged by the Beloved / To forget about things, / And remain at His side, / To gaze at Him in solitude / Before the awakening of dawn.*

why our elders said that it is not possible to see the face of God without dying. That face gazing at us belongs to an infinite Love, and is telling us an infinite *I love you*; for Love's gazing is His way of talking, and He can talk of nothing but Love. Love's dialogue with His creature is about love, because Love always talks about Love; it is an infinite dialogue in which the human creature responds to Love with words of her own love. That response is made possible from the moment that Love was given to her (Rom 5:5) as her own; now Love equally belongs to both of them. This reality, of which one cannot speak, arouses the wonder of creation, which, in reverent silence, contemplates what only God could have imagined: the Creator in mutual exchange and self-giving of love with His human creature:

> *El sol que se asomaba*
> *despertando a las flores con un beso,*
> *al ver que te escuchaba*
> *en un suave embeleso,*
> *decidió demorarse más por eso.*[13]

---

[13] *CFC*, 70. *The sun that was breaking / To wake up the flowers with a kiss / Saw that I was with you / And, upon seeing my rapture, / Decided to delay its rising awhile.*

XV

THE BEATITUDES

(Meditation for All Saints Day)

Seeing the crowds, he went onto the mountain. And when he was seated his disciples came to him. Then he began to speak. This is what he taught them:

How blessed are the poor in spirit: the kingdom of Heaven is theirs. Blessed are the gentle: they shall have the earth as inheritance. Blessed are those who mourn: they shall be comforted. Blessed are those who hunger and thirst for uprightness: they shall have their fill. Blessed are the merciful: they shall have mercy shown them. Blessed are the pure in heart: they shall see God. Blessed are the peacemakers: they shall be recognised as children of God. Blessed are those who are persecuted in the cause of uprightness: the kingdom of Heaven is theirs.

Blessed are you when people abuse you and persecute you and speak all kinds of calumny against you falsely on my account. Rejoice and be glad, for your reward will be great in heaven; this is how they persecuted the prophets before you.

(Mt 5: 1–12)

Introduction

Today's gospel tells us about the beatitudes. Since beatitude means Perfect Happiness, today's message is one of Happiness; which seems quite logical, if we consider that today we commemorate the Feast of All Saints.

The beatitudes are like master lines which lay out the path of the gospel. Thus the human being who has most perfectly trodden it, the Blessed Virgin Mary, whenever she named herself, did so precisely with that title: Blessed (Lk 1:48).

And because Happiness, as we have already said many times, is the other face of Love, we may refer to the beatitudes as the core of the gospel, the Good News of the Love God feels for us. The gospel is the proclamation that God has requested our love and awaits our response, since love always calls for love. The gospel is a formal declaration of love with everything that implies. For instance, God, as is always the case with any declaration of love, assumes the risk of courting us with His Love, while yearningly waiting for our answer.

Perhaps the silence of God in prayer could be taken in this sense. At times when it seems as if there can be no greater silence — which might be the silence of absence— it may be rather that God, having courted our love, is waiting for our answer. He is waiting for it because either we have not answered yet, or our answer was not final (God only accepts definitive answers: 2 Cor 1: 19–20).

It is then our silence and not God's silence, which means that it is our turn to move in this struggle or chess game, to which our combat with God may be compared (Sg 2:4). The truth is that God never fails to respond to those who have given Him a definitive answer. There is a likeness between the darkness of prayer and the darkness of night: neither happens because the sun goes away, but because the Earth withdraws. God has spoken to us and is now yearning for our answer. His silence is thus the attitude of him who awaits some answer or for the door to be opened to him (Rev 3:20; Sg 5:2). Nevertheless, what has just been said may be true only to a certain extent. God may have other motives to remain silent; the abandonment of Christ on the cross, for instance, stands as a proof of it (Mt 27:46).

We have already said that we are dealing here with a formal declaration of love on the part of God, with all the characteristics any declaration of love entails. God adopts the humble attitude of him who courts the beloved: "If any one wants to be a follower of mine..." (Lk 9:23; Mt 16:24); "Look, I am standing at the door knocking..." (Rev 3:20). At other times His request becomes the tender pleading of him who risks everything out of love (Sg 5:2):

> *Open to me, my sister, my beloved,*
> *my dove, my perfect one,*
> *for my head is wet with dew,*
> *my hair with the drops of night.*

At times He bursts out with unchecked longings that spur Him to speak, to shout, with the imprudent impetus of love (Jn 7:37). Many a time even the request is like the whispering of the most fiery words of love, words only lovers can utter (Sg 2: 10.13, 2:14, 6:5, 7:7):

Come then my beloved, my lovely one, come...
Come my dove show me your face, let me hear your voice...
Turn your eyes away from me; they take me by assaultl...
How beautiful you are, my beloved, how beautiful you are!

The tender and soft plea, or the longing and demanding request which even rises to a cry, or the whisper, or the silence filled with expectation —these are all forms or moments of the declaration of love and of the way lovers express themselves. All of them appear in prayer, too, although in a much higher degree: the silence is quieter and more yearning, the whisper is more evocative, and the cry is more demanding and poignant. The expressive eloquence of such moments abides mostly in the intensity of love and in nothing else, so the whisper, as well as silence itself, can be more expressive than other manifestations of love. In prayer, the whisper is more eloquent even than open dialogue, for the former mainly differs from the latter in that it hardly uses words, or uses no words at all. In the latter case, the whisper must be interpreted (thus being almost equal to the silence of absence), and so it can only be surpassed by the ecstatic silence of contemplation in love. The interpretation of this whisper (since it is barely heard) must be compared sometimes to silence itself (and then we discover that it was not silence), and sometimes to the gestures or signs of love:

> *Bajando por la vega,*
> *en tardes silenciosas y serenas,*
> *el dulce aroma llega*
> *de lirios y azucenas,*
> *al son de una canción que se oye apenas.*[1]
>
> *Allí junto al Amado,*
> *en silencio de amor correspondido,*
> *estar quise a su lado,*
> *y díjome al oído,*
> *que Él también por mi amor estaba herido.*[2]

The ecstatic silence is not as much an absence as an interchange of love so intense that, from its very intensity, it must disregard words; for ecstatic silence is not caused by absence but, quite the contrary, by abundance of presence.

The Beatitudes and Joy

We have said that the core of the gospel is the Love of God offered to man. It is clearly stated by Jesus at the end of His farewell speech: 'Father, I have made your name known to them and will continue to make it known, so that the love with which you loved

---

[1] *CFC*, 35. *Walking down the fertile valley, / In the quiet and soundless afternoons, / Softly the wind blows / From the thickets of white lilies: / A hardly heard whisper of love.*

[2] *CFC*, 55. *There, together with my Beloved, / Requited with a silence of love, / I wanted to remain by His side, / And He whispered into my ear / That He for my love was wounded, too.*

me may be in them, and so that I may be in them" (Jn 17:26). The choir of the song of songs also sings after the Bridegroom and the bride: "Daughters of Zion, come and see King Solomon, wearing the diadem with which his mother crowned him on his wedding day, on the day of his heart's joy" (3:11). And John the Baptist said: "It is the bridegroom who has the bride; and yet, the bridegroom's friend, who stands there and listens to him, is filled with joy at the bridegroom's voice. This is the joy I feel, and it is complete" (Jn 3:29). In brief, the Holy Scripture strings together those great themes such as Love, engagements, weddings, the bride and the groom, the heart's joy and complete Joy.

Joy is brought about in us, as its first and most characteristic fruit, by Love (Gal 5:22). That Joy is the awareness of Love living within us, the feeling that plenitude has invaded us (thus we are satiated, with a satisfaction which is not Joy yet, but is indispensable for it to come), and that we are stared at and desired. That is to say, Joy is also the feeling that we have been, at last, recognized. For when modern man persists so much in his right to be recognized, he is listening to an inner desire of a profound nature unknown to him: what he really wants is to be recognized, that is, contemplated. Accordingly, plenitude will not derive from man seeing himself filled with *things*, as much as from the fact that *somebody* is facing him and contemplating him in all he is, giving him his true worth. Man needs to be looked at by somebody: it is (mutual) contemplation that causes Love, and plenitude and Joy along with it. The truth is that Love is not caused by things or with things as a medium; Love can only happen and exist among persons, as is the case with God (supposing we can talk in this fashion, for God is all Love), where the Holy Spirit proceeds from the Father and the Son. It is interesting to see that the Marxist attitude, contrary to contemplation, runs parallel to its refusal to recognize the human being as truly a person. And that is the real attitude of all philosophies of immanence: a rejection of contemplation, refusing to see the world and things as they are in themselves, with a reality that is self–evident to us. Consequently, for those philosophers, man would be the sole creator.

The beatitudes are Joy because they are not a search for happiness, but for Love. Joy is not granted to those who search for it, but exclusively to those concerned with Love; it is curiously capricious, and it likes to give itself only to those who, forgetting about it, choose rather to share the destiny of the Beloved, of Jesus who, "for the sake of the joy which lay ahead of him, he endured the cross, disregarding the shame of it, and has taken his seat at the right of God's throne" (Heb 12:2). If having fun is the aim of our life, we condemn ourselves never to reach it. Notice that people laugh less all the time: the young think themselves compelled to be in anguish, children are increasingly reluctant to offer open smiles and hearty laughter, and the strange sadness of people, surroundings, cities under Marxism is well known. It would be interesting, for instance, to study the probable connection of the negative — motive force of the Hegelian dialectic— and hatred —motive force of the clash between classes— with the absence of Joy. Materialist civilization has betrayed mankind, especially the young, by making the cross disappear. If there is no sacrifice —in the Christian sense of the term— the way to Happiness is shut for good, because there is no Joy without Love and there is no Love without sharing the Beloved's existence. Thus this civilization, by keeping children and the young from knowing about sacrifice and the way of the beatitudes dooms them never to find Joy. In this sense, it is a significant fact that mere social–minded and *this–worldly* Catholicism hardly offers any form of preaching beyond denunciation and anger, rather than announcing the good news of great Joy (Lk 2:10).

Joy is the other side of Love. But because Love has been given to us in Jesus, Joy for us cannot be anything else than seeing Jesus; or rather, seeing Him and being seen by Him: "But I shall see you again, and your hearts will be full of joy, and that joy no one shall take from you" (Jn 16:22). If each beatitude is a promise of Joy, it is so because each one is a way of approaching the Lord. For instance, the poor are those who have given up everything and have only Jesus. The meek and humble are those of peaceful heart, because the love for Jesus is the only thing that matters to them, and through Jesus the love for all people; thus they achieve freedom of the spirit and the true possession of the earth: "Everything belongs to you, whether it is Paul, or Apollos, or Cephas, the world, life or death, the present or the future. All belong to you; but you belong to Christ and Christ belongs to God" (1 Cor 3: 21–23). Those who mourn are comforted because their tears are caused by the Beloved's presence, or perhaps by the feeling of His absence: whatever it may be, they are tears of Joy because they are tears of love. The pure in heart are those who have given up their hearts to God, and have received, as in exchange, God's heart. The peacemakers are those who radiate peace and insert it in people's hearts, precisely because having their own filled with Christ, they in turn find their own hearts overflowing with peace: "For he is the peace between us" (Eph 2:14). And then the happiest of all, the merciful; those who forgive always, because their Joy does not let them take any offense, and because they take no account of their personal sufferings, but only those of Him Who forgave everything on the cross.

All of them, the poor, the meek, the peacemakers, those who weep, the hungry for justice, are the ones who really have fallen in love with the Lord and have given everything for His sake; that is why they are poor, suffering, meek, peacemakers, pure of heart, and hungering for justice. Consider that Joy does not come into our lives because we are poor, but because, when we detach ourselves from our possessions, we are more able to possess the real treasure: Jesus (Mt 13:44). We do not feel Joy because we mourn, but because our weeping is one of Love. Joy is not having a pure heart, but it comes when, thanks to that purity, our heart is transformed into a closed garden and a sealed fountain (Sg 4:12), into which only the Bridegroom is allowed entrance (Sg 5:1):

> *I come into my garden,*
> *my sister, my promised bride,*
> *I pick my myrrh and my balsam,*
> *I eat my honey and honeycomb,*
> *I drink my wine and my milk.*

The beatitudes clear the way for us to see the Bridegroom (Lk 10:23), and to be with Him (Sg 2:6); and that is what Joy consists of. That is why the beatitudes amount to Joy.

And Joy is the first-fruit of heaven, the feeling of the Beloved's nearness, the weeping for His absence. Joy abides in our smallness: when we cannot love the Beloved more intensely; when we have spent the night of our life fishing and caught almost nothing, when we have not wept enough, when we still have not given everything. Nevertheless, Joy is there, with us, as a sort of privilege solely granted to those who are small and weak, to those who at least tried or were faithful in small things. Since smallness is of our nature, that is what we can offer to God; He never expected any kind of grandeur from us, His own was sufficient. Saint Paul was happy in his weakness (2 Cor 13:9); and the good servant, who was trustworthy in small things, could come into his master's Happiness (Mt 25:21). We arrive thus at Joy through a way the world does not understand, for we feel happy when knowing that we are small. I feel happier when I see myself becoming smaller, and even more when I see Christ steadily growing in your life. It is then that I understand the Apostle's saying that we can feel the Joy of seeing ourselves weak, whereas the others are strong; I also understand now what the Lord meant when He talked about those who are faithful in small things, which seems to signify that we can only be faithful in our smallness.

That is why the proclamation of the beatitudes —the proclamation of Joy— really is a summoning of the little ones of this world: the poor, the humble, people who mourn, and those who are persecuted, they all are called to Joy. Thus to say that Christianity preaches resignation to the little ones of this world in exchange for a future heaven, is not to have understood the gospel. Resignation has nothing to do with Joy, whereas the beatitudes are a convocation to Joy here and now. They who make that accusation tend to forget that, although as far as its plenitude is concerned, the Kingdom is eschatological, it has already started in us. On the contrary, we can, correctly, define as real resignation the Marxist pretense that man should renounce his dignity and liberty while waiting for a society without classes or State —and no one knows when that will come. In this sense, to say, as Marxism argues, that liberty identifies itself with necessity, or with the consciousness of that necessity, leaves the problem unsolved, when it does not give the impression of merely playing with words. Between Marxist resignation and Christian Joy, or between Marxist eschatology and the eschatology of the Kingdom —already started within us Christians— there is the same distance as that existing between hoping in man (and his promises) and hoping in God (and His promises). Besides, we have seen the promises of Joy become real in authentic Christians, the saints, whereas we are still waiting to see it in authentic Marxists. Confronted with Happiness, Marxism must resign itself to an attitude of searching and waiting (if we suppose that by happiness it refers to the absence of needs, the perfect harmony of man and Nature, etc; things which, according to Marxist doctrine, will be realized in the future *classless* society). Meanwhile, that Joy is already actual for us. It is legitimate, then, to question who really preaches resignation. Christian Waiting —which is a theological virtue— is a real and actual virtue, and in this sense is quite thoroughly opposite to a utopia —taking this word in its modern and not pejorative sense— and to an anachronism. It is an attitude based in reality, one embracing actual and present realities. It is true that this virtue, in so far it is waiting and hoping, is also a *not yet*, but that is so in reference to a plenitude (and not to an absence of reality) which has already begun and is capable of satisfying man. We would not understand the gospel at all, if we think of Christian Waiting as a mere bundle of promises for the future. The Lord said that the Kingdom of God is already among us (Lk 17:21; cf. 10:9). Conversely, the Marxist utopia is no more than a promise for the future; yet we know what it can promise and give in the here and now.

The Beatitudes and Music

It can be said that the sermon which contains the beatitudes is a Song to Joy. Singing, as well as the music which usually accompanies it, is the greatest effort of humanity in our attempt to express that which is ineffable. We have said that the beatitudes are Joy, and that Joy is the other side of Love. Now singing or music are voice, heart, rhythm and harmony, poetry and beauty, all together trying to talk about Love and to talk to Love, seeking to utter the unutterable — the undescribable— and to reach the unreachable. Singing, as well as music, is a desperate attempt to go beyond the spoken language, to get the heart to express itself as it would wish to. It is an attempt doomed to fail, but which is always wonderful, for what it achieves suffices to justify it. It can be said that the beatitudes become a genuine song, or a genuine chant if you prefer, not so much for their rhythm, refrain, parallels and contrasts, as for what they want to be: an unbelievable effort to weave, in extremely beautiful human language, a hymn to Joy and thus to Love.

Let us recall the remarkable presence of music and singing in the Bible. Some of its most important characters were musicians or singers. In the Old Testament, for instance, King David used to sing and dance in front of the Ark of the Covenant, as well as to compose psalms (the word itself refers to a composition specifically made to be sung) which take an important place among the books of the Old Testament. The Song of Songs, which perhaps is the most beautiful of the sacred books, is explicitly a song. The most important and exceptional creature in the entire Bible, the Holy Virgin Mary, can be found singing a wonderful song, the *Magnificat*. The psalms, the hymns, the Song of Songs, the angelical choirs in that Holy Night at Bethlehem, the *Magnificat*, the *Benedictus*, the beatitudes, the presentation of the Kingdom of heaven as a wedding feast with its joyful choirs of maidens awaiting the Beloved's coming, the Last Supper with its priestly prayer, Saint Paul's outburst filled with tenderness and yearnings, the triumphant hymns of the Apocalypse with its *new song*, they all make us think of music and songs in the background of the whole Bible. The Bible, indeed, starts with the first rhythms of Genesis narrating the creation with a refrain repeating that God saw that everything was good; it finishes with the last, joyful cry which closes the Apocalypse: "The Spirit and the Bride say, 'Come!' Let everyone who listens answer, 'Come!'... The one who attests these things says: I am indeed coming soon. Amen; come Lord Jesus" (Rev 22: 17.20). The saints also continue that tradition of songs: Saint Francis of Assisi was a singer, composer of the Canticle to Brother Sun. He was a man who went into ecstasy over the grasshopper's chirpings, or over the silent concert played by the stars in the tranquil summer nights. He sang to all the creatures: to brother fire, to sister water, and to his brothers the birds. A canticle is also the most beautiful lyric poetry written in Spanish, *The Spiritual Canticle* by Saint John of the Cross.

And so it should be, due to the insufficiency of human language to express Love; one must fall back on songs and music. It has always been easier singing to Love than talking about It. Consequently, the bride of the Song (1:4) says:

> *The king has brought me into his rooms;*
> *you will be our joy and our gladness.*
> *We shall praise your love more than wine.*

Heavenly music is unlike earthly music; we must use analogies if we want to talk about it. One who hears it will always feel alien to earthly things from then on. Any worldly music will seem deficient: "What no ear has heard," said Saint Paul (1 Cor 2:9); "It is not that, it is not that...!" so the unfortunate wandering musician of Bécquer's novel, *El Miserere*, shouted in desperation.

Music knocks at our soul's door, and, later, leaves her with a longing and with the exclamation of disappointment, "It is not that." For earthly music, when it is authentic, is suggestive; it evokes feelings of Kindness, of Beauty, and of Truth in us. Threefold is the way in which music acts upon us: telling us about the existence of what it evokes, showing us somehow the way to it, and giving us the first fruit of it. But earthly music does it all in a very small degree, which makes possible the distortion of its content, as we shall see later. On the contrary, heavenly music does not evoke anything, it takes us immediately into the presence of Kindness, Beauty, and Truth. Heavenly music, indeed, to the extent it is possible for us to hear it and talk about it in this world, is the very overflowing of Kindness, Truth, and Beauty overtaking our soul (it would be impossible and in fact illicit to talk about what is heard in Heaven: (2 Cor 12:4). In reality, more than talking to us about beauty, showing us the truth, or giving us kindness, what that music does is to introduce us to them, into their plenitude and without restraint of any kind (Jn 3:34). Heavenly music needs no mediation, for the Presence there of Kindness and Beauty is already music; and because evoking its sounds are of no avail to us now, silence is the better expression of that music. The Beloved's Presence there and His silent gaze say everything. Earthly music is a *not yet*, while the heavenly one is an *already* within the great symphony of Christian Waiting. But that *not yet* is, nevertheless, a first fruit, and that *already* is not plenitude as yet. That is why heavenly music, to the extent it is heard on earth, is always under tension. It brings us into the Beloved's presence, but, for the time being, it does not take us to the Joy of the mutual possession in love which, once it is achieved, will not be disturbed, since it is already plenitude. As a matter of fact, the Beloved's presence is called, in this world, to fade away, widening, by so doing, the wound of love His presence has inflicted upon us and, at the same time, makes the future enjoyment of love much more intense. This stanza tells us about the Beloved's presence, of a glance which means everything in the silence of love, of absences, sighs and longings for the definite return of the Bridegroom:

> *Y luego me miraste*
> *y en silencio dijiste que me amabas;*
> *y cuando, al fin, me hallaste*
> *y ya conmigo estabas,*
> *al par de mis sollozos, suspirabas.*[3]

Heavenly music, in so far as it is heard here on earth as a *not yet*, depends on hearing, too. That is important, because Christian witness is one of faith, and thus it depends likewise on hearing: "But it is in that way faith comes, from hearing" (Rom 10:17). That is the reason we can bear witness only to what we have heard from the Father (Jn 8:26; 15:15). By the same token, we cannot say anything about Jesus except what the Spirit tells us about Him (Jn 16: 13–15; 1 Jn 2: 20.27). This hearing undoubtedly refers to the word, and also to the harmony and beauty of things, and to the song of creation proclaiming God's deeds (Ps 18:2; cf. Rom 1:20). If we do not know how to listen to the music of things, we shall not be able to know God. In the same way, we ought to learn to perceive beauty, to be somehow capable of grasping Beauty. For that reason, music cannot be understood unless one carries it in the heart. I enthuse over the misty, blurred cockcrow before the

---

[3] *CFC*, 116. *And then you looked at me / And in silence you told me your love, / And afterwards you left me, / And I saw you were no longer there / And sighing for your absence you left me.*

lights of the early dawn. One does not know where it comes from, but it evokes, wrapped in the sunrise mystery, something distant: life which goes on in the astonishment of the coming new day. I shed tears at the music of caged birds, singing to a freedom they have never known. The lark's singing calling her mate, the animals' singing, are also songs of love. As is the symphony orchestrated by the million voices of the little animals which fill with life the tranquil and pleasant summer nights. In midsummer I like to wander around in the mountains and to listen to the music of some nearby brook. Water springs forth there from the depths of the earth singing, but it does not tell us where it comes from, nor what paths it has flowed through before seeing the light. Although I regard the music of wind as more beautiful, that wind becomes music when it passes through the subtle labyrinths of man-made instruments, a craft mastered by mankind, according to the fable, since the god Pan brightened the woods with his flute. The wind sings its fairest music when left on its own —when it puts on airs, one might say— or else when it passes through man's heart. It is then that the wind intones its best sounds, and then that its insinuating, talkative voice sings to the beauty of things; for all things have been known, kissed and caressed by the wind. It is the wind which makes it possible for the trees of the forest to kiss each other and to tell each other their secrets. The wind assists them with its breath and its singing voice; without them trees could not fall in love, nor breed, nor yield fruits later in spring. Where there is no singing nor dialogue there is no love, and there is no life without love, neither then nor now, neither later nor tomorrow.

In singing, music and word blend their boundaries; music becomes word, and word music. That is why songs talk to us and words sound like music to our ears. And there is the pause, too, the soundlessness of silence among the sonorous flowing of notes. Without it, chords could not be distinguished, the contrast among various sounds would not be emphasized, the symphony would be impossible, and there would be no room for the beating of the heart and the breathing of the listener. Music cannot exist without silence, and silence is meaningful only when it aids in our hearing music. Word, music, song, silence, all mingling into one: the symphony of the hymn to Beauty and to Kindness. All this is captured in this stanza of Saint John of the Cross:

> *La noche sosegada*
> *en par de los levantes de la aurora,*
> *la música callada,*
> *la soledad sonora,*
> *la cena que recrea y enamora.*[4]

Words were like this when man and woman were created, before words were stained by lies. Human language was then a transparent song, simple and unadorned, which reflected the beauty (the reality) of things; consequently, it could give them a name (Gen 2:19). The commonplace came afterwards, in the form of artificial, false, and distorted language, which does not correspond to the heart's truth. Sometimes it does not even pass through the heart, becoming thus a mere noise of words. The danger of the commonplace lurks always inside and outside us: at times we accept it from others, at other times we contrive it, and fling it into the world. The commonplace does not say or explain anything, but it puts our minds at ease with

---

[4]Saint John of the Cross, *Spiritual Canticle*, stanza 14: *The tranquil night / At the time of the rising dawn, / The silent music, / The sounding solitude, / The supper that refreshes and deepens love.*

a mere noise of words, making us petty. Simplicity is holiness, and holiness tends to return to the first ways of speaking God taught man: in the beginning was the Word.

We have forgotten that manner of speaking. It is difficult for us to get rid of artificial language when talking to ourselves. For instance, even though we readily affirm that God loves us, we are far from really believing it. Should we really believe that God loves us (1 Jn 4:16), we would be convinced that Love Himself is in love with us, and that He can love us with the same or greater intensity with which He loved Paul or Francis of Assisi. If we do not believe it so, we are diminishing Love, and then love —especially God's Love— has become a commonplace for us. Accordingly, the Christian should be a person of natural speech: that which springs from the heart and sounds like music. It is that simple speech which treads the almost imperceptible line in which, as I have said, the voice and the harmony of beauty become one song. Sacred preaching, for example, would need nothing else to be efficacious.

The world acts wittingly when it works to destroy youth's sensitivity. If there is no sensitivity, the ways of access to Love are blocked, because, at the present time, God can only be known though perception of the beauty of created things. It is probable that the modern corruption of the art of singing and of music did not happen by chance. A certain class of modern music is exactly the opposite of art and genuine music. No other epithet could be given, for instance, to shrill music, led by some contorting, dreadful idol dressed like a clown. The same could be said about political protest songs; they represent the manipulation of music in order to use it as a vehicle to spread political ideologies, many of them outrageous. Here we are far from Art and Aesthetics, far from *pulchrum* as the showing out and apprehension of beauty. That should not surprise us. It has happened because the makers of such music have lost sight of the reality —the being— of things; beauty, as well as kindness and truth, are only the forms in which being itself appears. Once being is lost, all its forms of self-manifestation go with it. The tragedy of Marxism, as the culminating philosophy of immanence, lies here: if there is no being, there is no Aesthetic; if there is no Truth, Kindness, and Beauty (the two last do not exist even as human realities for Marxism), there is no Art either. Futile have been the efforts of some ideologists, like Lukács, to prove the opposite. One could sing to beauty —think of music, poetry, literature— but one cannot sing to the Party's ordinances. Art in itself is independent; it does not withstand any subordination except the one imposed upon it by the radiance and harmony of being.

We refer here to being as it is, not to being as it is imagined by man. Music, as well as poetry and Plastic art, surrender themselves only to beauty, which is the same as saying to being. They do not surrender to what is distorted and formless —the latter taken in a philosophical sense, that is to say, without form. Neither do they surrender to manipulation or falsification on the part of man, in order to enslave others; falsehood hides truth, thus rendering the manifestation of being impossible. There are probably Marxist poets, or at least those who call themselves so, but a Marxist poetry is not possible. The poetry found in some Marxist works is there in so far as it comes from reality, but not because it reflects the ideology. We ought not to forget that evil has no entity by itself; it is a parasite which needs the good for its existence. Should evil not appear as *being* and *truth*, it would not appear at all. The different attempts to justify a Marxist Art or Aesthetic are contradictory in themselves and represent the last tribute that, against its will, Marxism pays to Truth, Kindness, and Beauty, in one word, to being. Even the devil, though unwillingly, must disguise himself as truth and good if he wants to be heeded; to be sure, he will have a hard time inside that disguise, for it supposes another surrender before the Being as Being.

The Beatitudes and Poverty

Poverty is the first beatitude. The poor are the first to receive the news about Happiness. In other words, Poverty is the first way which leads us to Jesus.

It seems logical if we consider that He was the poorest of the poor: nobody, having as much as He, has ever renounced so much as He has or has humbled himself to the extent He has. Saint Paul said of Jesus, "Although he was rich, he became poor for our sake" (2 Cor 8:9). "For our sake" means out of love for us. Consequently, it is necessary first to be in love, then to become poor. Only love can move somebody to become poor, and only Poverty can lead the way towards Love. Let us recall that poverty is a virtue, and as such it requires a willing *becoming poor*; for if there is no option freely assumed in love, there is no virtue. That is why nobody would consciously mistake Poverty for misery or for mere lack or want. Notice that what we have just said places us at the most remote point from Marxist ideology, which fosters hatred —class struggle— as the way for man to get rid of poverty.

Christian poverty is a situation of sheer indigence chosen out of love. There is a passage in the gospel, the story of the poverty-stricken widow who gave to the treasure of the Temple two small coins (Mk 12: 41–44; Lk 21: 1–4), which warns us of a dangerous attitude: giving God things we can spare. It is a danger that is on the prowl for us when we have many things. The poverty-stricken widow, on the contrary, had little, and she generously gave it.

Some modern ways of living Christian faith give the impression of following that attitude of giving God what one can dispense with. Pastoral efforts aimed at youth, for instance, are for some reduced to organizing groups of boys and girls in order to pass the time. Some Eucharistic celebrations stress psychological and sociological aspects, forgetting all about the ontological character of Sacrifice and Banquet in the Mass. Leaving to one side the serious questions that lie at the bottom of such an attitude, the alibi that this merry-making Catholicism carries with it is designed to make many believe that they are giving God what they were supposed to. But the truth is that these people never really committed themselves to God. Undoubtedly, this sort of Catholicism, in order to provide an alibi for itself, will employ widely a jargon that refers to generosity — to Christian commitment, say— but which is mere words with no reality behind them except a political or worldly one. The giving of oneself to God out of love is completely obliterated here; it has been supplanted by a misuse of God in order to achieve dark interests of which the mildest that could be said about them is that they are purely human.

It is important not to have many things if one wants to live a Christian life. The poor widow had little, and she gave it in spite of the fact that she needed it to live. Others had much, and they gave only what they could spare. Since a self-giving to the Lord and a following after Him demand that we get rid of all things, it seems that in order to achieve those goals, it is better to possess little rather than much; and that is what the Lord means to say:

when we possess one sole thing only, then we will be ready to give it up, that is to say, to give up all completely.

We may keep, at least for the time being, one thing alone. For we must have at least one hope so that we can live for it; besides, if we did not have that hope, we could not give it up. Eventually, however, we arrive at the point where we can give up the only thing we have and keep nothing: "... but she in her poverty has put in all she had to live on." It is then that we begin really to be poor.

The beautiful thing about Love appears when we have given God all we had to live on, the only thing we possessed, that which was our life, the only hope we were looking forward to. Those who attain that goal are the truly poor, that is to say, the really joyful. They are those who have nothing but God, who have chosen Him instead of things. When we surrender what our life consists of, and which gives meaning to it, when we lose our life for God's sake, that is when He becomes our life (Sg 3: 3–4):

> *I came upon the watchmen—*
> *those who go on their rounds in the city;*
> *"Have you seen my sweetheart?"*
> *Barely had I passed them*
> *when I found my sweetheart.*

The gospel tells us that the Lord had nowhere to lay his head. As for the bride of the Song, she could at last find the Bridegroom when she left everybody and everything; then she could say (Sg 2:16):

> *My love is mine and I am his;*

also (Sg 6:3; 7:11):

> *I belong to my love, and my love to me;*
> *I belong to my love*
> *and his desire is for me.*

The great adventure of Love earnestly begins and is consummated in Poverty. For Love, as we have said many times, is completeness, and demands the entire self–giving of oneself to the other, beyond and above all. Love comes at the moment we believe seriously that we are going to find Happiness in the Other as a Person, in the Beloved's gaze which is contemplating us, not things. Things can neither look nor smile at us, nor can they freely and willingly surrender to us. That is why we call this love for the Beloved an adventure, because it goes beyond all things. Even more, it is an adventure in which there is both risk and danger. The danger is a logical consequence of responding to Love with Poverty in an answer that is total and affirmative. For instance: if you tell Him that you are going to make up with your heart for all the lack of love in the world, Love will give Himself to you in the same way, resting upon you all the weight of His Infinity. Then, pure Love Himself, enamored Love, will move toward you with no obstacle interfering, as if saying to each one of you: I also want to love you with all the love I offered others and which they rejected: I now grant all that love to you.

The answer depends on us, whereas the first earnest request belonged to Love, for He loved us first: "Let us love, then, because he first loved us" (1 Jn 4:19). That statement that God loved us first ought to signify that Love was in love with me before time even existed, before any sort of before, since the forever of eternity. In other words, He never, not for a single moment, did not love me with that intense love. For He loved me before any moment came into existence. He also loved me when time came to be, and there were a *before* and an *after*, and one moment was followed by another. He always loved me, through time, and through eternity. He loved me previous to any before; He loves me in the *now*, and will continue to love me in the *after*. Man has not been able to pin–point the moment at which the *now* occurs, because at the same instant it is said it has already passed. Man always talks about the unfolding and the becoming, but that is because he has never understood the always, the *tota simul* of eternity, even less the *perfecta possessio*. If man wants to understand that, he should comprehend Love. For Him there was no moment before now in which He did not love, or was not loving me; nor will there be a later moment in which He will stop loving me. Love loves in time, but existed before it and will continue beyond it. Love always was and shall always be: love never comes to an end (1 Cor 13:8).

Our poverty will not hinder our affirmative answer to Love. Quite the opposite, since love calls for our indigence; it is precisely our poverty that makes an intimate dialogue with Love possible. In prayer, for instance, our poverty becomes an obstacle only when we do not accept it. We refer here to absolute poverty, which also includes the incapacity to pray. Our poverty can also become an obstacle to prayer when we unconsciously attribute our own limitations to God, thinking that He is like us and loves in the same way that we do. Our answer to God in prayer must be that of poor and humble ones, not the perfect answer of those who have already arrived at the final goal. We still are on our way; there is nothing wrong in this, for we just accept the fact that we have not yet achieved the end. Only God has already arrived at the end, and has done so since forever. For us, His creatures, it is not only good to go on walking, it is also lovely. For our final meeting with Him depends on walking and constant searching. This is the meaning of the stanza:

> *Si vas hacia el otero*
> *deja que te acompañe, peregrino,*
> *a ver si el que yo quiero*
> *nos da a beber su vino*
> *en acabando juntos el camino.*[5]

Our life is a walking toward the hill, toward the holy mountain of God. It is good for us to do that pilgrimage in fellowship with our brothers: let me join you, pilgrim. That verse is a plea of love, because it refers to a pilgrimage of love, and love cannot be imposed on anybody. Then, once we have completed our way together, we shall finally meet the Love of the Beloved, ''For your love–making is sweeter than wine" (Sg 1:2). Our life, in the meantime, is a searching (Jn 1:38), a constant walking on the way, ''You know the way to the place where I am going" (Jn 14:4). The Lord Himself wanted to be like us in this respect, ''If you loved me you would be glad that I AM GOING to the Father" (Jn 14:28); He told us that his very existence was a Way (Jn 14:6). We cannot be happy upon reaching the goal if we have not journeyed; we cannot feel the happiness of resting if we have never been tired. Rain itself is most fair after drought; dawn seems more beautiful because the night is past; the sun would not rise had it not set. We cannot discover what silence wishes to

---

[5] *CFC*, 1. *If you are walking toward the lonely hill / Let me join you, pilgrim, / May he whom I love / Give us a drink of his wine / As we complete together our journey.*

whisper to us if the noises of the world have not deafened us before: "You will be sorrowful, but your sorrow will turn to joy" (Jn 16:20).

Now it happens that when we are looking for silence in order to search only for God, we face our internal voices and distractions that disturb our peace and our heart's serenity. As a consequence we grow sad, wishing those voices to be destroyed, as was the case with the bride of the Song (2:15):

> *Catch the foxes for us,*
> *the little foxes*
> *that make havoc of the vineyards,*
> *for our vineyards are in fruit.*

But the truth is that most of the time we should not worry about it, they are only little foxes. More important than to destroy them is to understand that they are part of us, because we have not yet reached the end of the road. Victory is achieved here through patience and accepting our own poverty, always remembering that we cannot love God unless we also love ourselves. Our cries shall not drive away those little foxes that make havoc of our vineyard; only the conjuring voice of the Beloved will do it (Sg 3:5; 8:4):

> *I charge you,*
> *daughters of Jerusalem,*
> *by gazelles and wild does,*
> *do not rouse, do not wake my beloved*
> *before she pleases.*

We shall never overcome distractions until we are overtaken by the Beloved voice. Then, and only then, all shall cease (Sg 2:6; 8:3):

> *His left arm is under my head,*
> *his right embraces me.*

In the intimate dealings with God our prayer consists of, distraction will gradually fade away as we become poorer. The less things we possess, the less we will be concerned about them. When we have nothing, then only God shall be our life, and we shall live in Perfect Happiness; then, what was said in the Song (2:16; 6:3) will become reality,

> *My love is mine and I am his.*

I have often told you that things do not bring about Happiness. If they do, it is only when received as gifts from the Beloved, gifts that speak to us about Him. Thus we are back at the same point: Happiness is the Beloved. For he who seeks to possess things is only acting selfishly. In reality, Happiness —let me stress it— is solely found at the moment we turn ourself towards the other, or, if you prefer, when we see ourselves in the gaze of the other. In the Trinity, the Father contemplates Himself in the Son, the Son contemplates Himself in the Father, and both breathe out the same breath of love: the Holy Spirit. God wants us to look at the other —our neighbor— in like manner, so that we may learn to discover Him, the Totally Other. If we confine ourselves to looking at ourselves, we become incapable of loving, of feeling Perfect Happiness, even of seeing or comprehending anything. The Happiness of our inner world is unknown to us. The only way in which we can, to some degree, bring it to view, is by looking at the Other, at God. Only He can make us feel it, since it is in itself ineffable. What I mean is that only God can tell us about God, His presence within us, and even about ourselves: "The Spirit himself joins with our spirit to bear witness that we are children of God" (Rom 8:16). The Happiness of our inner world —which is the expression of our love affair with God— is now incomprehensible and inexplicable in its entirety to us, but it becomes real and expresses itself though the other and in the Other, as the poem goes:

> *Mi amado, las estrellas,*
> *el mar que besan proas de mil naves,*
> *los ojos de doncellas,*
> *el canto de las aves,*
> *aquello que te dije y que tú sabes.*[6]

In these lines, love is called the most beautiful thing, and the dialogue which expresses the love between God and humans is ineffable. Nothing can be compared to it: not the stars, nor the blue of the sea, nor the clear gaze of virginal purity. They all are surpassed by "that," what I told you and you know, when we communicate our love to each other. It is said to be "that" because it cannot be put into words, not even by the heart of the enamored soul who uttered it. Thus it adds "and you know," because only God apprehends it and fully understands it as it is, in all its beauty. God is love, but the depths of the indwelling Love, even of our participation in love, are unknown to us. Only the Spirit can look with impunity into the depths of the abyss of Love (1 Cor 2:10).

---

[6] *CFC*, 67. *My beloved, the stars, / The sea kissed by the prows of a thousand ships, / The maidens' eyes, / The singing of birds, / What I told you and you well know.*

The Beatitudes and Suffering

The charm and beauty of the beatitude about suffering are in its expression as paradox: blessed are those who mourn. Indeed, Perfect Joy belongs to those who weep.

The reason has been given before. Weeping may be an expression of happiness for the very reason that it may be an expression of Love, and Love becomes a Presence which groans in ways that cannot be put into words (Rom 8:26). Saint Peter wept bitterly out of love (Mt 26:75), and the Jews who accompanied Jesus to Lazarus' tomb rightly connected Jesus' weeping with love: "Jesus wept; and the Jews said, 'See how much he loved him!'" (Jn 11: 35–36). The gift of tears is one of the gifts of the Spirit of Love, and eyes radiantly glittering with tears can weep of love. Thus if weeping may accompany Love, it also may accompany Joy.

Weeping may reveal the happiness of union with the Beloved. Or it may unveil the suffering for His absence, and then it is also happiness, precisely because it is love. Therefore, weeping out of love, or for love, is always Joy.

Weeping, so long as we are pilgrims, is a way for Love to express that we do not possess Love yet. Besides, it is through our eyes that we weep, and we know that the dialogue of intimacy between two who surrender to each other is hastily *uttered* through a mutual enamored looking. Weeping, Joy, and Love are given us together now in our lives. For Love, while showing itself through the eyes —a much better instrument for it than words— is sometimes noiseless, and at other times is the sound of weepings. Weeping for Joy, precisely because it is a weeping of Love: blessed are those who weep. It is a Love which weeps because it is perfect, and at the same time, because it has not yet reached the end of the journey.

A perfect Love may still be an itinerant one, whereas Love that has reached the end is a Love of placid peace, of the total and tranquil possession which knows neither absences nor weeping. When the bride achieves this stage she says, referring to the Bridegroom, "His left hand is under my head, his right embraces me" (Sg 2:6; cf. 8:3).

But this longing of love that is expressed by weeping belongs to both lovers, to the Bridegroom as well:

> *En noches silenciosas*
> *del sueño de los niños guardadoras,*
> *tras aves voladoras*
> *al aire de las brisas rondadoras*
> *en auras rumorosas;*
> *por pasos escondidos*
> *de bosques olvidados*
> *de rosas y de lirios florecidos...,*
> *allí busqué al Amado*
> *y a todos fui con ansias preguntando,*
> *y todos me han contado*
> *que estábame aguardando*
> *y con llanto de amores suspirando.*[7]

In the dialogue of love, the bride will surely complain to the Groom about His absences, and of her seeing Him only in the darkness of faith; perhaps she will go so far as to ask why He is also weeping. In the dialogue of love, the Groom will answer to the bride:

---

[7] *CFC*, 4. *The silent nights / Watching the sleeping children, / The murmuring waters, / The flying birds, / The kiss of the musing breeze... / I looked for my Beloved among them / And to them all I longingly questioned, / And they all have told me / That He was awaiting me / Sighing with enamored weepings.*

I am shedding tears because of that, because your eyes cannot see mine yet.

The bride of the Song said that she was dying with love (2:5), and the Bridegroom, in His turn, replied that it was she with her eyes who was killing Him with love. Thus He said (1:15; 4:1; 4:9; 6:5):

> *How beautiful you are, my beloved,*
> *how beautiful you are!*
> *Your eyes are doves.*
> *How beautiful you are, my beloved,*
> *how beautiful you are!*
> *Your eyes are doves, behind your veil.*
> *You ravish my heart,*
> *my sister, my promised bride,*
> *you ravish my heart*
> *with a single one of your glances.*
> *Turn your eyes away from me,*
> *they take me by assault!*

''How beautiful are your eyes behind your veil...!" The Bridegroom may allude here to the veil that tears of love cast on our eyes. Or perhaps He means the veil of faith, which still conceals the Bridegroom and makes us cry for His absence. That is why the bride said: I know, Lord, that you are there, for my heart tells me of your presence; but I cannot see you, as if a veil stood between us. And the Bridegroom replied: ''How beautiful you are, my beloved, how beautiful you are...!" Yes, ''your eyes are doves behind your veil....''

Weeping out of love is a joyful shedding of tears which brings us Perfect Joy. Blessed are those who weep. In the declining evening of our life, in the dark but serene night, while we are waiting for the Bridegroom's arrival, our weeping is the only way which takes us to happiness.

Sometimes we weep for others, who also weep in their turn but perhaps with no joy: "Be sad with those in sorrow," said the Apostle (Rom 12:15). But even then our weeping is joyful; after all, shedding tears for others is like a step forward toward giving our life for them, which, according to the Lord, is the greatest proof of love. Remember, too, that the first fruits of love are those of Happiness.

Love speaks within us with groans that cannot be put into words. One weeps for love of the Beloved: because His presence stirs up our joy or because His absence fills us with longing. One weeps out of love for others. But there is always Love. And one weeps with the eyes, because Love consists of turning oneself to the other to gaze at him. Thus weeping is always done with Joy, "Blessed are you who are weeping now" (Lk 6:21). We come into this world crying and leave it shedding our last tears: surely because an earthly life which starts and ends by weeping must be a life spent in love. That is why those who never loved never learned how to weep. Love speaks inside us with groans that cannot be put into words because it is strong as Death (Sg 8:6), which we can understand in all its meanings: love is immensely great and powerful, enormously intense and strong. Thus large hearts only are capable of real weeping; stingy people do not cry, at the most they whimper or howl with fear. There is reason here why God became man: because He had never wept over us: "As he drew near and came in sight of the city he shed tears over it" (Lk 19:41); "Jesus wept; and the Jews said, 'See how much he loved him!'" (Jn 11: 35–36).

The Beatitudes and the Truth

To say beatitude is to say Love. And the beatitudes point to the way of the love between man and God, a road leading to Perfect Happiness.

Our Lord proclaimed the beatitudes on the top of a mountain. Perhaps He meant to tell us that if we want to comprehend them we have to climb high above the plains to breathe clean air. Indeed, He was not understood by many, and even fewer grasped the depth of His teaching. Many a man came after Him in History pretending to possess the secret of happiness. All types of formulas were tested here, and with great enthusiasm at first, only to be abandoned later on, amongst disappointments and often with pain: 'I have come in the name of my Father and you refuse to accept me; if someone else should come in his own name you would accept him" (Jn 5:43). We are now in need of some men and women willing to return to the mountain of the beatitudes to listen again to the Master's voice, which speaks of God's love for Man and of Man's love for God.

The beatitudes are God's Love challenge. This statement places us at the antipodes of Gnostic Christians and of those who reduce Christianity to almost nothing. The only problem with them is their refusal, or incapacity, to understand the Love of God; they think it too much for man to believe, that it cannot happen, that, at all cost, a more *reasonable* explanation fitting human standards must be found. It would be interesting to find what lies underneath the rejection of doctrines such as obedience to the Teaching Authority, the virginity of our Blessed Mother, the real Presence of Jesus Christ in the Eucharist, or the divinity of Christ, to mention some examples. Modern man, according to the opinion of some, can admit only things adapted to the parameters of human reason. Nevertheless, never before have so many irrational things been accepted as they are now, which makes us think that *irrationality* is not the only motive behind the rejection we are talking about. What lies at the bottom of this mentality is a rejection of God and of His Love; man, following decisions made from a certain point of view, has proclaimed himself god.

Gnostic–Rational Christianity, that today has become sociological and political, first reduces divine love to human love, and then it finally makes human love and mankind itself disappear. What is left of man in Marxism? Marxism does not believe in Christian love or justice; it does not even want to hear about them. In reality, it does not want to make people better or more righteous, it wants to make them gods. But it pretends it will obtain that condition not by lifting them to heaven, but by bringing heaven down to earth and imposing the principle that man depends exclusively on himself. The different varieties of Progressive Christianity proclaim theirs a concern for humanity, which has been long forgotten by those who have spent their life looking at heaven. The proclamation is good, for it sets at ease the conscience, and appeals to many. But the problem still stands. For nobody has ever proved that anyone who is not concerned about God can be really concerned about man. The facts, indeed, would prove just the opposite, but they cannot do it, because men have decided that facts prove nothing. When the devil talked to man for the first time, according to the account in the Bible, he appeared to be one concerned for the human race, and his deceptive arguments dealt with such concern: the human race had to be raised and, along with it, the possibility of being like God, of achieving an independent knowledge of good and evil, etc. We see here how speeches prove nothing, for they may be dreadfully deceiving. The course to follow is to examine the results, which is precisely what the gospel insists on: "You will be able to tell them by their fruits" (Mt 7:20). The Lord Himself abided by that norm: "Then even if you refuse to believe in me, at least believe in the work I do" (Jn 10:38; cf. 5:36; 10:25). But today who wants to examine results, fruits, works or facts? Man no longer wishes to submit his thinking to the facts; quite the contrary, he has decided that there is no other reality than the one his own thinking wills.

In the meantime, God's Love is there, offered to man. A Love that cannot be grasped by *progressive*, mundane Christians, nor by those who proclaim themselves as possessing the Spirit, if that Spirit is not the Spirit of Jesus. The Spirit also submits to proof of His authenticity, and this proof passes through the cross: "When the Spirit of truth comes... he will glorify me, since all he reveals to you will be taken from what is mine" (Jn 16:14). For the Spirit never comes to speak of Himself (Jn 16:13), but about Jesus, in order to take us to the Father through Him. He would not be the Spirit of Truth if He led us by a different road than the one Jesus trod (Jn 14: 5–7.26): the way of the cross. The cross of Christ has many aspects: one is obedience and fidelity to the Church. Jesus gave His Spirit on the cross (Lk 23:46; Jn 19:30), a Spirit of truth and humility who, consequently, submits Himself to the Church to be authenticated. The Spirit certainly blows where He pleases (Jn 3:8), but not in the manner He pleases —at least not in the meaning given to that manner by some— because, being the Spirit of Jesus, He always blows toward the Father. The freedom of Spirit invoked by many can only mean one thing: The Spirit is supremely free, but He is always the Spirit of the Lord, and nothing else. The Apostle expressed that reality in an accurate and brief formula: "Where the Spirit of the Lord is, there is freedom" (2 Cor 3:17; cf. Rom 8:9). Thus one should say that the Spirit not only submits Himself to authentication, but rather that He demands it. This is the only way the Spirit bears witness to Himself, a witness which is the only true one (Rom 8:16). When men themselves, going astray from the ways we have just mentioned, pretend to possess the Spirit, then we ought to consider that witness borne only by men has no guarantee of being true (Jn 5:34). The Spirit of Jesus takes on the cross precisely because it is the Spirit of Jesus, and hence Spirit of obedience, humility, victimization, and docility. Before being a gift of tongues or healing, the Spirit essentially is a gift of Love. To reduce Him to those or other *charismatic* manifestations is to stifle "the best way of all" (1 Cor 12:31) and consequently to "suffocate the Spirit" (1 Thess 5:19). For a Spirit that is not one of victimization is not then the Spirit of Jesus, nor the Spirit of Love, nor therefore the true Spirit. A long time ago, Saint John the Apostle wrote us a recommendation we seem to have forgotten: "My dear friends, not every spirit is to be trusted, but test the spirits to see whether they are from God, for many false prophets are at large in the world" (1 Jn 4:1).

The true Spirit of Love is not necessarily compelled to walk on festive paths —such festivity often takes on a diminished significance— displaying secondary charisma. The true movements of charismatic renewal will have to bear in mind Saint Paul's advice to the Corinthians: the Apostle warned them of over-estimating other charismas to the detriment of charity (1 Cor 12). And, so that they might know what true charity is, Paul supplied the Corinthians with criteria, which are equally valid for us (1 Cor 13).

It is not legitimate either to reduce the Message to a moralizing casuistry emphasizing fear. The Law, which must not be abolished, is meant to be fully fulfilled (Mt 5:17). The Christian is not under the law (Gal 5:18), though not against it either; he must go beyond it by fulfilling it with love: "Love is the fulfillment of the Law" (Rom 13:10).

The Beatitudes and Love

The annunciation of the message of the beatitudes, or of Perfect Joy, consists of this: God is Love, and He wants to have loving relations with Man. That is precisely the theme of the beginning of the Song of Songs (1:2):

> *Let him kiss me with the kisses of his mouth,*
> *for your love-making is sweeter than wine.*

The bride ardently desires to be kissed by the Groom with kisses of his mouth. Now, what does a kiss of love try to be? For a kiss, indeed, is mainly an attempt of being, of reaching something that is ineffable. In human love, the kiss is a mere attempt which fails in achieving plenitude and in reaching a totality it has been seeking. What it really wants is the interchange of the lovers' lives, that the lovers may be lost in each other. And that is only possible in divine love. That is what Saint Paul meant when he said, "Yet it is no longer I, but Christ living in me" (Gal 2:20). The Lord also said, "Whoever eats my flesh and drinks my blood lives in me and I live in that person... whoever eats me will also draw life from me" (Jn 6: 56–57).

What does it mean to live in the other, or to draw life from the other? If we pronounce those expressions seriously, it seems to us that we are at the threshold of the Mystery. We are too used to uttering words without going deeply into their meaning. The expression to live in the other may signify, for instance, the mutual change of hearts between lovers: heart for heart; or the eternal contemplation of one in the other in the reciprocal gaze of love; or the eternal and total possession of one by the other. Anyway, having said all this, all we are doing is trying to explain the Mystery with other words that never fully clarify it.

To understand that would be to understand Love, which can only be done fully by the Love that is only Love. Then we would also comprehend what the intimate dialogue of Love is: Love is just that, an eternal saying of mutual love between the two lovers. Love is a saying between two, precisely because it always proceeds from two.

The intimate dialogue of love begins in an intimacy with the other's name (Sg 1:3):

Your name is like oil poured out.

To pronounce the other's name is to be intimate with him in the sense of entering inside him, into his innermost I: *Jesus intuitus eum dilexit eum* (Mk 10:21). It is to provoke the gaze of the other person to come to rest upon our gaze, so that both may enjoy a mutual possession. Thus, pronouncing the name of the other person is, to some extent, to possess and to be possessed in a mutual surrender of love. The name is used to call the other person by using a word which bears all the wonder the other represents for the lover: "Your name is like oil poured out." And the other person is called because he is needed, desired, and the lover now depends on him. The bride can no longer live without the Bridegroom, but the Bridegroom cannot live without the bride either: "His desire is for me," said the bride of the Song referring to the Bridegroom (Sg 7:11); therefore, the love that torments the bride also torments the Bridegroom. Thus the fact is that God has wanted to love me, and now He cannot do without me. And that torment of love the Bridegroom suffers is the very same torment the bride undergoes. Perfect Joy is this: God has wanted to belong to me and He does belong to me now. His torments of love for me are not metaphorical but real; as real as the Being Who is God and is Love. In order to make me understand it, He became flesh in History, in Jesus and in His passion and death. Perfect Joy is possible from the moment I can be His friend (Jn 15: 13–15) and say His name, calling Him You; the moment my heart is able to hurt His; the moment He wishes to gaze at my eyes and feel that He dies with love (Sg 6:5). And all that is done in ardent longing (Lk 22:15). For the bride, Perfect Joy cannot be other than the feeling that she is dying of love for the Groom; the certainty that He is waiting for her ever since; the perception of His call coming from afar (Sg 2: 13–14):

> *Come then, my beloved, my lovely one, come.*
> *My dove, hiding in the clefts of the rock,*
> *in the coverts of the cliff.*

To this request she answers with a silence of love that forgets everything except the Beloved. The request and answer of love are made thus, when everything else has been silenced, in the unique place no one else can climb to, in spotless sites —white and blue— not trodden yet. The bride feels herself incapable of holding back her enamored answer, which comes forth with an impetus that leaves behind the very silence of things, clear things, yet forgotten:

> *Amado, en las brumosas*
> *laderas de montañas escarpadas,*
> *con cuevas de raposas*
> *y cimas plateadas*
> *en silencio de nieves olvidadas...*[8]

---

[8] *CFC*, 72. *My Beloved, the misty / Tops of the sheer mountains, / The dens of foxes, / The winged eagles, / The silence of the forgotten snowed peaks.*

The Song of Songs (1:2) speaks about the love between God and man, comparing it to a drunkenness of love:

For your love–making is sweeter than wine.

Love is inebriation, and some inebriation is also caused by drugs and wine. But the drug of love is much stronger, "For your love–making is sweeter than wine." Besides, love does not destroy, it gives life. On the contrary, any other drug destroys, for when man turns his back to Being, which is Love, he necessarily faces the horror and vertigo of that Void which is Nothingness. A Void —with a capital letter— which is worst than nothing —the latter, at least, would be nothing— since it is the consciousness of the Total Loss, of the No, of Absolute Negation. In other words: the realization that one had been destined for Love, for Absolute Love, and that one has lost it forever. The opposite happens with divine–human love, which is an incredible inebriation or madness of love. That is the reason why the message of the beatitudes, of the Christian life, can only be understood and lived by those able to fall in love. Christian life is a public announcement of Love issued for lovers; to think differently about it is to condemn Christianity and ourselves to disaster. I remember my early years and my classmates, my fellow seminarians, who were thrilled to wear their cassocks as soon as possible, to have people listening to their homilies or seeing them celebrating Mass. They are the same, unfortunately, who have become secularized and disappointed. Perhaps reality lost its focus: it should not have been a matter of becoming enthusiastic about things, not even with the priestly things we have mentioned, for nobody falls in love with things but with persons. The Love that unites the Father and the Son in God is also a Person, the Holy Spirit. The reason for that is that love, being something eminently personal and given, according to its nature, among persons, Love in essence had to be a hypostatic Love, a Person. To be enthusiastic about the things of God does not suffice, one must fall in love with God. Accordingly, if one has properly understood priesthood, for him things like Mass, preaching, hearing confessions are, regardless of all the thrill they entail, at the same time, and above all, a crucifixion: they ought to be performed out of love. Here enthusiasm for things, whatever they may be, will soon end in emptiness and despair. Human love can be misunderstood as well when persons are treated as if they were things. Should that happen, love is no longer possible. And nobody can live without Love. To falsify this meaning of Christian life as Love is to distort the Message of Jesus Christ and the content of the whole Revelation of the New Testament. The guilt here must be equally distributed to timorous and excessively legalistic Christians, to empty and over-sentimental piety, and to the *progressive* Christians exclusively concerned with worldly realities. The false Christians of the past, as well as the modern ones, are a clear demonstration of failure to fall in love with Love. They all willingly became incapable of speaking and struggling with Love.

Conclusion

I have told you that the beatitudes were first proclaimed on a mountain. The air is cleaner in the countryside, and things are seen more clearly, and even words and noises are better heard. So the bride of the Song says (7: 12–13):

Come, my love,
let us go to the fields.
We will spend the night in the villages,
and in the early morning we will go to the vineyards.
We will see if the vines are budding,
if their blossoms are opening,
if the pomegranate trees are in flower.
Then I shall give you
the gift of my love.

We have said that the beatitudes are Joy because they point at the road which leads to true Love. That Joy consists in knowing that God loves us and we love Him. It is Joy which, according to the beatitudes, is reserved for the poor, those who weep, the humble, the pure of heart, and the lovers of justice who are persecuted for justice's sake. But these people are officially accused as mad by the world. If God and the world are right, then Joy would be an exclusive privilege of the mad; though all depends on what one understands as madness. For the ancient world, according to Saint Paul's testimony (1 Cor 1:23), the God of the Christians was mad. A great part of the modern world has believed it to be so, too. In modern times, the world has made a huge effort to present a more *reasonable* God (we must mention here, for instance the philosophies of Kant, Hegel, and Spinoza). But then something singular happened: once God had become much more rational, He vanished. Thus there is just one logical conclusion: either God is mad, or He cannot exist. That is not surprising, indeed the reasonable God of human standards cannot be God. We rather think, therefore, of the beatitudes as something for mad people, leaving it for another time —which will coincide with the end of History— to find out what was mad and what was not. We accept being labeled as mad by the world, and we choose the road of the beatitudes; but it does not prevent us from seeing how a world that has exalted Reason above all is becoming less reasonable all the time.

We, at least, are fortunate because of God's madness. That madness has made it possible that a foolish, mad, infinite Love has loved us in a foolish, mad, enormous way, the way God does love us. Only a bottomless Love could love us in such a way. There are only incredible explanations for incredible foolishness.

For the same reason, if we want to comprehend the Heart of Christ —with which we are loved— we first must comprehend all the love and pain experienced by men and women. For all true love and all true suffering have passed through that Heart. Therefore, any talking about Christ that is not an enamored and crucified one becomes commonplace, and ends in profanation: "This people honors me only with lip-service, while their hearts are far from me" (Mt 15:8). All the books in the world would be insufficient; only He can tell us about Him.

Therefore, we, on our part, ought to clean our hearts. Let us seek the pure air of the mountain of the beatitudes, so that we may hear and comprehend them. Once there, we will be ready then to hear the Master's voice, to see the smile and contemplate the face which shall quench the thirst of our hearts forever, introducing us into the expressive and enamored Silence of a Perfect Joy which never ends.

XVI

THE WEDDING AT CANA

On the third day there was a wedding at Cana in Galilee. The mother of Jesus was there, and Jesus and his disciples had also been invited. And they ran out of wine, since the wine provided for the feast had all been used, and the mother of Jesus said to him, "They have no wine." Jesus said, "Woman, what do you want from me? My hour has not come yet." His mother said to the servants, "Do whatever he tells you."

There were six stone water jars standing there, meant for the ablutions that are customary among the Jews: each could hold twenty or thirty gallons. Jesus said to the servants, "Fill the jars with water," and they filled them to the brim. Then he said to them, "Draw some out now and take it to the president of the feast." They did this; the president tasted the water, and it had turned into wine. Having no idea where it came from —though the servants who had drawn the water knew— the president of the feast called the bridegroom and said, "Everyone serves good wine first and the worse wine when the guests are well wined; but you have kept the best wine till now." This was the first of Jesus' signs: it was at Cana in Galilee. He revealed his glory, and his disciples believed in him.

(Jn 2: 1–11)

The true content of the story of the wedding at Cana is the idea of Feast, the idea of Joy. This passage deals with what the feast of man is and could be. In order to do that, the feast of man appears paralleled, though not opposed, to the Feast of God. The text places both kinds of feasts on two levels, which develop simultaneously but at different heights, only to end up by telling us that the feast of man is impossible unless the Feast of God is celebrated along with it at the same time.

Both feasts are shown with their peculiar characteristics, which we are going to analyze so that we may understand their content and mutual interconnections. In the feast of man it is always possible, for instance, that the unforeseen and the unpleasant may appear at the least expected moment; in the one we are presently commenting upon, there was a lack of wine at the height of the banquet: "And they ran out of wine, since the wine provided for the feast had all been used, and the mother of Jesus said to him, 'They have no wine.'" Besides, in the feast of man, one always has to count with unfortunate or stingily made calculations: the man who presided over the feast pointed it out very clearly to the bridegroom: 'Everyone serves good wine first and the worse wine when the guests are well wined." There is no human feast, no matter how magnificent it may be, that can proceed without calculation, stinginess, or the decision *that should be enough*. For the abundance of overflowing and limitless Joy can only appear at the Feast of God, not at man's feast. That is so because there are always two guests attending the feast of man who are impossible to expel: the limit of time, since it has to end, and the limit of size, since it is finite.

Fortunately God takes part in the feast of man, not to annul it, but quite on the contrary, to make it possible, since God holds nothing against the feast of man. God wants it to become real, and He is prompt to intervene to raise the limitations that hinder man's feast from becoming a real Feast. In reality, God from the very beginning called man to Happiness, and Happiness is always enjoyed during the Feast. That is why, according to the passage upon which we are commenting, our Lord steps in, making possible a feast which had been doomed to fail: "Jesus said to the servants, 'Fill the jars with water,' and they filled them to the brim. Then he said to them, 'Draw some out now and take it to the president of the feast.' They did this; the president tasted the water, and it had turned into wine. Having no idea where it came from —though the servants who had drawn the water knew— the president of the feast called the bridegroom and said, 'Everyone serves good wine first and the worse wine when the guests are well wined; but you have kept the best wine till now.'" What is proper to the Feast of God is shown here: the text talks about weddings, guests, wine, happiness; and at the same time of plenitude, overflowing, wine of the best quality, and the incredible surprise that makes possible both Happiness and the culmination of the Feast. It seems, indeed, that the evangelist wanted to insist on those details: he mentions large jars of great capacity, which are to be completely filled, "to the brim" to be precise, and he ends up by telling us that the water turned into a wine of the finest quality.

The image of wine and the idea of plenitude are usually found together in the Bible. They signify that which is the most specific to the Feast in which the love between God and man is going to be celebrated. The Song of Songs expresses through the Groom something which is, simultaneously, some kind of order, invitation, summons, and even a summary of that which God calls man to (5:1):

> *I come into my garden,*
> *my sister, my promised bride,*
> *I pick my myrrh and my balsam,*
> *I eat my honey and my honeycomb,*
> *I drink my wine and my milk.*
> *Eat, friends, and drink,*
> *drink deep, my dearest friends.*

The Bridegroom goes to His garden to drink His wine. He goes to His fenced-in garden or to His sealed fountain, which represents the bride, so that He may become deeply drunk there, undoubtedly with an inebriation of Love. And then comes the Bridegroom's pressing invitation to His friends, "Eat, friends, and drink, drink deep, my dearest friends," which reminds us of what He said in another place: "I shall no longer call you servants, because a servant does not know his master's business; I call you friends, because I have made known to you everything I have learnt from my Father" (Jn 15:15). The invitation is to drink wine till the point of drunkenness: "Eat, friends, and drink, drink deep, my dearest friends." God is summoning mankind to the Feast of infinite Love. A Feast that opens the way to inebriation, plenitude, loss of the heart in the Beloved, madness and drunkenness of love, the complete surrender of the Bridegroom to the bride and of the bride to the Bridegroom. A Feast in which the inebriation of love takes place, causing, at the same time, elation, Perfect Happiness, loss of the senses, and the abandonment of all that is not Love. The Feast man is invited to by God is the Feast in which one experiences the Joy caused by tasting the best wine till the drunkenness of total Love: "There was a man who gave a great banquet, and he invited a large number of people. When the time for the banquet came, he sent his servant to say to those who had been invited, 'Come along: everything is ready now...'" (Lk 14: 16–17). "'Look, my banquet is all prepared, my oxen and fattened cattle have been slaughtered, everything is ready. Come to the wedding...'" (Mt 22:4). God is calling us to a Feast, to an abundance, to fullness, to overflowing Joy, to the inebriation of unlimited Love. That is why a great banquet is mentioned; a wedding banquet, with good wine, oxen and fattened cattle. And the text we are commenting on says that the jars destined to contain the wine were large, that they were filled to the brim, and that the wine later found in them was of the best quality. Now we understand why any effort to debase the gospel in an attempt to set it within temporal coordinates is a betrayal of the invitation God has made to man; it is the same as concocting a gospel without transcendence, consequently, an insignificant gospel. The images of wine and of inebriation are so constantly used in the Bible to signify the call to love uttered by Love, that Jesus compared the image of the vine to Himself: "I am the vine, you are the branches. Whoever remains in me, with me in him, bears fruit in plenty" (Jn 15:5). Accordingly, the wine which causes drunkenness is produced by Him, Who is the vine; and He is the cause of the drunkenness of Love, because He produces the fruit from which the wine comes. Love, indeed, never has its origin in itself, but in the two lovers who mutually exhale it: "When the Spirit of truth comes... he will not be speaking of his own accord, but will say only what he has been told" (Jn 16:13). Inebriation would be impossible without wine, and this could not exist apart from the vine, which produces it, and from the vinedresser who grows it ("My Father is the vinedresser" Jn 15:1).

Love also is that which turns the two lovers into beloveds at the same time; in other words, Love causes the lover to be, in his turn, beloved, and the beloved to be lover. Each one is, at the same time, a lover in himself, and the beloved regarding the other one; both are at once lovers and beloved. All this is possible because Love, though being distinct from them as persons who love each other, becomes one and the same with them in the identity of the one and only nature of love ("God is love" 1 Jn 4:8). Jesus is thus the cause of our inebriation of Love, inebriation to which we are pressingly called: "Jesus stood and cried out: 'Let anyone who is thirsty come to me! Let anyone who believes in me come and drink!'" (Jn 7:37). One might sum up the Christian message by saying that it is Joy brought about by the inebriation the wine of Love has caused, as can be seen in those other words of the Lord, "From now on, I tell you, I shall never again drink wine until the day I drink the new wine with you in the kingdom of my Father" (Mt 26:29).

Wine causes drunkenness and happiness, which in this case are the drunkenness and the Happiness of Love. On this earth Jesus drank that wine with those who were His own, and He shall drink it again in the Kingdom, more definitively then. That is why the words the Virgin addressed to her Son at the wedding at Cana —"They have no wine"— are the sad diagnosis of a situation which could perfectly be the present: there is no wine, so there is no Happiness. The Virgin's words touched the sore spot of the actual situation of a Christian life from which the Spirit of Jesus seems to be absent. It does not matter that today much is said about the Spirit. The first fruit of His presence is Joy (Gal 5:22), but the actual Christian world, whatever may be said in this respect, is a sad world, thus denoting an absence of the Spirit. When we affirm this, we are fully aware that today's fashion is to state the opposite, and that we shall be accused of despairing and ignoring the signs of the times. The Spirit, it is true, will never abandon the Church, but she may sometimes go through an extinction or kenosis of that Spirit. Actual Christianity is, to a great extent, under a strain. The general crisis of faith and morality particularly reaches to consecrated Christians. Some members of the Hierarchy are suffering an inferiority complex, at the same time that they praise the avant garde theologians who question the divinity of Jesus Christ. And even when, in an extreme case, they are softly admonished by that Hierarchy, the latter waste no time in apologizing for the admonishment, advising that those theologians are not really being punished, and remorsefully appearing as guilty for doing it. Today doubt is acclaimed while the certainty of faith is censured; suspicion is promoted whereas all forms of fidelity are held in contempt; truth is disguised by those who denounce the injustice and sins of the weak but keep silent about those of the powerful (arguing at the same time that they are denouncing the powerful and defending the oppressed). Many think that the Church of freedom and of the Spirit should no longer submit herself to the narrow frame of institutions, nor to the demands of any official Teaching. Meanwhile, those who openly hold these viewpoints are flattered by some members in charge of that official Teaching, who suffer their attacks when they should denounce them. But those members appear not to worry much about that matter.

The Lord calls those who are thirsty, with the promise that from those who come to Him shall flow streams of living water; Saint John explains that He is speaking of the Spirit which those who believed in him were to receive (Jn 7: 37–39). We are dealing here with God overflowing us with His Love (Rom 5:5). We have been invited to a (wedding) banquet, so that we become inebriated in it by drinking the wine that is Love: "Eat, friends, and drink, drink deep, my dearest friends." Because God wanted to give us His love, He presented us with His Love, "So that the love with which you loved me may be in them, and so that I may be in them" (Jn 17:26). God is so madly in love with us that He wants us to live with Him that mutual surrender of which the marital one is but a remote figure: "As the bridegroom rejoices in his bride, so will your God rejoice in you" (Is 62:5). But that surrender, that inebriation of Love, that Joy ought to be reciprocal: "I exult for joy in Yahweh, my soul rejoices in my God... like a bride adorned in her jewels" (Is 61:10). As we have said many times, since Love is a matter of two and comes from two, Love is also the reciprocal looking of two lovers gazing at each other. That is why the Bridegroom says things such as (Jn 16:22; Sg 4:9; 6:5; Hos 2:19):

> *I shall see you again,*
> *and your hearts will be full of joy.*
>
> *You ravish my heart*
> *with a single one of your glances...*
>
> *Turn your eyes away from me,*
> *they take me by assault!*
>
> *I shall betroth you to myself forever,*
> *I shall betroth you in uprightness and justice,*
> *and faithful love and tenderness.*
> *Yes, I shall betroth you to myself in loyalty*
> *and in the knowledge of Yahweh.*

And the bride in her turn, too (Sg 5:12; 8:10):

*His eyes are like doves
beside the water–courses,
bathing themselves in milk,
perching on a fountain–rim.*

Under his eyes I have found true peace.

Some theologians, though they admit that the Holy Spirit is *nexus duorum*, a bond or tie that links the Father and the Son, point out that this formulation may present difficulties in reaching through it for an attempt to explain the mystery of the procession of the third divine Person, warning, at the same time, of some danger of anthropomorphism. According to them, that which unites two who love each other cannot be precisely their real act of loving, because each one lives his own act of loving, which would demand two loves or two acts of loving. But, their reasoning continues, at the origin of the Holy Spirit there is but one act, one sole principle of expiration common to the Father and to the Son. Sure enough, they have grounds for the objection, but I would dare to venture the suggestion that perhaps it is not necessary to establish two acts of loving in God in order to attempt some explanation of the procession of the third Person. The danger of anthropomorphism does certainly exist, and because it is subtle and is always lurking, it can slide into the thinking of those who make the objection as well.

Perhaps they try to explain Love (that is God: 1 Jn 4:8) through human love and that which happens in it. It is true that the third Person proceeds from only one principle of expiration. But in God the act of love between the two lovers is one and the same, which is made possible thanks to the unity in the essence of the Persons; there are two lovers, but only one act of love. We should bear in mind that we are attempting to say something about Love (that is

God), and not to explain what human love is, which is but a figure of, or participation, in the divine Love (although we can pass from one to the other while leaning on the analogy). The act of love can never be single in human love, that is in created love; the reason is that since created love is not a perfect love, it is not Love but a participation in Him. I believe that we should not set out with created love, for there is a danger of anthropomorphism here, too. In God, the Holy Spirit, or, if we so prefer, the Love between the Father and the Son, is different from both of them as Person (this is the only way Love can exist); but at the same time it is the same and only act of love, which proceeds from them both, because His essence is identical to Theirs. Now we understand why it is said that love unites and is an element of union, because there is only one act of love in the mystery of the Trinitarian life. In God, Who is perfect Love, unity is perfected in His one essence (the Holy Spirit is rightly said to be the Principle of unity in the Church, and as the soul or Principle that joins all the members in the Mystical Body). It cannot be the same with creatures, and consequently love can never achieve a complete identification among them; never mind that husband and wife are said to be *one and the same* in matrimony (let us notice how here love is again presented as an element of union and *striving for* making one of the two lovers). But what cannot be given among creatures is a reality in God. Let us keep in mind that we are talking about Love; to explain that mystery would amount to explaining the mystery of the Trinity, the mystery of God Himself. God is Love because the sole act in which both the Father and the Son love each other is exactly like their essence (the same essence, numerically one). And because it is one Perfect, Total Act, infinite as well as the essence, it begets one total Love. Now Love is given among Persons; God is Love by essence, consequently Love must also be a Person in God. This Person is not also a Lover (He is rather the Love the other two Persons profess for each other). Since He has identical essence to the other two, He possesses the same intelligence and the same will (numerically one) as the other two do. Since He is opposed to the Father and to the Son, as far as their mutual relationships are concerned, as Persons that love each other, He Himself is another Person. For that reason, when God gives us His Love, the Gift that the third Person is (the Holy Spirit, the Lord, the Giver of Life), that third Person is never given alone —it would have no sense, for love is not possible without lovers— for when He inhabits us, the indwelling of the other two Persons is inevitably present: "Anyone who loves me will keep my word, and my Father will love him, and we shall come to him and make a home in him" (Jn 14:23). This text is concerned with the Son Who can be loved (and consequently is able to love), with the Father Who can love (and consequently can be loved), and with the Love they both can give and have received (involving here created love, which requires the presence in the creatures of uncreated Love): two Lovers and Love. That is why Holy Scripture commonly talks about the love of the Father for us or about ours for Him; or about the love of the Son for us and ours for Him; but it does not say that the Spirit loves us: for this Person is not so much Lover as Love Himself, although identical in essence with the other two divine Persons.

The Spirit that is Love has been given to us. That is possible because He is essentially a Gift, a Present. When it is said that we are made gods it also means that we are made love, possessed and overwhelmed by Love; we are made like Him and share Him to the same extent that we share the divine nature. If it can be said in the Holy Scripture, "You are gods —and scripture cannot be set aside" (Jn 10: 34–35), then it also can be said that we are made love. Love has been given to us for us to become love, and therefore for us to give ourselves. Consequently, keeping our lives instead of giving them would be exactly contrary to God and to His plans for us: "Anyone who tries to preserve his life will lose it; and anyone who loses it will keep it safe" (Lk 17:33). And Saint Paul said that it was not he who lived, but Christ living in him (Gal 2:20). In reality, none of us lives for himself (Rom 14: 7–8). God's plan was to make us rich (1 Cor 1:5; 2 Cor 8:9) granting us, therefore, the possibility of giving up everything; only through freely embraced poverty can we feel that Perfect Joy which lies in giving more than in receiving (Acts 20:35). Therefore, Poverty and richness may be said to be interchangeable, to the extent that Poverty blends with richness or becomes one with it (Rev 2:9). Poverty can be said, by the same token, to be the virtue closest to charity, for he who out of love gave up everything would open his heart to Love; then total Poverty would open the floodgates to total Love, for Love consists of total giving or total surrender to the other: to be lost in the Beloved.

The Feast of God is the feast of our wedding to Him. In it, as we have seen, His Spirit, His Love, is given to us. And the Spirit is Fire; fire is the highest degree of warmth, the fastest agitation of the molecules forming a substance: stirring, movement, vitality... God is Spirit and Fire because He is infinite Life. We have been endowed with an infinite longing, vitality, elation and enthusiasm: "I have come so that they may have life and have it to the full" (Jn 10:10). Therefore, God's life inside us, the life of grace, is anything but passivity. The kingdom of God inside us is the yeast that leavens the whole dough, the mustard seed that becomes a big tree, the seed that grows nobody knows how, while the sower sleeps, the seed that yields a hundredfold, the group of virgins who go out to meet the Bridegroom, the great banquet with the fattened cattle, the treasure found in the field, the pearl of great value, the dragnet that is hauled ashore containing all kinds of fish. The Kingdom of God inside us is the Feast of God at the wedding at Cana, presided over by Jesus and His Mother, to which we have been invited along with His disciples ("Jesus and his disciples had also been invited"). Once there, we shall find that we were not mere guests: it is the feast of our own wedding! Indeed, have you noticed that the names of the couple are not mentioned? Because it is really our own wedding feast: ''The jealousy that I feel for you is, you see, God's own jealousy: I gave you all in marriage to a single husband, a virgin pure for presentation to Christ'' (2 Cor 11:2). God's life in us cannot be anger, but Love; it cannot be tepidity either, but infinite longing and vitality. For Love is infinite vitality, since it is a self-giving to the other in totality and a receiving in the same way. All idea of passivity is thus excluded; therefore, I think the use of that term in mystical theology is not very fortunate.

Contemplative prayer —let us notice the permanent deficiency of human language to express these realities— is given by God; it cannot be otherwise, since created love is but a participation in the divine life, the presence of the Non-Created Love within us. But that does not imply that man's role in it is restricted to a mere contemplative, receiving, passive attitude. The statement that in contemplative prayer man is less active than God, granted, of course, the predominant character of God here, is not true either. What I am trying to say is that in contemplation both God as well as man strive hard utterly to give themselves to each other. Love has no room for passivity, in the sense that love is a total, continuous, consciously and fully wanted (mutual) self-giving. Love is, at least, as much to give as to receive, and this mutual giving being a pure and intense act, it cannot be mere passivity. Love is jointly exhaled by two in only one active principle. Should one of the Lovers fail to do it, there would be no Love. Now if we apply that to human love we must point out a great number of exceptions, but at any rate there must always be two lovers. On the other hand, to say that contemplative prayer is mainly passive is to know little or nothing of the riches of compassion God can grant in it. The intimate sharing in the sufferings and death of Christ are quite far from contemplative passivity, terms that, moreover, do not seem too congenial to Saint Paul's expression about making up in our own body all the hardships that still have to be undergone by Christ (Col 1:24). Certainly these all are manners of speaking, in the simple attempt of somehow getting nearer to the mystery, always taking into account the deficiency of human language. Nevertheless, I want to stress the point that contemplation is the highest state of vitality, effort, and personal realization of himself that a person can achieve in this world. If a human being is, above all, intelligence and will, he never understands nor loves more intently than in contemplation. The greatest love is shown by freely laying down one's own life (Jn 15:13), which is the highest degree of giving; that is not precisely passivity. We discover here the incredible thing about our dialogue with God: we have been granted the possibility of giving something to God, Who wants to be in need of us, to become poor and a beggar for our love. The dialogue with God means the possibility of addressing God as *you*, of reciprocity, of giving and receiving. It is true that all is grace in contemplation, but a grace that supposes or creates reality, otherwise it would be a senseless grace.

Always, little people have tried time and again to cut down the gospel. Today's great heresy is the same that has always existed: gnosticism, the attempt to replace the Feast of God with an ordinary human feast (to finally destroy it as a feast). The man who presided over the feast admitted that the wine he was given to taste was excellent, furnishing a logical explanation from his point of view: the cunning groom had kept the best wine for a final surprise. Nonetheless, the explanation was wrong. It is very amusing, for instance, to read essays about the personality or poetry of Saint John of the Cross: all they contain are literary and psychological explanations, the influence of the time he lived in, the historical and social conditions, etc. Less amusing are the twisted explanations of some theologians endeavoring to prove that Jesus Christ is a human person. The gospel mindfully points out that what really happened was that the waiter in charge of the feast did not know where the wine came from, and that is precisely what happens with those renowned theologians: they have no faith. And we may assume, though the gospel does not expressly say it, that the servants laughed at the credible, *reasonable*, and logical explanation of the waiter, because, as the gospel does say, they knew where the wine had come from. We are among those servants who knew the true explanation, very grateful to God for His great gift of our faith and the no less great gift of His own Love. The implacable divine logic is present too; it seems to disregard man, and rightly so, when he is intent on destroying the divine Feast and runs out of wine ("Woman, what do you want from me?"). Fortunately, the persistence of the Blessed Mother with her faith and confidence in Jesus intervened: now we see that the Virgin and the saints can destroy human stubbornness and defeat the divine logic. At the same time we bear in mind, of course, that the Virgin and the saints, who are God's masterpieces, also are included in the divine plans and logic. Indeed, God's logic, ways and thoughts go far beyond the thinking, logic and ways of man.

INDEX OF QUOTATIONS
OF THE
NEW TESTAMENT

Matthew

3: 14, **57, 197**
4: 5, **18**
5: 1–12, **271**
    3, **40, 95, 251**
    5, **123, 143**
    8, **141, 229**
    13, **28**
    14, **210**
    14–16, **88**
    15, **19, 178**
    15–16, **210**
    16, **110, 183**
    17, **307**
    19, **209**
6: 7, **166**
    9, **33**
    22, **141**
    23, **141**
7: 6, **89**
    7, **35**
    8, **263**
    20, **306**
    23, **106, 125**
8: 17, **54**
    26, **241**
9: 15, **107**
10: 9–10, **29, 38**
    14, **89**
    23, **89, 98**
    24, **87**
    24–25, **57**
    34, **36**
    35, **74**
    39, **152**
11: 2–6, **24, 202**
    4, **209**
    6, **57**
    25, **84, 116, 250**
    25–26, **230**
    28, **191**
    28–30, **192**
12: 20–21, **144**
    43, **95**
13: 8, **43**
    44, **280**
15: 8, **314**
    26, **89**
    32, **68**
16: 1–4, **15**
    24, **29, 274**
    26, **120**
17: 21, **164**
18: 3, **87, 116, 250**
    4, **250**
19: 29, **105, 132**
20: 6–7, **191**
    8, **87**
    16, **102**
    22, **154**

21: 22, **35, 246**
22: 2–14, **102**
    4, **320**
23: 8, **87, 120**
24: 12, **20**
    24, **27**
    28, **72**
    30, **27**
    36, **20**
    42–44, **118**
    48–51, **114**
25: 1–13, **99, 175, 231**
    14–30, **188**
    21, **281**
    24–25, **249**
26: 6–13, **67**
    29, **321**
    37–38, **57**
    75, **300**
27: 46, **274**
28: 19, **98**
    19–20, **18**

Mark

1: 1–8, **195**
   29–39, **91**
3: 20, **192**
   31–35, **224**
4: 40, **241**

5: 3, **94**
   38–39, **71**
   40, **72**
7: 37, **93**
8: 22–26, **75**
9: 18, **95**
   50, **19**
10: 15, **116, 250**
    21, **309**
11: 24, **35, 246**
12: 27, **95**
    41–44, **291**
    44, **192**
13: 22, **27**
    32–36, **118**
14: 3–9, **67**
15: 28, **54**
16: 15, **98**

Luke

1: 48, **273**
2: 10, **144, 279**
3: 16, **159**
4: 16, **18**
   18–21, **144**
5: 5, **192**
6: 20, **250**
   21, **303**
   21–23, **123**

38, **35**, **105**
7: 11–15, **61**
18–23, **24**
23, **57**
44–46, **106**
8: 37–39, **89**
9: 23, **274**
10: 9, **282**
17–20, **31**
21, **116**
23, **280**
41, **120**
42, **39**
11: 14, **95**
12: 14, **25**
35, **78**, **231**
35–36, **178**
36, **217**, **223**
37, **232**
38, **232**
48, **35**
49, **110**, **159**, **160**
13: 25, **125**
14: 16–17, **320**
23, **79**
26–27, **87**
15: 16, **35**
17: 21, **282**
33, **327**
18: 1, **162**

8, **20**
11, **55**
19: 1–8, **45**
13, **191**
41, **303**
21: 1–4, **291**
19, **87**
34–36, **118**
22: 15, **310**
23: 8, **18**
46, **306**
24: 13–35, **136**
32, **78**

John

1: 3, **48**
4–5, **185**
6–8, **207**
9, **77**
12, **44**
14, **209**
16, **60**
19–28, **207**
38, **296**
39, **60**
41, **79**
45–46, **79**
2: 1–11, **315**
17, **79**
3: 8, **162**, **306**

    11, **141**
    14, **23**
    16, **150**
    18, **72**
    29, **108, 277**
    34, **285**
 4: 6, **192**
    36, **192**
    42, **52**
 5: 17, **190**
    25, **72**
    34, **307**
    36, **18, 306**
    43, **304**
 6: 44, **101**
    56, **44**
    56–57, **308**
    57, **48**
    63, **177**
 7: 37, **274, 321**
    37–39, **322**
    46, **78**
 8: 1–11, **67**
    7, **59**
    11, **60**
    12, **77, 82, 210**
    18, **18**
    23, **19**
    26, **286**
    28, **23**

    44, **240**
    46, **54**
 9: 1–3, **94**
    1–38, **168**
    4, **87**
10: 2–5, **158**
    5, **73**
    10, **131, 139, 226, 327**
    25, **18, 306**
    34–35, **326**
    37–38, **18**
    38, **306**
11: 9, **87**
    25, **73**
    28, **137**
    33, **68**
    35–36, **300, 303**
12: 1–8, **67**
    24, **55, 164, 226**
    24–25, **149**
    32–33, **23**
    35, **88**
    46, **77**
13: 1, **24, 27, 111, 128**
    21, **247**
    35, **24**
14: 4, **296**
    5–7, **306**
    6, **57, 143, 296**
    12, **43**

12–14, **246**
16–17, **160**
17, **211**
20, **127**
21, **137, 161, 230**
23, **104, 326**
26, **120, 306**
27, **36**
28, **296**
15: 1, **320**
5, **132, 320**
8, **132**
10–11, **145**
11, **95, 172**
13, **24, 27, 151, 255, 329**
13–15, **310**
15, **44, 106, 159, 247, 286, 319**
16, **101, 132**
19, **19, 28**
20, **43**
26, **160**
16: 6–7, **154, 160**
13, **85, 257, 306, 320**
13–14, **160**
13–15, **286**
14, **306**
20, **297**
22, **95, 279, 323**

23, **35**
24, **172, 246**
33, **259**
17: 6, **33**
13, **95, 172**
15, **41**
16, **28**
21, **127**
21–23, **245**
23, **127**
26, **127, 160, 245, 248, 277, 323**
18: 37, **161**
19: 30, **27, 306**
20: 24–29, **142**
21: 1–7, **138**

Acts of the Apostles

1: 1, **209**
7, **20**
8, **98**
21–22, **54**
3: 5–6, **34**
6, **33, 38**
4: 12, **33, 37**
32, **245**
6: 2–4, **79**
20: 35, **134, 227, 248, 327**
22: 20, **29**

Romans

1: 19, **22**
   20, **286**
5: 5, **269, 322**
   8, **164**
   14, **56**
6: 2–4, **57**
   3, **23, 147**
   3–5, **147**
   6, **56**
   8, **147**
   10, **94**
   11, **147**
   14, **94**
8: 3, **56**
   9, **306**
   15, **162**
   16, **299, 307**
   26, **122, 300**
9: 3, **70**
10: 14, **209**
    15, **98, 144**
    17, **51, 209, 286**
12: 1, **147, 148**
    15, **303**
13: 10, **307**
14: 7, **48, 226**
    7–8, **147, 327**

1 Corinthians

1: 5, **327**
   17–18, **153**
   21–23, **23**
   23, **153, 313**
   25, **218**
   26–29, **29**
2: 9, **109, 284**
   10, **299**
   10–12, **171**
   14, **22**
3: 21–23, **279**
7: 29, **98**
10: 13, **237**
12: —, **307**
    11, **162**
    31, **307**
13: —, **307**
    1–3, **112**
    3, **25**
    7, **26, 67**
    8, **225, 295**
    12, **87, 138, 229**
    13, **225**
15: 8, **60**

2 Corinthians

1: 19–20, **273**
3: 17, **162, 306**
4: 6, **229**
5: 2, **191**
   14, **120**
   14–15, **226**
   15, **48, 147**
   21, **56, 94**
6: 6, **23**
8: 9, **56, 250, 291, 327**
11: 2, **328**
12: 4, **285**
13: 9, **281**

Galatians

2: 19, **23**
   20, **48, 106, 125, 210, 226, 245, 308, 327**
3: 14, **26**
4: 4–5, **151**
   19, **87**
5: 6, **26**
   18, **307**
   22, **44, 144, 277, 321**
   23, **26**
   24, **23**
6: 14, **23**

Ephesians

1: 22, **151**
2: 14, **279**
3: 17, **26**
4: 15–16, **151**
5: 2, **147**
   8, **110, 178**
   25, **132**
   32, **132**
6: 12, **38**
   16, **43**

Philippians

1: 21, **47**
   21–23, **139**
2: 5, **59, 69, 147**
   7–8, **146**
   8, **56**
   9–10, **37**
3: 1, **153**
   20, **191**
   21, **94**
4: 4, **144**

Colossians

1: 16–17, **48**
   18, **151**

24, **54, 329**
2: 9, **229**
  20, **147**
3: 3, **147**
4: 12, **104**

1 Tessalonians

5: 16, **144**
  17, **162**
  19, **307**

2 Tessalonians

2: 7, **20**
  9–10, **27**

1 Timothy

1: 19, **26**
2: 4, **50**
6: 12–13, **30**

2 Timothy

2: 9, **182**
4: 2, **77**
  7, **87**
  8, **114**

Hebrews

2: 18, **237**
4: 12, **14**
  15, **56**
5: 1, **146**
  1–3, **56**
  5, **56**
  7, **69, 122**
7: 27, **149**
9: 22, **55, 150**
10: 37, **118**
11: 1, **142**
  6, **26**
12: 2, **278**
  29, **138**
13: 14, **25**
4: 3, **156**

1 Peter

2: 5, **147**
  9, **147, 151**
3: 18, **56**
4: 7, **163**

2 Peter

    1: 4, **127**

1 John

    1: 1–3, **141**
       3, **81**
       3–4, **82**
       7, **77**
    2: 20, **85, 286**
       27, **85, 286**
    3: 5, **94**
       16, **27**
    4: 1, **307**
       5, **26**
       8, **217, 241, 321, 324**
       9, **150**
       16, **127, 128, 218, 289**
       18, **21, 241**
       19, **164, 294**
    5: 2, **111**
       4, **22**
       7–9, **18**

Revelation

    1: 5, **29**
       6, **147**
       8, **57, 118**
       15, **166**

    2: 9, **327**
       13, **33**
       17, **215**
       18, **166**
       19, **26**
    3: 8, **33**
       15–16, **240**
       17, **35**
       20, **50, 97, 157, 217, 274**
    5: 10, **147**
    6: 9, **29**
    13: 13–15, **27**
    19: 7, **109**
       9, **109**
    20: 6, **147**
    21: 4, **59**
       8, **242**
       9, **185**
       23, **130**
    22: 17, **114, 284**
       20, **114, 133, 235, 284**

BOOKS OF THE BIBLE

Acts, Acts of the Apostles	**Jn**, John	**1 Pet**, 1 Peter
Amos, Amos	**1 Jn**, 1 John	**2 Pet**, 2 Peter
Bar, Baruch	**2 Jn**, 2 John	**Phil**, Philippians
1 Chron, 1 Chronicles	**3 Jn**, 3 John	**Philem**, Philemon
2 Chron, 2 Chronicles	**Job**, Job	**Prov**, Proverbs
Col, Colossians	**Joel**, Joel	**Ps**, Psalms
1 Cor, 1 Corinthians	**Jon**, Jonah	**Rev**, Revelation
2 Cor, 2 Corinthians	**Josh**, Joshua	**Rom**, Romans
Dan, Daniel	**Jud**, Judith	**Ruth**, Ruth
Deut, Deuteronomy	**Jude**, Jude	**1 Sam**, 1 Samuel
Eccles, Ecclesiastes	**Judg**, Judges	**2 Sam**, 2 Samuel
Eph, Ephesians	**1 Kings**, 1 Kings	**Sg**, Song of Songs
Esther, Esther	**2 Kings**, 2 Kings	**Sir**, Sirach
Ex, Exodus	**Lam**, Lamentations	**1 Thess**, 1 Thessalonians
Ezek, Ezekiel	**Lev**, Leviticus	**2 Thess**, 2 Thessalonians
Ezra, Ezra	**Lk**, Luke	**1 Tim**, 1 Timothy
Gal, Galatians	**1 Mac**, 1 Maccabees	**2 Tim**, 2 Timothy
Gen, Genesis	**2 Mac**, 2 Maccabees	**Tit**, Titus
Hab, Habakkuk	**Mal**, Malachi	**Tob**, Tobit
Hag, Haggai	**Mic**, Micah	**Wis**, Wisdom
Heb, Hebrews	**Mk**, Mark	**Zech**, Zechariah
Hos, Hosea	**Mt**, Matthew	**Zep**, Zephaniah
Is, Isaiah	**Nahum**, Nahum	
Jas, James	**Neh**, Nehemiah	
Jer, Jeremiah	**Num**, Numbers	
	Obad, Obadiah	

CONTENTS

The Feast of Man
and the Feast of God

Foreword	7
The Signs which the World Demands	15
The Name of Jesus	31
Zacchaeus	45
The Resurrection of the Young Man of Nain	61
The Blind Man at Bethsaida	75
A Day in the Life of the Lord	91
Parable of the Ten Virgins	99
The Disciples on the Road to Emmaus	135
With Trimmed Lamps	175
Christian Work	187
Saint John the Baptist	195
Witnesses to the Love of God	207
Hope, the Virtue of Overflowing Joy	219
Ways Toward True Love	237
The Beatitudes	271
The Wedding at Cana	315

www.ingramcontent.com/pod-product-compliance
Lightning Source LLC
Chambersburg PA
CBHW060413010526
44107CB00006B/682